Joseph Conrad's
Heart of Darkness

A CASEBOOK

Recent titles in
CASEBOOKS IN CRITICISM

JOSEPH CONRAD'S
Heart of Darkness

◆ ◆ ◆

A CASEBOOK

Edited by
Gene M. Moore

OXFORD
UNIVERSITY PRESS
2004

OXFORD
UNIVERSITY PRESS

Oxford   New York
Auckland   Bangkok   Buenos Aires   Cape Town   Chennai
Dar es Salaam   Delhi   Hong Kong   Istanbul   Karachi   Kolkata
Kuala Lumpur   Madrid   Melbourne   Mexico City   Mumbai
Nairobi   São Paulo   Shanghai   Taipei   Tokyo   Toronto

Copyright © 2004 by Oxford University Press, Inc.

Published by Oxford University Press, Inc.
198 Madison Avenue, New York, New York 10016

www.oup.com

Oxford is a registered trademark of Oxford University Press

Library of Congress Cataloging-in-Publication Data
Joseph Conrad's Heart of darkness : a casebook / edited by Gene M. Moore.
p.   cm. — (Casebooks in criticism)
Includes bibliographical references.
ISBN 0-19-515995-0; 0-19-515996-9 (pbk.)
1. Conrad, Joseph, 1857–1924. Heart of darkness. 2. Psychological
fiction, English—History and criticism. 3. Africa—in literature.
I. Moore, Gene M., 1948–   II. Series.
PR6005.O4H476 2004
823'.912—dc21   2003009868

1 3 5 7 9 8 6 4 2

Printed in the United States of America
on acid-free paper

Credits

Max Beerbohm, "The Feast," from *A Christmas Garland* (London: Heinemann, 1912), pp. 125–30. Copyright © by the Estate of Max Beerbohm. Reprinted by permission of London Management.

Patrick Brantlinger, "Victorians and Africans: The Genealogy of the Myth of the Dark Continent," originally published in *Critical Inquiry* 12, no. 1 (Autumn 1985): 166–203. Copyright © 1985 by the University of Chicago. Reprinted with permission of the author and the University of Chicago Press.

Linda Costanzo Cahir, "Narratological Parallels in Joseph Conrad's *Heart of Darkness* and Francis Ford Coppola's *Apocalypse Now*," originally published in *Literature/Film Quarterly* 20, no. 3 (1992): 181–87. Reprinted with permission.

Cyril Clemens, "A Chat with Joseph Conrad," originally published in *Hobbies: The Magazine for Collectors* (January 1966): 85, 88, 92. Reprinted with permission of *Antiques & Collecting Magazine*.

Joseph Conrad, "An Outpost of Progress," from *Tales of Unrest* (London: T. Fisher Unwin, 1898), pp. 124–70.

David Denby, "Jungle Fever," originally published in *The New Yorker*, 6 November 1995, pp. 118–29. Reprinted with permission of the author.

Arthur Conan Doyle, *The Crime of the Congo* (Garden City, N.Y.: Doubleday, Page, 1909), pp. 3–21.

G. F. W. Hope, "Joseph Conrad's First Cruise in the *Nellie*," originally published in *The Conradian* 25, no. 2 (Autumn 2000): 42–52. Reprinted with permission of the Harry Ransom Humanities Research Center, University of Texas at Austin.

Marion Michael and Wilkes Berry, "The Typescript of 'The Heart of Darkness,'" originally published in *Conradiana* 12, no. 2 (1980): 147–55. Copyright © 1980 by the Textual Studies Institute, Department of English, Texas Tech University. Reprinted with permission of the authors and of Texas Tech University Press.

Zdzisław Najder, "To the End of the Night," from *Joseph Conrad: A Chronicle*, translated by Halina Carroll-Najder (Cambridge: Cambridge University Press, 1983), pp. 123–39. Revised and reprinted with permission of the author.

Nina Pelikan Straus, "The Exclusion of the Intended from Secret Sharing in Conrad's *Heart of Darkness*," originally published in *Novel: A Forum on Fiction* 20, no. 2 (Winter 1987): 123–37. Copyright © 1987 by NOVEL Corp. Reprinted with permission.

Ian Watt, "Conrad's Impressionism," from *Conrad in the Nineteenth Century* (Berkeley: University of California Press, 1979), pp. 169–80. Copyright © 1979 by Ian Watt. Reprinted with permission.

Rino Zhuwarara, "*Heart of Darkness* Revisited: The African Response," originally published in *Kunapipi* 16, no. 3 (1994): 21–37. Reprinted with permission of the author.

Contents

Joseph Conrad's
Heart of Darkness

A CASEBOOK

Introduction

GENE M. MOORE

✦ ✦ ✦

"AND THIS ALSO," said Marlow suddenly, "has been one of the dark places of the earth." If there is a moral to *Heart of Darkness*, it lies perhaps in these words, with which Marlow breaks the silence of a little yacht becalmed on the Thames estuary awaiting the turn of the tide. Marlow then proceeds to tell the entire story of *Heart of Darkness* in miniature, as the tale of a young Roman sent off to the blank edges of the known world "nineteen hundred years ago—the other day," there to confront the "utter savagery" of a primeval England. London has been one of the dark places; the swamps of the Thames were a Congo for the Romans; and the final words of the story drape the entire modern world in a brooding projection of its darkness: "The offing was barred by a black bank of clouds, and the tranquil waterway leading to the uttermost ends of the earth flowed sombre under an overcast sky—seemed to lead into the heart of an immense darkness."

The shifting nature and location of this "darkness" have largely determined the course of response to Conrad's tale over the years.

Is this a story about the horrors of African colonialism, or Belgian colonialism, or colonialism in general? Is it essentially a symbolic modern descent into the hell of Vergil or Dante? Is it about the psychological or atavistic horror of unrestrained libido, or about the impossibility of storytelling? Was Conrad a "bloody racist," as Chinua Achebe has claimed, or the author of what Adam Hochschild describes as "one of the most scathing indictments of imperialism in all literature"? The story combines elements from many genres, and has been described by Cedric Watts as "a mixture of oblique autobiography, traveller's yarn, adventure story, psychological odyssey, political satire, symbolic prose-poem, black comedy, spiritual melodrama, and sceptical meditation" (45).

Given its power to evoke a remarkable range of intense responses, it seems odd that Conrad never made large claims for *Heart of Darkness*. Accepting William Blackwood's invitation to contribute to the thousandth issue of *Blackwood's Edinburgh Magazine*, he expressed reservations about whether the subject he proposed to treat would "commend itself," but insisted that "The criminality of inefficiency and pure selfishness when tackling the civilizing work in Africa is a justifiable idea" (Davies 2: 139–40). When "The Heart of Darkness" began appearing in three installments in the spring of 1899, its artistry appealed to Conrad's literary friends, but it was hardly a popular success. In 1902, when Blackwood published the story together with "Youth" and "The End of the Tether," Conrad titled the volume *Youth: A Narrative, and Two Other Stories*, and of the three stories, *Heart of Darkness* received the least attention from reviewers.

Thereafter, and for the rest of Conrad's life, the story received no special attention either from readers or from Conrad himself, although a few literary echoes may be found in works like H. G. Wells's *Tono-Bungay* (1908), a satire of commercialism involving the exploitation of radioactive "quap" from an African island. The brief references to the story scattered through Conrad's later correspondence are almost entirely of a factual or practical sort, offering a manuscript for sale or arranging for a translation. The general disregard for the story is signaled by the fact that the first translations (into French and German) did not appear until 1924, the year of Conrad's death. Two years later, in *Joseph Conrad in the Congo*, Conrad's friend G. Jean-Aubry published a first sketch of the story's biographical sources.

But *Heart of Darkness* continued to find readers, among them Orson Welles, who adapted the story twice for radio and took it as the basis for an ambitious Hollywood film that was never finished; when the project ran over budget and was scrapped, Welles made *Citizen Kane* instead. Conrad's academic reputation can be dated from 1948, when F. R. Leavis, the most influential British critic of his generation, argued that Conrad's best work belonged to what he called the "great tradition" in English literature. Leavis considered *Heart of Darkness* only a "minor work" and complained of its "adjectival insistence upon inexpressible and incomprehensible mystery" (177); but *The Great Tradition* admitted Conrad to the academic canon and sanctioned his work as a proper subject for literary criticism. According to Leavis, only four English authors had achieved such "greatness": two women (Jane Austen and George Eliot) and two immigrants (Henry James and Conrad).

By the 1950s psychological criticism was dominant in American universities, and Conrad's life and works were interpreted in universalizing or archetypal terms that had little to do with history or colonialism and everything to do with moral or mythic introspection. In *Conrad the Novelist* (1958), Albert J. Guerard called the novella "Conrad's longest journey into self" (33), and subsequent generations of critics have extended this line of inquiry. In the same period, Thomas Moser's "achievement and decline" thesis narrowed the canon of Conrad studies, dismissing the earliest Malay works as well as the later historical novels, but acknowledging the importance of *Heart of Darkness* in spite of its many flaws.

As structuralism succeeded psychology as the dominant critical paradigm of the 1960s and 1970s, the stylistic indeterminacies of which Leavis had complained were reclaimed as positive strengths, signs that Conrad had inscribed the aporias of postmodernity into the cumbrous texture of his style. Tzvetan Todorov described the ambiguous "void" represented by Kurtz at the heart of Conrad's tale, and Peter Brooks would later explore the notion that Conrad, like Kurtz, had written an "unreadable report." At the same time, the cultural and historical aspects of Conrad's work were also being investigated: in 1971 Norman Sherry published the first scholarly account of Conrad's African sources in the opening chapters of *Conrad's Western World*, and in 1979 Ian Watt's *Conrad in the Nineteenth Century* provided a magisterial account of Conrad's early career in its multiple cultural contexts.

Nevertheless, these approaches all shared a silent assumption that the meaning of *Heart of Darkness* had nothing to do with the reality of Africa, which seemed to have served Conrad merely as an exotic backdrop for more important or "universal" self-confrontations. This dismissal of Africa as a place unworthy of history or culture so angered the novelist Chinua Achebe that in 1977 he published an attack on Conrad that changed the very nature of Conrad studies. In "An Image of Africa," Achebe accused Conrad of being a "bloody racist" who "had a problem with niggers"; and he argued that *Heart of Darkness* should be dropped from the canon as an "offensive and totally deplorable book," a story "in which the very humanity of black people is called in question" (Achebe, in Hamner, 124–26). Achebe cited examples of Conrad's (or Marlow's) callous and demeaning portrayal of African characters whose very real sufferings far outweighed the moral discomforts of a self-absorbed adventurer. His evidence restored Africa to the map of Conrad studies, and outlawed the comfortable notion that "Africa is merely a setting for the disintegration of the mind of Mr. Kurtz" (Hamner 124).

Achebe's attack demanded a reply, and critics scrambled to find ways of proving that Conrad was *not* a racist. Some of these replies and subsequent commentaries are listed in the Suggested Reading section at the back of this volume (see Firchow, Hamner, Mongia, Watt, and Watts, among others). Achebe has also softened his own language somewhat, concluding the revised version of his essay published in the third Norton Critical Edition of *Heart of Darkness* with an acknowledgment that "Conrad saw and condemned the evil of imperial exploitation but was strangely unaware of the racism on which it sharpened its iron tooth" (Achebe, in Conrad

[1988], 262). Achebe is apparently unaware that the words *racist* and *racism* did not exist during Conrad's lifetime; the first usages recorded in the *Oxford English Dictionary* date from the 1930s, and even their predecessor, *racialism*, was unknown before 1907. Doubtless racism by any other name is no less offensive; but it is perhaps not entirely strange that Conrad could complain of "the vilest scramble for loot that ever disfigured the history of human conscience" ("Geography" 17), yet fail to deplore a prejudice that was as yet nameless in both English and French.

Of course the value of Achebe's work does not depend on such details; in taking Conrad as a symbol of the "best" literature the West can offer on the subject of Africa, Achebe has raised vital questions that go far beyond Conrad studies to involve postcolonial and cultural theory more generally. Although his essay is not reprinted in the present volume, it is readily available in many casebooks and anthologies, including current editions of the *Norton Anthology of English Literature*. Indeed, its fame is so great that it sometimes appears to represent a unanimous African condemnation of *Heart of Darkness*. To correct this bias, the present volume includes an essay by Rino Zhuwarara, who, while generally agreeing with Achebe's criticism of Conrad, argues that it is also necessary for African readers to become "sensitized to how peoples of other nations perceive Africa." The heart of Conrad's darkness lies not only in Africa or in ancient London, but also in the bosom of the beholder, male or female, black or white.

THE SELECTIONS IN THIS CASEBOOK attempt to strike a balance between historical background materials and essays representing a number of major theoretical approaches. The cutting edge of literary criticism seems to swing (like Poe's fatal pendulum) between formal and cultural-historical approaches every twenty years or so, as for example recently from Deconstructionism to New Historicism, although both form and content remain indispensable (and ultimately indivisible) elements of a full understanding of any work of art. In preparing this volume, I have tried to avoid recycling the classic texts that figure in previous casebooks, and have chosen where possible to introduce new or neglected materials into the discussion.

Conrad's other and earlier African story, "An Outpost of Progress," remains in many ways the best of all introductions to *Heart of Darkness*, since it tells basically the same tale in a more condensed and accessible form, like a brisk overture preceding a symphony. Conrad's bitterly ironic exposé of the demoralizing effects of isolation on a pair of ordinary time servers offers a preliminary sketch of what the same conditions might do to a remarkable genius like Kurtz. There are uncanny textual echoes as well: Makola's "Come along, Mr. Kayerts. He is dead" eerily foreshadows the announcement that "Mistah Kurtz—he dead." "An Outpost of Progress" was Conrad's own favorite among all his stories, and although he spoke of it as "the lightest part of the loot" he brought out of Africa ("Author's Note" vii), it remains a deeply troubling and subversive work. As Brian W. Shaffer has argued, each of the two African stories extends and amplifies the criticism expressed in the other, and they need to be studied together for a full understanding of the meaning of Conrad's encounter with Africa. The text printed here reproduces the original spelling and punctuation from the first English edition of *Tales of Unrest* (London: T. Fisher Unwin, 1898), pp. 124–70.

The "darkness" of Africa was an established myth in Victorian England well before Conrad's journey, as Patrick Brantlinger shows in "Victorians and Africans: The Genealogy of the Myth of the Dark Continent." This wide-ranging survey of Victorian attitudes reminds us of the contexts of abolitionism and humanitarianism that made it possible for adventurers like Henry Morton Stanley and imperialists like King Leopold II to conceal the outrages and abuses that accompanied their purported philanthropy. After all, as David Brion Davis reminds us, "It was not the enslavers who colonized and subjugated Africa, but the European liberators" (xvii).

In 1909, Sir Arthur Conan Doyle published *The Crime of the Congo*, a scathing indictment of what we would now call the human-rights abuses perpetrated by the agents of Western progress and civilization. The ivory-grabbing witnessed by Conrad in

1890 had been followed by the rubber boom, when it became customary to hold families hostage while the men were sent into the bush to gather wild latex, and failures to meet quotas were punished with amputations and mutilations. Conrad's friend Roger Casement was sent inland to report on the atrocities, and the publicity surrounding his report to Parliament in 1904, reinforced by the efforts of the Congo Reform Association, which Casement founded with Edmund Dene Morel, ultimately forced King Leopold to transfer responsibility for the Congo to the Belgian government (and to destroy the archives of the Congo Free State). A vivid recent account of these events is available in Adam Hochschild's book *King Leopold's Ghost*; but the first two chapters of Doyle's volume are reprinted here to provide a capsule history of the origins and development of the Congo Free State in the words of a great writer who took up the cause of the Reform Association. The text printed here is that of the first American edition (Garden City, N.Y.: Doubleday, Page, 1909), pp. 3–21.

Much has been written about Conrad's own African journey and about possible historical models for the character of Kurtz, but almost no attention has been paid to the historical sources of the frame-tale of *Heart of Darkness*. There is no doubt that the model for the Director of Companies was George Fountaine Weare Hope (1854–1930), one of Conrad's oldest English friends. Hope owned a little yacht called the *Nellie* and invited Conrad to join him in the summer of 1889 for a cruise on the Thames estuary together with two other friends, the accountant W. B. Keen and the lawyer E. G. Mears. In 1958 a typescript of Hope's memoir, entitled *Friend of Conrad*, was prepared by J. R. Nicholas Ross. It remained unpublished, although excerpts were cited by some of Conrad's biographers, and in 1971 Ross's typescript was acquired by the Harry Ransom Humanities Research Center at the University of Texas at Austin. *Friend of Conrad* was published for the first time in 2000 in a special issue of *The Conradian*, which was also released separately under the title of *Conrad Between the Lines: Documents in a Life* (Amsterdam: Rodopi, 2000). Hope's little-known account of the cruise in the *Nellie* is the "true" story behind the frame-tale of *Heart of Darkness*, and it is reprinted here in the hope that scholars will seek to understand the "darkness" of the tale not only on the Congo River but also in the well-trafficked waters of Victorian England.

Zdzisław Najder's *Joseph Conrad: A Chronicle* is generally regarded as the best of the available Conrad biographies for many reasons, not least because of the author's familiarity with Conrad's Polish background. The chapter dealing with Conrad's African journey, "To the End of the Night," relies heavily on Conrad's own accounts in his notebooks and letters, and illustrates the differences between the facts of Conrad's journey and the adventures of his fictional counterpart. The author has kindly revised and updated a number of references especially for this casebook.

It is important to remember that *Heart of Darkness* did not spring full-blown from the head of Conrad like Athena from the head of Zeus, but was the ultimate result of a process of composition and revision. Surviving fragments of manuscript and typescript bear documentary witness to this process and testify to the incidents and accidents that conditioned it, including a number of typing errors apparently made by Conrad's wife amid the distractions of caring for their one-year-old son, Borys, who in later years would remember the machine in question as "a monolithic typewriter called a Yost" that was too heavy to be lifted without help (Borys Conrad 12). The resulting document is examined by Marion Michael and Wilkes Berry in "The Typescript of 'The Heart of Darkness,'" which, while cataloging many details of spelling and punctuation, reminds us that literary works are always in some sense the result of a social process of textual production that can never be free from errors and editorial arbitrations.

Given Conrad's fame and the amount of attention paid to his distinctive style, it seems odd that he should have received so few tributes in the form of parodies—far fewer, for example, than Ernest Hemingway or William Faulkner. Max Beerbohm's "The Feast" is the most famous of all Conrad parodies, and is reproduced here both for the sake of comic relief and to call attention to the importance of parody as a means of identifying the distinctive features of an author's individual style. In true Conradian fashion, the ironies of "The Feast" are integral to the very structure of this compact little anecdote, which Mr. Williams opens with the complaint that he has been "eaten up." The cumbersome adjectives in post-position demonstrate the extent to which Conrad was indebted to French authors like Guy de Maupassant not only for narrative structures and frames but even for the very rhythms of his sentences. Ford Madox Ford often described the extent to which French classics served as subtexts to Conrad's works, and Yves Hervouet managed to document an amazing number of these intertextual references in *The French Face of Joseph Conrad*.

Among Ian Watt's many contributions to Conrad studies is the term "delayed decoding," which is commonly used to describe Conrad's habit of describing events impressionistically before identifying what "really" happened. The term was first introduced in 1972 with remarkable modesty and circumscription, as a local device "peculiar [. . .] to Conrad in his early phase" (28). However, it soon became evident to Watt and to many others that the term could not be limited only to Conrad's early work. The excerpt titled "Conrad's Impressionism" reprinted here is taken from Watt's *Conrad in the Nineteenth Century* and can be seen as a definitive statement of the importance of "delayed decoding" in understanding the nature and originality of Conrad's art.

If the notion of "darkness" has proved susceptible to wide-ranging interpretations by literary critics, the idea of "horror" has had a comparable appeal for filmmakers. At least ten film or television adaptations of *Heart of Darkness* have been made in the course of the last half-century, including parodies and spoofs as well as serious efforts. None were ever filmed in the Congo, and only one (by director Ettore Scola) used African locations. The greatest and most daring of these films is surely Francis Ford Coppola's *Apocalypse Now* (1979), which is "structured on" *Heart of Darkness* but transplants the action from colonial Africa to the Vietnam War. In "Narratological Parallels in Joseph Conrad's *Heart of Darkness* and Francis Ford Coppola's *Apocalypse Now*," Linda Costanzo Cahir studies the ways in which Conrad's text and Coppola's film share a similar narrative structure despite the differences in their stories.

Chinua Achebe's iconoclastic essay exposed Conrad's story to criticism from other quarters, and feminist critics were quick to charge that Conrad was not only a racist but also a sexist, noting Marlow's patronizing and dismissive treatment of women. This accusation implicitly echoed the complaints of earlier psychological critics that Conrad could not portray women convincingly and was unable to deal with what Moser called the "uncongenial subject" of love. In "The Exclusion of the Intended from Secret Sharing in Conrad's *Heart of Darkness*," Nina Pelikan Straus argues that Marlow's refusal to share the truth about Kurtz's death with his Intended is based not on a heroic or gentlemanly desire to protect her, but on his need to protect himself and preserve the exclusively masculine order that governs throughout the story.

In "*Heart of Darkness* Revisited: The African Response," Rino Zhuwarara surveys African commentaries on Conrad's work in the context of Edwardian adventure fiction and appreciates the ironies and narrative strategies that "almost rescue" Conrad's story from becoming "a political romance in the Rider Haggard school of imperialist propaganda." Highlighting aspects of the narrative that would puzzle African readers, Zhuwarara admires Conrad's resistance to imperialism but nevertheless finds him guilty of a "rather lazy over-dependence on metaphors and stereotypes which have been used to justify the physical and spiritual mutilation of non-whites." The essay provides a cautionary commentary on *Heart of Darkness* in the wake of the "Achebe controversy."

In the final essay in this collection, "Jungle Fever," David Denby chronicles the reactions of students reading Conrad's story in the context of a Literature Humanities course taught by James Shapiro at Columbia University. Denby summarizes recent trends in Conrad criticism and examines them in the light of the vividly personal responses of students, concluding that "Conrad will never be dropped from the reading lists. Achebe's and [Edward] Said's anguish only confirms his centrality to the modern age."

English was Conrad's third language, and he never managed to speak it without a thick accent that at times made him incomprehensible even to his private secretary. When he was invited to speak in New York in May 1923, the clerks assigned by F. N. Doubleday to record his speech were unable to follow what he said. Accordingly, he gave very few interviews in English, none of them containing any significant discussion of *Heart of Darkness*. The one notable exception is a curious interview recorded by Cyril Clemens (1902–1999), a tenth cousin of Mark Twain who devoted his career to boosting Twain's international reputation. Unpublished before 1966, the interview is said to have taken place at Oswalds, Conrad's home near Canterbury, and allusions to Conrad's "recent visit to America" indicate that the year must have been 1923, shortly after Conrad's return from New York on 9 June. Yet Conrad's correspondence makes no mention of a young American guest named Clemens, nor is the name recorded anywhere in connection with Hugh Walpole. Clemens made a grand tour of Europe in the spring of 1930 to organize international support for his Mark Twain Society, but I can find no evidence of an earlier visit in 1923. Moreover, Sir Gilbert Parker, whom Conrad mentions as a favorite author whose work he can quote at length from memory (and with near-perfect accuracy, from the eighth paragraph of chapter 13 of *The Right of Way*), is mentioned nowhere else in Conrad's letters or recorded conversations. In other words, the interview may be a forgery, though it must be said that Conrad's "voice" sounds plausible enough. One tantalizing possibility—or plausibility—is that Clemens was among the many young readers who heard Conrad talking about his works in America, and that when he came to prepare his recollections for publication years later, he transposed the setting and invented a more personal relationship for the sake of dramatic effect. The bibliographical record does show that in May 1924 the New York journal *Mentor* published a brief account of Conrad's American tour entitled "Conrad Pays Tribute to Mark Twain" in which Conrad singled out *The Mississippi Pilot* for special praise.

Marlow's journey to the heart of darkness leads him to the

edges of the map, the limits of experience, and the blanks at the center of our presumptive knowledge of the world and of ourselves. This casebook is meant to serve as a rough map or guide to this multidimensional territory, in the hope of illuminating at least some of its darkness.

Works Cited

Achebe, Chinua. "An Image of Africa." In *Joseph Conrad: Third World Perspectives*, edited by Robert Hamner. Washington, D.C.: Three Continents, 1990, pp. 119–29. Revised version in Conrad, *Heart of Darkness*, edited by Robert Kimbrough. New York: Norton, 1988, pp. 251–62.

Brooks, Peter. "An Unreadable Report: *Heart of Darkness*." In Brooks, *Reading for the Plot: Design and Intention in Narrative*. New York: Knopf; Oxford: Clarendon, 1984, pp. 28–63.

Conrad, Borys. *My Father: Joseph Conrad*. London: Calder & Boyars, 1970.

Conrad, Joseph. "Author's Note" to *Tales of Unrest*. 1898. London: Dent's Collected Edition, 1947, pp. v–ix.

——. "Geography and Some Explorers." In *Last Essays*. 1926. London: Dent's Collected Edition, 1955, pp. 1–21.

——. *Heart of Darkness*. 1902. Edited by Robert Kimbrough. New York: Norton, 1988.

Davies, Laurence, et al., eds. *The Collected Letters of Joseph Conrad*. 6 vols. to date. Cambridge: Cambridge University Press, 1983–.

Davis, David Brion. *Slavery and Human Progress*. New York: Oxford University Press, 1984.

Guerard, Albert J. *Conrad the Novelist*. Cambridge, Mass.: Harvard University Press, 1958.

Hamner, Robert, ed. *Joseph Conrad: Third World Perspectives*. Washington, D.C.: Three Continents, 1990.

Hervouet, Yves. *The French Face of Joseph Conrad*. Cambridge: Cambridge University Press, 1990.

Hochschild, Adam. *King Leopold's Ghost*. Boston and New York: Houghton Mifflin, 1998.

Hope, G. F. W. "Friend of Conrad." *The Conradian* 25, no. 2 (2000): 1–56. Also as *Conrad Between the Lines: Documents in a Life*, edited by Gene M. Moore, Allan H. Simmons, and J. H. Stape. Amsterdam and Atlanta: Rodopi, 2000, pp. 1–56.

Leavis, F. R. *The Great Tradition* London: Chatto & Windus, 1948.

Moser, Thomas. *Joseph Conrad: Achievement and Decline.* Cambridge, Mass.: Harvard University Press, 1957.

Najder, Zdzisław. *Joseph Conrad: A Chronicle.* New Brunswick, N.J.: Rutgers University Press, 1983.

Shaffer, Brian W. "Progress and Civilization and All the Virtues': Teaching *Heart of Darkness* via 'An Outpost of Progress.' " *Conradiana* 24, no. 3 (1992): 219–31.

Sherry, Norman. *Conrad's Western World.* Cambridge: Cambridge University Press, 1971.

Todorov, Tzvetan. "Knowledge in the Void: *Heart of Darkness.*" 1975. Translated by Walter C. Putnam III. *Conradiana* 21, no. 3 (1989): 161–72.

Watt, Ian. *Conrad in the Nineteenth Century.* Berkeley and Los Angeles: University of California Press, 1979.

———. "Pink Toads and Yellow Curs: An Impressionist Narrative Device in *Lord Jim.*" In *Joseph Conrad Colloquy in Poland, 5–12 September 1972,* edited by Róża Jabłkowska. Wrocław: Ossolineum, 1975, pp. 11–31.

Watts, Cedric. "Heart of Darkness." In *The Cambridge Companion to Joseph Conrad,* edited by J. H. Stape. Cambridge: Cambridge University Press, 1996, pp. 45–62.

An Outpost of Progress

JOSEPH CONRAD

◆   ◆   ◆

I.

There were two white men in charge of the trading station. Kayerts, the chief, was short and fat; Carlier, the assistant, was tall, with a large head and a very broad trunk perched upon a long pair of thin legs. The third man on the staff was a Sierra Leone nigger, who maintained that his name was Henry Price. However, for some reason or other, the natives down the river had given him the name of Makola, and it stuck to him through all his wanderings about the country. He spoke English and French with a warbling accent, wrote a beautiful hand, understood bookkeeping, and cherished in his innermost heart the worship of evil spirits. His wife was a negress from Loanda, very large and very noisy. Three children rolled about in sunshine before the door of his low, shed-like dwelling. Makola, taciturn and impenetrable, despised the two white men. He had charge of a small clay storehouse with a dried-grass roof, and pretended to keep a correct account of beads, cotton cloth, red kerchiefs, brass wire, and other trade goods it contained. Besides the storehouse and Makola's hut, there was only one large building in the cleared ground of the station. It was built neatly of reeds, with a verandah on all the four sides. There were three rooms in it. The one in the middle was the living-room, and had two rough tables and a few stools in it. The other two were the bedrooms for the white men. Each had a bedstead and a mosquito net for all furniture. The plank floor was littered with the belongings of the white men; open half-empty boxes, torn wearing apparel, old boots; all the things dirty, and all the things broken, that accumulate mysteriously round untidy men. There was also another dwelling-place some distance away from the buildings. In it, under a tall cross much out of the perpendicular, slept the man who had seen the beginning of all this; who had planned and had watched the construction of this outpost of progress. He had been, at home, an unsuccessful painter who, weary of pursuing fame on an empty stomach, had gone out there through high protections. He had been the first chief of that station. Makola had watched the energetic artist die of fever in the just finished house with his usual kind of "I told you so" indifference. Then, for a time, he dwelt alone with his family, his account books, and the Evil Spirit that rules the lands under the equator. He got on very well with his god. Perhaps he had propitiated him by a promise of more white men to play with, by and by. At any rate the director of the Great Trading Company, coming up in a steamer that resembled an enormous sardine box with a flat-roofed shed erected on it, found the station in good order, and Makola as usual quietly diligent. The director had the cross put up over the first agent's grave, and appointed Kayerts to the post. Carlier was told off as second in charge. The director was a man ruthless and efficient, who at times, but very imperceptibly, indulged in grim humour. He made a speech to Kayerts and Carlier, pointing out to them the promising aspect of their station. The nearest trading-post was about three hundred miles away. It was an exceptional opportunity for them to distinguish themselves and to earn percentages on the trade. This appointment was a favour done to beginners. Kayerts was moved almost to tears by his director's kindness. He would, he said, by doing his best, try to justify the flattering confidence, &c., &c. Kayerts had been in the Administration of the Telegraphs, and knew how to express himself correctly. Carlier, an ex-non-commissioned officer of cavalry in an army guaranteed from harm by several European Powers, was less impressed. If there were commissions to get, so much the better; and, trailing a sulky glance over the river, the forests, the impenetrable bush that seemed to cut off the station from the rest of the world, he muttered between his teeth, "We shall see, very soon."

Next day, some bales of cotton goods and a few cases of provisions having been thrown on shore, the sardine-box steamer went off, not to return for another six months. On the deck the director touched his cap to the two agents, who stood on the bank waving their hats, and turning to an old servant of the Company on his passage to headquarters, said, "Look at those two imbeciles. They must be mad at home to send me such specimens. I told those fellows to plant a vegetable garden, build new storehouses and fences, and construct a landing-stage. I bet nothing will be done! They won't know how to begin. I always thought the station on this river useless, and they just fit the station!"

"They will form themselves there," said the old stager with a quiet smile.

"At any rate, I am rid of them for six months," retorted the director.

The two men watched the steamer round the bend, then, ascending arm in arm the slope of the bank, returned to the station. They had been in this vast and dark country only a very short time, and as yet always in the midst of other white men, under the eye and guidance of their superiors. And now, dull as they were to the subtle influences of surroundings, they felt themselves very much alone, when suddenly left unassisted to face the wilderness; a wilderness rendered more strange, more incomprehensible by the mysterious glimpses of the vigorous life it contained. They were two perfectly insignificant and incapable individuals, whose existence is only rendered possible through the high organisation of civilised crowds. Few men realise that their life, the very essence of their character, their capabilities and their audacities, are only the expression of their belief in the safety of their surroundings. The courage, the composure, the confidence; the emotions and principles; every great and every insignificant thought belongs not to the individual but to the crowd: to the crowd that believes blindly in the irresistible force of its institutions and of its morals, in the power of its police and of its opinion. But the contact with pure unmitigated savagery, with primitive nature and primitive man, brings sudden and profound trouble into the heart. To the sentiment of being alone of one's kind, to the clear perception of the loneliness of one's thoughts, of one's sensations—to the negation of the habitual, which is safe, there is added the affirmation of the unusual, which is dangerous; a suggestion of things vague, uncontrollable, and repulsive, whose discomposing intrusion excites the imagination and tries the civilised nerves of the foolish and the wise alike.

Kayerts and Carlier walked arm in arm, drawing close to one another as children do in the dark; and they had the same, not altogether unpleasant, sense of danger which one half suspects to be imaginary. They chatted persistently in familiar tones. "Our station is prettily situated," said one. The other assented with enthusiasm, enlarging volubly on the beauties of the situation. Then they passed near the grave. "Poor devil!" said Kayerts. "He died of fever, didn't he?" muttered Carlier, stopping short. "Why," retorted Kayerts, with indignation, "I've been told that the fellow exposed himself recklessly to the sun. The climate here, everybody says, is not at all worse than at home, as long as you keep out of the sun. Do you hear that, Carlier? I am chief here, and my orders are that you should not expose yourself to the sun!" He assumed his superiority jocularly, but his meaning was serious. The idea that he would, perhaps, have to bury Carlier and remain alone, gave him an inward shiver. He felt suddenly that this Carlier was more precious to him here, in the centre of Africa, than a brother could be anywhere else. Carlier, entering into the spirit of the thing, made a military salute and answered in a brisk tone, "Your orders shall be attended to, chief!" Then he burst out laughing, slapped Kayerts on the back and shouted, "We shall let life run easily here! Just sit still and gather in the ivory those

savages will bring. This country has its good points, after all!"
They both laughed loudly while Carlier thought: "That poor Kayerts; he is so fat and unhealthy. It would be awful if I had to
bury him here. He is a man I respect. . . ." Before they reached
the verandah of their house they called one another "my dear
fellow."

The first day they were very active, pottering about with ham-
mers and nails and red calico, to put up curtains, make their
house habitable and pretty; resolved to settle down comfortably
to their new life. For them an impossible task. To grapple effectually with even purely material problems requires more serenity
of mind and more lofty courage than people generally imagine.
No two beings could have been more unfitted for such a struggle.
Society, not from any tenderness, but because of its strange needs,
had taken care of those two men, forbidding them all independent thought, all initiative, all departure from routine; and forbidding it under pain of death. They could only live on condition
of being machines. And now, released from the fostering care of
men with pens behind the ears, or of men with gold lace on the
sleeves, they were like those lifelong prisoners who, liberated after
many years, do not know what use to make of their freedom.
They did not know what use to make of their faculties, being
both, through want of practice, incapable of independent
thought.

At the end of two months Kayerts often would say, "If it was
not for my Melie, you wouldn't catch me here." Melie was his
daughter. He had thrown up his post in the Administration of
the Telegraphs, though he had been for seventeen years perfectly
happy there, to earn a dowry for his girl. His wife was dead, and
the child was being brought up by his sisters. He regretted the
streets, the pavements, the cafés, his friends of many years; all
the things he used to see, day after day; all the thoughts suggested
by familiar things—the thoughts effortless, monotonous, and
soothing of a Government clerk; he regretted all the gossip, the
small enmities, the mild venom, and the little jokes of Government offices. "If I had had a decent brother-in-law," Carlier would
remark, "a fellow with a heart, I would not be here." He had left

the army and had made himself so obnoxious to his family by his laziness and impudence, that an exasperated brother-in-law had made superhuman efforts to procure him an appointment in the Company as a second-class agent. Having not a penny in the world, he was compelled to accept this means of livelihood as soon as it became quite clear to him that there was nothing more to squeeze out of his relations. He, like Kayerts, regretted his old life. He regretted the clink of sabre and spurs on a fine afternoon, the barrack-room witticisms, the girls of garrison towns; but, besides, he had also a sense of grievance. He was evidently a much ill-used man. This made him moody, at times. But the two men got on well together in the fellowship of their stupidity and laziness. Together they did nothing, absolutely nothing, and enjoyed the sense of the idleness for which they were paid. And in time they came to feel something resembling affection for one another.

They lived like blind men in a large room, aware only of what came in contact with them (and of that only imperfectly), but unable to see the general aspect of things. The river, the forest, all the great land throbbing with life, were like a great emptiness. Even the brilliant sunshine disclosed nothing intelligible. Things appeared and disappeared before their eyes in an unconnected and aimless kind of way. The river seemed to come from nowhere and flow nowhither. It flowed through a void. Out of that void, at times, came canoes, and men with spears in their hands would suddenly crowd the yard of the station. They were naked, glossy black, ornamented with snowy shells and glistening brass wire, perfect of limb. They made an uncouth babbling noise when they spoke, moved in a stately manner, and sent quick, wild glances out of their startled, never-resting eyes. Those warriors would squat in long rows, four or more deep, before the verandah, while their chiefs bargained for hours with Makola over an elephant tusk. Kayerts sat on his chair and looked down on the proceedings, understanding nothing. He stared at them with his round blue eyes, called out to Carlier, "Here, look! look at that fellow there—and that other one, to the left. Did you ever such a face? Oh, the funny brute!"

Carlier, smoking native tobacco in a short wooden pipe, would swagger up twirling his moustaches, and, surveying the warriors with haughty indulgence, would say—

"Fine animals. Brought any bone? Yes? It's not any too soon. Look at the muscles of that fellow—third from the end. I wouldn't care to get a punch on the nose from him. Fine arms, but legs no good below the knee. Couldn't make cavalry men of them." And after glancing down complacently at his own shanks, he always concluded: "Pah! Don't they stink! You, Makola! Take that herd over to the fetish" (the storehouse was in every station called the fetish, perhaps because of the spirit of civilisation it contained) "and give them up some of the rubbish you keep there. I'd rather see it full of bone than full of rags."

Kayerts approved.

"Yes, yes! Go and finish that palaver over there, Mr. Makola. I will come round when you are ready, to weigh the tusk. We must be careful." Then, turning to his companion: "This is the tribe that lives down the river; they are rather aromatic. I remember, they had been once before here. D'ye hear that row? What a fellow has got to put up with in this dog of a country! My head is split."

Such profitable visits were rare. For days the two pioneers of trade and progress would look on their empty courtyard in the vibrating brilliance of vertical sunshine. Below the high bank, the silent river flowed on glittering and steady. On the sands in the middle of the stream, hippos and alligators sunned themselves side by side. And stretching away in all directions, surrounding the insignificant cleared spot of the trading post, immense forests, hiding fateful complications of fantastic life, lay in the eloquent silence of mute greatness. The two men understood nothing, cared for nothing but for the passage of days that separated them from the steamer's return. Their predecessor had left some torn books. They took up these wrecks of novels, and, as they had never read anything of the kind before, they were surprised and amused. Then during long days there were interminable and silly discussions about plots and personages. In the centre of Africa they made acquaintance of Richelieu and of d'Artagnan, of

Hawk's Eye and of Father Goriot, and of many other people. All
these imaginary personages became subjects for gossip as if they
had been living friends. They discounted their virtues, suspected
their motives, decried their successes; were scandalised at their
duplicity or were doubtful about their courage. The accounts of
crimes filled them with indignation, while tender or pathetic passages moved them deeply. Carlier cleared his throat and said in
a soldierly voice, "What nonsense!" Kayerts, his round eyes suf-
fused with tears, his fat cheeks quivering, rubbed his bald head,
and declared, "This is a splendid book. I had no idea there were
such clever fellows in the world." They also found some old
copies of a home paper. That print discussed what it was pleased
to call "Our Colonial Expansion" in high-flown language. It spoke
much of the rights and duties of civilisation, of the sacredness of
the civilising work, and extolled the merits of those who went
about bringing light, and faith, and commerce to the dark places
of the earth. Carlier and Kayerts read, wondered, and began to
think better of themselves. Carlier said one evening, waving his
hand about, "In a hundred years, there will be perhaps a town
here. Quays, and warehouses, and barracks, and—and—billiard-
rooms. Civilisation, my boy, and virtue—and all. And then, chaps
will read that two good fellows, Kayerts and Carlier, were the
first civilised men to live in this very spot!" Kayerts nodded, "Yes,
it is a consolation to think of that." They seemed to forget their
dead predecessor; but, early one day, Carlier went out and re-
planted the cross firmly. "It used to make me squint whenever I
walked that way," he explained to Kayerts over the morning coffee. "It made me squint, leaning over so much. So I just planted
it upright. And solid, I promise you! I suspended myself with
both hands to the cross-piece. Not a move. Oh, I did that properly."

At times Gobila came to see them. Gobila was the chief of the
neighbouring villages. He was a gray-headed savage, thin and
black, with a white cloth round his loins and a mangy panther
skin hanging over his back. He came up with long strides of his
skeleton legs, swinging a staff as tall as himself, and, entering the

common room of the station, would squat on his heels to the left of the door. There he sat, watching Kayerts, and now and then making a speech which the other did not understand. Kayerts, without interrupting his occupation, would from time to time say in a friendly manner: "How goes it, you old image?" and they would smile at one another. The two whites had a liking for that old and incomprehensible creature, and called him Father Gobila. Gobila's manner was paternal, and he seemed really to love all white men. They all appeared to him very young, indistinguishably alike (except for stature), and he knew that they were all brothers, and also immortal. The death of the artist, who was the first white man whom he knew intimately, did not disturb this belief, because he was firmly convinced that the white stranger had pretended to die and got himself buried for some mysterious purpose of his own, into which it was useless to inquire. Perhaps it was his way of going home to his own country? At any rate, these were his brothers, and he transferred his absurd affection to them. They returned it in a way. Carlier slapped him on the back, and recklessly struck off matches for his amusement. Kayerts was always ready to let him have a sniff at the ammonia bottle. In short, they behaved just like that other white creature that had hidden itself in a hole in the ground. Gobila considered them attentively. Perhaps they were the same being with the other—or one of them was. He couldn't decide—clear up that mystery; but he remained always very friendly. In consequence of that friendship the women of Gobila's village walked in single file through the reedy grass, bringing every morning to the station, fowls, and sweet potatoes, and palm wine, and sometimes a goat. The Company never provisions the stations fully, and the agents required those local supplies to live. They had them through the good-will of Gobila, and lived well. Now and then one of them had a bout of fever, and the other nursed him with gentle devotion. They did not think much of it. It left them weaker, and their appearance changed for the worse. Carlier was hollow-eyed and irritable. Kayerts showed a drawn, flabby face above the rotundity of his stomach, which gave him a weird aspect. But being constantly together, they did not notice the change that took place gradually in their appearance, and also in their dispositions.

Five months passed in that way.

Then, one morning, as Kayerts and Carlier, lounging in their chairs under the verandah, talked about the approaching visit of the steamer, a knot of armed men came out of the forest and advanced towards the station. They were strangers to that part of the country. They were tall, slight, draped classically from neck to heel in blue fringed cloths, and carried percussion muskets over their bare right shoulders. Makola showed signs of excitement, and ran out of the storehouse (where he spent all his days) to meet these visitors. They came into the courtyard and looked about them with steady, scornful glances. Their leader, a powerful and determined-looking negro with bloodshot eyes, stood in front of the verandah and made a long speech. He gesticulated much, and ceased very suddenly.

There was something in his intonation, in the sounds of the long sentences he used, that startled the two whites. It was like a reminiscence of something not exactly familiar, and yet resembling the speech of civilised men. It sounded like one of those impossible languages which sometimes we hear in our dreams.

"What lingo is that?" said the amazed Carlier. "In the first moment I fancied the fellow was going to speak French. Anyway, it is a different kind of gibberish to what we ever heard."

"Yes," replied Kayerts. "Hey, Makola, what does he say? Where do they come from? Who are they?"

But Makola, who seemed to be standing on hot bricks, answered hurriedly, "I don't know. They come from very far. Perhaps Mrs. Price will understand. They are perhaps bad men."

The leader, after waiting for a while, said something sharply to Makola, who shook his head. Then the man, after looking round, noticed Makola's hut and walked over there. The next moment Mrs. Makola was heard speaking with great volubility. The other strangers—they were six in all—strolled about with an air of ease, put their heads through the door of the storeroom, congregated round the grave, pointed understandingly at the cross, and generally made themselves at home.

"I don't like those chaps—and, I say, Kayerts, they must be from the coast; they've got firearms," observed the sagacious Carlier.

Kayerts also did not like those chaps. They both, for the first time, became aware that they lived in conditions where the unusual may be dangerous, and that there was no power on earth outside of themselves to stand between them and the unusual. They became uneasy, went in and loaded their revolvers. Kayerts said, "We must order Makola to tell them to go away before dark."

The strangers left in the afternoon, after eating a meal prepared for them by Mrs. Makola. The immense woman was excited, and talked much with the visitors. She rattled away shrilly, pointing here and there at the forests and at the river. Makola sat apart and watched. At times he got up and whispered to his wife. He accompanied the strangers across the ravine at the back of the station-ground, and returned slowly looking very thoughtful. When questioned by the white men he was very strange, seemed not to understand, seemed to have forgotten French— seemed to have forgotten how to speak altogether. Kayerts and Carlier agreed that the nigger had had too much palm wine.

There was some talk about keeping a watch in turn, but in the evening everything seemed so quiet and peaceful that they retired as usual. All night they were disturbed by a lot of drumming in the villages. A deep, rapid roll near by would be followed by another far off—then all ceased. Soon short appeals would rattle out here and there, then all mingle together, increase, become vigorous and sustained, would spread out over the forest, roll through the night, unbroken and ceaseless, near and far, as if the whole land had been one immense drum booming out steadily an appeal to heaven. And through the deep and tremendous noise sudden yells that resembled snatches of songs from a madhouse darted shrill and high in discordant jets of sound which seemed to rush far above the earth and drive all peace from under the stars.

Carlier and Kayerts slept badly. They both thought they had heard shots fired during the night—but they could not agree as to the direction. In the morning Makola was gone somewhere. He returned about noon with one of yesterday's strangers, and eluded all Kayerts' attempts to close with him: had become deaf apparently. Kayerts wondered. Carlier, who had been fishing off the bank, came back and remarked while he showed his catch, "The niggers seem to be in a deuce of a stir; I wonder what's up. I saw about fifteen canoes cross the river during the two hours I was there fishing." Kayerts, worried, said, "Isn't this Makola very queer to-day?" Carlier advised, "Keep all our men together in case of some trouble."

II.

There were ten station men who had been left by the Director. Those fellows, having engaged themselves to the Company for six months (without having any idea of a month in particular and only a very faint notion of time in general), had been serving the cause of progress for upwards of two years. Belonging to a tribe from a very distant part of this land of darkness and sorrow, they did not run away, naturally supposing that as wandering strangers they would be killed by the inhabitants of the country; in which they were right. They lived in straw huts on the slope of a ravine overgrown with reedy grass, just behind the station buildings. They were not happy, regretting the festive incantations, the sorceries, the human sacrifices of their own land; where they also had parents, brothers, sisters, admired chiefs, respected magicians, loved friends, and other ties supposed generally to be human. Besides, the rice rations served out by the Company did not agree with them, being a food unknown to their land, and to which they could not get used. Consequently they were unhealthy and miserable. Had they been of any other tribe they would have made up their minds to die—for nothing is easier to certain savages than suicide—and so have escaped from the puzzling difficulties of existence. But belonging, as they did, to a warlike tribe with filed teeth, they had more grit, and went on stupidly living through disease and sorrow. They did very little work, and had lost their splendid physique. Carlier and Kayerts doctored them assiduously without being able to bring them back into condition again. They were mustered every morning and told off to different tasks—grass-cutting, fence-building, tree-felling, &c., &c., which no power on earth could induce them to execute efficiently. The two whites had practically very little control over them.

In the afternoon Makola came over to the big house and found Kayerts watching three heavy columns of smoke rising above the forests. "What is that?" asked Kayerts. "Some villages burn," answered Makola, who seemed to have regained his wits. Then he said abruptly: "We have got very little ivory; bad six months' trading. Do you like get a little more ivory?"

"Yes," said Kayerts, eagerly. He thought of percentages which were low.

"Those men who came yesterday are traders from Loanda who have got more ivory than they can carry home. Shall I buy? I know their camp."

"Certainly," said Kayerts. "What are those traders?"

"Bad fellows," said Makola, indifferently. "They fight with people, and catch women and children. They are bad men, and got guns. There is a great disturbance in the country. Do you want ivory?"

"Yes," said Kayerts. Makola said nothing for a while. Then: "Those workmen of ours are no good at all," he muttered, looking round. "Station in very bad order, sir. Director will growl. Better get a fine lot of ivory, then he say nothing."

"I can't help it; the men won't work," said Kayerts. "When will you get that ivory?"

"Very soon," said Makola. "Perhaps to-night. You leave it to me, and keep indoors, sir. I think you had better give some palm wine to our men to make a dance this evening. Enjoy themselves. Work better to-morrow. There's plenty palm wine—gone a little sour."

Kayerts said yes, and Makola, with his own hands, carried the big calabashes to the door of his hut. They stood there till the evening, and Mrs. Makola looked into every one. The men got them at sunset. When Kayerts and Carlier retired, a big bonfire was flaring before the men's huts. They could hear their shouts and drumming. Some men from Gobila's village had joined the station hands, and the entertainment was a great success.

In the middle of the night, Carlier waking suddenly, heard a man shout loudly; then a shot was fired. Only one. Carlier ran out and met Kayerts on the verandah. They were both startled. As they went across the yard to call Makola, they saw shadows moving in the night. One of them cried, "Don't shoot! It's me, Price." Then Makola appeared close to them. "Go back, go back, please," he urged, "you spoil all." "There are strange men about," said Carlier. "Never mind; I know," said Makola. Then he whispered, "All right. Bring ivory. Say nothing! I know my business." The two white men reluctantly went back to the house, but did not sleep. They heard footsteps, whispers, some groans. It seemed as if a lot of men came in, dumped heavy things on the ground, squabbled a long time, then went away. They lay on their hard beds and thought: "This Makola is invaluable." In the morning Carlier came out, very sleepy, and pulled at the cord of the big bell. The station hands mustered every morning to the sound of the bell. That morning nobody came. Kayerts turned out also, yawning. Across the yard they saw Makola come out of his hut, a tin basin of soapy water in his hand. Makola, a civilised nigger, was very neat in his person. He threw the soapsuds skilfully over a wretched little yellow cur he had, then turning his face to the agent's house, he shouted from the distance, "All the men gone last night!"

They heard him plainly, but in their surprise they both yelled out together: "What!" Then they stared at one another. "We are in a proper fix now," growled Carlier. "It's incredible!" muttered Kayerts. "I will go to the huts and see," said Carlier, striding off. Makola coming up found Kayerts standing alone.

"I can hardly believe it," said Kayerts, tearfully. "We took care of them as if they had been our children."

"They went with the coast people," said Makola after a moment of hesitation.

"What do I care with whom they went—the ungrateful brutes!" exclaimed the other. Then with sudden suspicion, and looking hard at Makola, he added: "What do you know about it?"

Makola moved his shoulders, looking down on the ground. "What do I know? I think only. Will you come and look at the ivory I've got there? It is a fine lot. You never saw such."

He moved towards the store. Kayerts followed him mechanically, thinking about the incredible desertion of the men. On the ground before the door of the fetish lay six splendid tusks.

"What did you give for it?" asked Kayerts, after surveying the lot with satisfaction.

"No regular trade," said Makola. "They brought the ivory and gave it to me. I told them to take what they most wanted in the station. It is a beautiful lot. No station can show such tusks. Those traders wanted carriers badly, and our men were no good here. No trade, no entry in books; all correct."

Kayerts nearly burst with indignation. "Why!" he shouted, "I believe you have sold our men for these tusks!" Makola stood impassive and silent. "I—I—will—I," stuttered Kayerts. "You fiend!" he yelled out.

"I did the best for you and the Company," said Makola, imperturbably. "Why you shout so much? Look at this tusk."

"I dismiss you! I will report you—I won't look at the tusk. I forbid you to touch them. I order you to throw them into the river. You—you!"

"You very red, Mr. Kayerts. If you are so irritable in the sun, you will get fever and die—like the first chief!" pronounced Makola impressively.

They stood still, contemplating one another with intense eyes, as if they had been looking with effort across immense distances. Kayerts shivered. Makola had meant no more than he said, but his words seemed to Kayerts full of ominous menace! He turned sharply and went away to the house. Makola retired into the bosom of his family; and the tusks, left lying before the store, looked very large and valuable in the sunshine.

Carlier came back on the verandah. "They're all gone, hey?" asked Kayerts from the far end of the common room in a muffled voice. "You did not find anybody?"

"Oh, yes," said Carlier, "I found one of Gobila's people lying dead before the huts—shot through the body. We heard that shot last night."

Kayerts came out quickly. He found his companion staring grimly over the yard at the tusks, away by the store. They both sat in silence for a while. Then Kayerts related his conversation with Makola. Carlier said nothing. At the midday meal they ate very little. They hardly exchanged a word that day. A great silence seemed to lie heavily over the station and press on their lips. Makola did not open the store; he spent the day playing with his children. He lay full-length on a mat outside his door, and the youngsters sat on his chest and clambered all over him. It was a touching picture. Mrs. Makola was busy cooking all day, as usual. The white men made a somewhat better meal in the evening. Afterwards, Carlier smoking his pipe strolled over to the store; he stood for a long time over the tusks, touched one or two with his foot, even tried to lift the largest one by its small end. He came back to his chief, who had not stirred from the verandah, threw himself in the chair and said—

"I can see it! They were pounced upon while they slept heavily after drinking all that palm wine you've allowed Makola to give them. A put-up job! See? The worst is, some of Gobila's people were there, and got carried off too, no doubt. The least drunk woke up, and got shot for his sobriety. This is a funny country. What will you do now?"

"We can't touch it, of course," said Kayerts.

"Of course not," assented Carlier.

"Slavery is an awful thing," stammered out Kayerts in an unsteady voice.

"Frightful—the sufferings," grunted Carlier, with conviction.

They believed their words. Everybody shows a respectful deference to certain sounds that he and his fellows can make. But about feelings people really know nothing. We talk with indignation or enthusiasm; we talk about oppression, cruelty, crime, devotion, self-sacrifice, virtue, and we know nothing real beyond the words. Nobody knows what suffering or sacrifice mean— except, perhaps the victims of the mysterious purpose of these illusions.

Next morning they saw Makola very busy setting up in the yard the big scales used for weighing ivory. By and by Carlier said: "What's that filthy scoundrel up to?" and lounged out into the yard. Kayerts followed. They stood watching. Makola took no notice. When the balance was swung true, he tried to lift a tusk into the scale. It was too heavy. He looked up helplessly without a word, and for a minute they stood round that balance as mute and still as three statues. Suddenly Carlier said: "Catch hold of the other end, Makola—you beast!" and together they swung the tusk up. Kayerts trembled in every limb. He muttered, "I say! O! I say!" and putting his hand in his pocket found there a dirty bit of paper and the stump of a pencil. He turned his back on the others, as if about to do something tricky, and noted stealthily the weights which Carlier shouted out to him with unnecessary loudness. When all was over Makola whispered to himself: "The sun's very strong here for the tusks." Carlier said to Kayerts in a careless tone: "I say, chief, I might just as well give him a lift with this lot into the store."

As they were going back to the house Kayerts observed with a sigh: "It had to be done." And Carlier said: "It's deplorable, but, the men being Company's men, the ivory is Company's ivory. We must look after it." "I will report to the Director, of course," said Kayerts. "Of course; let him decide," approved Carlier.

At mid-day they made a hearty meal. Kayerts sighed from time to time. Whenever they mentioned Makola's name they always added to it an opprobrious epithet. It eased their conscience. Makola gave himself a half-holiday, and bathed his children in the river. No one from Gobila's villages came near the station that day. No one came the next day, and the next, nor for a whole week. Gobila's people might have been dead and buried for any sign of life they gave. But they were only mourning for those

they had lost by the witchcraft of white men, who had brought
wicked people into their country. The wicked people were gone,
but fear remained. Fear always remains. A man may destroy
everything within himself, love and hate and belief, and even
doubt; but as long as he clings to life he cannot destroy fear: the
fear, subtle, indestructible, and terrible, that pervades his being;
that tinges his thoughts; that lurks in his heart; that watches on
his lips the struggle of his last breath. In his fear, the mild old
Gobila offered extra human sacrifices to all the Evil Spirits that
had taken possession of his white friends. His heart was heavy.
Some warriors spoke about burning and killing, but the cautious
old savage dissuaded them. Who could foresee the woe those
mysterious creatures, if irritated, might bring? They should be left
alone. Perhaps in time they would disappear into the earth as the
first one had disappeared. His people must keep away from them,
and hope for the best.

Kayerts and Carlier did not disappear, but remained above on
this earth, that, somehow, they fancied had become bigger and
very empty. It was not the absolute and dumb solitude of the
post that impressed them so much as an inarticulate feeling that
something from within them was gone, something that worked
for their safety, and had kept the wilderness from interfering with
their hearts. The images of home; the memory of people like
them, of men that thought and felt as they used to think and
feel, receded into distances made indistinct by the glare of un-
clouded sunshine. And out of the great silence of the surrounding
wilderness, its very hopelessness and savagery seemed to approach
them nearer, to draw them gently, to look upon them, to en-
velop them with a solicitude irresistible, familiar, and disgusting.

Days lengthened into weeks, then into months. Gobila's people
drummed and yelled to every new moon, as of yore, but kept
away from the station. Makola and Carlier tried once in a canoe
to open communications, but were received with a shower of
arrows, and had to fly back to the station for dear life. That
attempt set the country up and down the river into an uproar
that could be very distinctly heard for days. The steamer was late.
At first they spoke of delay jauntily, then anxiously, then gloom-

ily. The matter was becoming serious. Stores were running short. Carlier cast his lines off the bank, but the river was low, and the fish kept out in the stream. They dared not stroll far away from the station to shoot. Moreover, there was no game in the impenetrable forest. Once Carlier shot a hippo in the river. They had no boat to secure it, and it sank. When it floated up it drifted away, and Gobila's people secured the carcase. It was the occasion for a national holiday, but Carlier had a fit of rage over it, and talked about the necessity of exterminating all the niggers before the country could be made habitable. Kayerts mooned about silently; spent hours looking at the portrait of his Melie. It represented a little girl with long bleached tresses and a rather sour face. His legs were much swollen, and he could hardly walk. Carlier, undermined by fever, could not swagger any more, but kept tottering about, still with a devil-may-care air, as became a man who remembered his crack regiment. He had become hoarse, sarcastic, and inclined to say unpleasant things. He called it "being frank with you." They had long ago reckoned their percentages on trade, including in them that last deal of "this infamous Makola." They had also concluded not to say anything about it. Kayerts hesitated at first—was afraid of the Director.

"He has seen worse things done on the quiet," maintained Carlier, with a hoarse laugh. "Trust him! He won't thank you if you blab. He is no better than you or me. Who will talk if we hold our tongues? There is nobody here."

That was the root of the trouble! There was nobody there; and being left there alone with their weakness, they became daily more like a pair of accomplices than like a couple of devoted friends. They had heard nothing from home for eight months. Every evening they said, "To-morrow we shall see the steamer." But one of the Company's steamers had been wrecked, and the Director was busy with the other, relieving very distant and important stations on the main river. He thought that the useless station, and the useless men, could wait. Meantime Kayerts and Carlier lived on rice boiled without salt, and cursed the Company, all Africa, and the day they were born. One must have lived on such diet to discover what ghastly trouble the necessity of swallowing one's food may become. There was literally nothing else in the station but rice and coffee; they drank the coffee without sugar. The last fifteen lumps Kayerts had solemnly locked away in his box, together with a half-bottle of Cognac, "in case of sickness," he explained. Carlier approved. "When one is sick," he said, "any little extra like that is cheering."

They waited. Rank grass began to sprout over the courtyard. The bell never rang now. Days passed, silent, exasperating, and slow. When the two men spoke, they snarled; and their silences were bitter, as if tinged by the bitterness of their thoughts.

One day after a lunch of boiled rice, Carlier put down his cup untasted, and said: "Hang it all! Let's have a decent cup of coffee for once. Bring out that sugar, Kayerts!"

"For the sick," muttered Kayerts, without looking up.

"For the sick," mocked Carlier. "Bosh! . . . Well! I am sick."

"You are no more sick than I am, and I go without," said Kayerts in a peaceful tone.

"Come! out with that sugar, you stingy old slave-dealer."

Kayerts looked up quickly. Carlier was smiling with marked insolence. And suddenly it seemed to Kayerts that he had never seen that man before. Who was he? He knew nothing about him. What was he capable of? There was a surprising flash of violent emotion within him, as if in the presence of something undreamt-of, dangerous, and final. But he managed to pronounce with composure—

"That joke is in very bad taste. Don't repeat it."

"Joke!" said Carlier, hitching himself forward on his seat. "I am hungry—I am sick—I don't joke! I hate hypocrites. You are a hypocrite. You are a slave-dealer. I am a slave-dealer. There's nothing but slave-dealers in this cursed country. I mean to have sugar in my coffee to-day, anyhow!"

"I forbid you to speak to me in that way," said Kayerts with a fair show of resolution.

"You!—What?" shouted Carlier, jumping up.

Kayerts stood up also. "I am your chief," he began, trying to master the shakiness of his voice.

"What?" yelled the other. "Who's chief? There's no chief here.

There's nothing here: there's nothing but you and I. Fetch the sugar—you pot-bellied ass."

"Hold your tongue. Go out of this room," screamed Kayerts. "I dismiss you—you scoundrel!"

Carlier swung a stool. All at once he looked dangerously in earnest. "You flabby, good-for-nothing civilian—take that!" he howled.

Kayerts dropped under the table, and the stool struck the grass inner wall of the room. Then, as Carlier was trying to upset the table, Kayerts in desperation made a blind rush, head low, like a cornered pig would do, and over-turning his friend, bolted along the verandah, and into his room. He locked the door, snatched his revolver, and stood panting. In less than a minute Carlier was kicking at the door furiously, howling, "If you don't bring out that sugar, I will shoot you at sight, like a dog. Now then— one—two—three. You won't? I will show you who's the master."

Kayerts thought the door would fall in, and scrambled through the square hole that served for a window in his room. There was then the whole breadth of the house between them. But the other was apparently not strong enough to break in the door, and Kayerts heard him running round. Then he also began to run laboriously on his swollen legs. He ran as quickly as he could, grasping the revolver, and unable yet to understand what was happening to him. He saw in succession Makola's house, the store, the river, the ravine, and the low bushes; and he saw all those things again as he ran for the second time round the house. Then again they flashed past him. That morning he could not have walked a yard without a groan.

And now he ran. He ran fast enough to keep out of sight of the other man.

Then as, weak and desperate, he thought, "Before I finish the next round I shall die," he heard the other man stumble heavily, then stop. He stopped also. He had the back and Carlier the front of the house, as before. He heard him drop into a chair cursing, and suddenly his own legs gave way, and he slid down into a sitting posture with his back to the wall. His mouth was as dry as a cinder, and his face was wet with perspiration—and tears.

What was it all about? He thought it must be a horrible illusion; he thought he was dreaming; he thought he was going mad! After a while he collected his senses. What did they quarrel about? That sugar! How absurd! He would give it to him—didn't want it himself. And he began scrambling to his feet with a sudden feeling of security. But before he had fairly stood upright, a common-sense reflection occurred to him and drove him back into despair. He thought: "If I give way now to that brute of a soldier, he will begin this horror again to-morrow—and the day after—every day—raise other pretensions, trample on me, torture me, make me his slave—and I will be lost! Lost! The steamer may not come for days—may never come." He shook so that he had to sit down on the floor again. He shivered forlornly. He felt he could not, would not move any more. He was completely distracted by the sudden perception that the position was without issue—that death and life had in a moment become equally difficult and terrible.

All at once he heard the other push his chair back; and he leaped to his feet with extreme facility. He listened and got confused. Must run again! Right or left? He heard footsteps. He darted to the left, grasping his revolver, and at the very same instant, as it seemed to him, they came into violent collision. Both shouted with surprise. A loud explosion took place between them; a roar of red fire, thick smoke; and Kayerts, deafened and blinded, rushed back thinking: "I am hit—it's all over." He expected the other to come round—to gloat over his agony. He caught hold of an upright of the roof—"All over!" Then he heard a crashing fall on the other side of the house, as if somebody had tumbled headlong over a chair—then silence. Nothing more happened. He did not die. Only his shoulder felt as if it had been badly wrenched, and he had lost his revolver. He was disarmed and helpless! He waited for his fate. The other man made no sound. It was a stratagem. He was stalking him now! Along what side? Perhaps he was taking aim this very minute!

After a few moments of an agony frightful and absurd, he decided to go and meet his doom. He was prepared for every surrender. He turned the corner, steadying himself with one hand on the wall; made a few paces, and nearly swooned. He had seen on the floor, protruding past the other corner, a pair of turned-up feet. A pair of white naked feet in red slippers. He felt deadly sick, and stood for a time in profound darkness. Then Makola appeared before him, saying quietly: "Come along, Mr. Kayerts. He is dead." He burst into tears of gratitude; a loud, sobbing fit of crying. After a time he found himself sitting in a chair and looking at Carlier, who lay stretched on his back. Makola was kneeling over the body.

"Is this your revolver?" asked Makola, getting up.

"Yes," said Kayerts; then he added very quickly, "He ran after me to shoot me—you saw!"

"Yes, I saw," said Makola. "There is only one revolver; where's his?"

"Don't know," whispered Kayerts in a voice that had become suddenly very faint.

"I will go and look for it," said the other, gently. He made the round along the verandah, while Kayerts sat still and looked at the corpse. Makola came back empty-handed, stood in deep thought, then stepped quietly into the dead man's room, and came out directly with a revolver, which he held up before Kayerts. Kayerts shut his eyes. Everything was going round. He found life more terrible and difficult than death. He had shot an un-armed man.

After meditating for a while, Makola said softly, pointing at the dead man who lay there with his right eye blown out—

"He died of fever." Kayerts looked at him with a stony stare. "Yes," repeated Makola, thoughtfully, stepping over the corpse, "I think he died of fever. Bury him to-morrow."

And he went away slowly to his expectant wife, leaving the two white men alone on the verandah.

Night came, and Kayerts sat unmoving on his chair. He sat quiet as if he had taken a dose of opium. The violence of the emotions he had passed through produced a feeling of exhausted serenity. He had plumbed in one short afternoon the depths of horror and despair, and now found repose in the conviction that life had no more secrets for him: neither had death! He sat by the corpse thinking; thinking very actively, thinking very new thoughts. He seemed to have broken loose from himself altogether. His old thoughts, convictions, likes and dislikes, things he respected and things he abhorred, appeared in their true light at last! Appeared contemptible and childish, false and ridiculous. He revelled in his new wisdom while he sat by the man he had killed. He argued with himself about all things under heaven with that kind of wrong-headed lucidity which may be observed in some lunatics. Incidentally he reflected that the fellow dead there had been a noxious beast anyway; that men died every day in thousands; perhaps in hundreds of thousands—who could tell?— and that in the number, that one death could not possibly make any difference; couldn't have any importance, at least to a thinking creature. He, Kayerts, was a thinking creature. He had been all his life, till that moment, a believer in a lot of nonsense like the rest of mankind—who are fools; but now he thought! He knew! He was at peace; he was familiar with the highest wisdom! Then he tried to imagine himself dead, and Carlier sitting in his chair watching him; and his attempt met with such unexpected success, that in a very few moments he became not at all sure who was dead and who was alive. This extraordinary achievement of his fancy startled him, however, and by a clever and timely effort of mind he saved himself just in time from becoming Carlier. His heart thumped, and he felt hot all over at the thought of that danger. Carlier! What a beastly thing! To compose his now disturbed nerves—and no wonder!—he tried to whistle a little. Then, suddenly, he fell asleep, or thought he had slept; but at any rate there was a fog, and somebody had whistled in the fog.

He stood up. The day had come, and a heavy mist had descended upon the land: the mist penetrating, enveloping, and silent; the morning mist of tropical lands; the mist that clings and kills; the mist white and deadly, immaculate and poisonous. He stood up, saw the body, and threw his arms above his head with a cry like that of a man who, waking from a trance, finds himself immured forever in a tomb. "*Help! . . . My God!*"

A shriek inhuman, vibrating and sudden, pierced like a sharp dart the white shroud of that land of sorrow. Three short, impatient screeches followed, and then, for a time, the fog-wreaths rolled on, undisturbed, through a formidable silence. Then many more shrieks, rapid and piercing, like the yells of some exasperated and ruthless creature, rent the air. Progress was calling to Kayerts from the river. Progress and civilisation and all the virtues. Society was calling to its accomplished child to come, to be taken care of, to be instructed, to be judged, to be condemned; it called him to return to that rubbish heap from which he had wandered away, so that justice could be done.

Kayerts heard and understood. He stumbled out of the verandah, leaving the other man quite alone for the first time since they had been thrown there together. He groped his way through the fog, calling in his ignorance upon the invisible heaven to undo its work. Makola flitted by in the mist, shouting as he ran—

"Steamer! Steamer! They can't see. They whistle for the station. I go ring the bell. Go down to the landing, sir. I ring."

He disappeared. Kayerts stood still. He looked upwards; the fog rolled low over his head. He looked round like a man who has lost his way; and he saw a dark smudge, a cross-shaped stain, upon the shifting purity of the mist. As he began to stumble towards it, the station bell rang in a tumultuous peal its answer to the impatient clamour of the steamer.

THE MANAGING DIRECTOR of the Great Civilising Company (since we know that civilisation follows trade) landed first, and incontinently lost sight of the steamer. The fog down by the river was exceedingly dense; above, at the station, the bell rang unceasing and brazen.

The Director shouted loudly to the steamer:

"There is nobody down to meet us; there may be something wrong, though they are ringing. You had better come, too!"

And he began to toil up the steep bank. The captain and the engine-driver of the boat followed behind. As they scrambled up the fog thinned, and they could see their Director a good way ahead. Suddenly they saw him start forward, calling to them over his shoulder:—"Run! Run to the house! I've found one of them. Run, look for the other!"

He had found one of them! And even he, the man of varied and startling experience, was somewhat discomposed by the manner of this finding. He stood and fumbled in his pockets (for a knife) while he faced Kayerts, who was hanging by a leather strap from the cross. He had evidently climbed the grave, which was high and narrow, and after tying the end of the strap to the arm, had swung himself off. His toes were only a couple of inches above the ground; his arms hung stiffly down; he seemed to be standing rigidly at attention, but with one purple cheek playfully posed on the shoulder. And, irreverently, he was putting out a swollen tongue at his Managing Director.

Victorians and Africans

The Genealogy of the Myth of the Dark Continent

PATRICK BRANTLINGER

♦   ♦   ♦

IN *HEART OF DARKNESS*, Marlow says that Africa is no longer the "blank space" on the map that he had once daydreamed over. "It had got filled since my boyhood with rivers and lakes and names.... It had become a place of darkness."[1] Marlow is right: Africa grew "dark" as Victorian explorers, missionaries, and scientists flooded it with light, because the light was refracted through an imperialist ideology that urged the abolition of "savage customs" in the name of civilization. As a product of that ideology, the myth of the Dark Continent developed during the transition from the main British campaign against the slave trade, which culminated in the outlawing of slavery in all British territory in 1833, to the imperialist partitioning of Africa which dominated the final quarter of the nineteenth century.

The transition from the altruism of the antislavery movement to the cynicism of empire building involved a transvaluation of values that might be appropriately described in the genealogical language of Michel Foucault. Edward Said's Foucauldian analysis in *Orientalism*, based on a theory of discourse as strategies of power and subjection, inclusion and exclusion, the voiced and the silenced, suggests the kind of approach I am taking here. For middle- and upper-class Victorians, dominant over a vast working-class majority at home and over increasing millions of "uncivilized" peoples of "inferior" races abroad, power was self-validating. There might be many stages of social evolution and many seemingly bizarre customs and "superstitions" in the world, but there was only one "civilization," one path of "progress," one "true religion." "Anarchy" was many-tongued; "culture" spoke with one voice. Said writes of "the power of culture by virtue of its elevated or superior position to authorize, to dominate, to legitimate, demote, interdict, and validate: in short, the power of culture to be an agent of, and perhaps the main agency for, powerful differentiation within its domain and beyond it too." At home, culture might often seem threatened by anarchy: through Chartism, trade unionism, and socialism, the alternative voices of the working class could at least be heard by anyone who cared to listen. Abroad, the culture of the "conquering race" seemed unchallenged: in imperialist discourse the voices of the dominated are represented almost entirely by their silence, their absence. If Said is right that "the critic is responsible to a degree for articulating those voices dominated, displaced, or silenced" by the authority of a dominant culture, the place to begin is with a critique of that culture. This, according to Foucault, is the function of "genealogy," which seeks to analyze "the various systems of subjection: not the anticipatory power of meaning, but the hazardous play of dominations."[2]

Paradoxically, abolitionism contained the seeds of empire. If we accept the general outline of Eric Williams' thesis in *Capitalism and Slavery* that abolition was not purely altruistic but was as economically conditioned as Britain's later empire building in Africa, the contradiction between the ideologies of antislavery and imperialism seems more apparent than real. Although the idealism that motivated the great abolitionists such as William Wilberforce and Thomas Clarkson is unquestionable, Williams argues that Britain could *afford* to legislate against the slave trade only after that trade had helped to provide the surplus capital necessary for industrial "take-off." Britain had lost much of its slave-owning territory as a result of the American Revolution; as the leading industrial power in the world, Britain found in abolition a way to work against the interests of its rivals who were still heavily involved in colonial slavery and a plantation economy.[3]

The British abolitionist program entailed deeper and deeper involvement in Africa—the creation of Sierra Leone as a haven for freed slaves was just a start—but British abolitionists before the 1840s were neither jingoists nor deliberate expansionists. Humanitarianism applied to Africa, however, did point insistently toward imperialism.[4] By mid-century, the success of the antislavery movement, the impact of the great Victorian explorers, and the merger of racist and evolutionary doctrines in the social sciences had combined to give the British public a widely shared view of Africa that demanded imperialization on moral, religious, and scientific grounds. It is this view that I have called the myth of the Dark Continent; by mythology I mean a form of modern, secularized, "depoliticized speech" (to adopt Roland Barthes' phrase)—discourse which treats its subject as universally accepted, scientifically established, and therefore no longer open to criticism by a political or theoretical opposition. In *The Idea of Race in Science: Great Britain, 1800–1960*, Nancy Stepan writes:

> A fundamental question about the history of racism in the first half of the nineteenth century is why it was that, just as the battle against slavery was being won by abolitionists, the war against racism was being lost. The Negro was legally freed by the Emancipation Act of 1833, but in the British mind he was still mentally, morally and physically a slave.[5]

It is this "fundamental question" which a genealogy of the myth of the Dark Continent can help to answer.

1

From the 1790s to the 1840s, the most influential kind of writing about Africa was abolitionist propaganda (see fig. 1). Most of the great Romantics wrote poems against what William Wordsworth

FIG. 1 Typical of abolitionist propaganda were the
publications of the Leeds Anti-Slavery Society.

in *The Prelude* called "the traffickers in Negro blood." William
Blake's "Little Black Boy" is probably the most familiar of these:

> My mother bore me in the southern wild,
> And I am black, but O! my soul is white;
> White as an angel is the English child;
> But I am black as if bereav'd of light.[6]

To Blake's poem can be added Coleridge's "Greek Prize Ode on
the Slave Trade," Wordsworth's "Sonnet to Thomas Clarkson,"
and a number of stanzas and poems by both Byron and Shelley.
Several of Robert Southey's poems deal with the slave trade, including the final stanza of his poem "To Horror":

> Horror! I call thee yet once more!
> Bear me to that accursed shore,
> Where on the stake the Negro writhes.[7]

Quite apart from the similarity between Southey's "Dark Horror"
and Conrad's "The horror! The horror!" a century later, I want
to make two main points about the literature of the antislavery
tradition.[8]

First, antislavery writing involves the revelation of atrocities.
Simon Legree's beating Uncle Tom to death is only the most
familiar example. Abolitionist propaganda depicted in excruciating
detail the barbaric practices of slave traders and owners in Africa,
during the infamous middle passage, and in the southern states
and West Indies. The constant association of Africa with the inhuman violence of the slave trade, of course, did much to darken
its landscape even during the Romantic period. The exposé style
of abolitionist propaganda, moreover, influenced much British
writing about Africa well after slavery had ceased to be an urgent
issue. Though not directly about slavery, an exposé purpose is
evident in *Heart of Darkness* and also, for example, in Olive Schreiner's fictional diatribe against Cecil Rhodes, *Trooper Peter Halket of
Mashonaland* (1897). The frontispiece to Schreiner's novel is a photograph showing white Rhodesians with three lynched Mashona

FIG. 2 Frontispiece, Olive Schreiner, *Trooper Peter Halket of Mashonaland,*
1897.

rebels—unfortunately a summary of much of the history of
southern Africa (fig. 2).

The second main point about antislavery literature is that the
Romantics, unlike the Victorians, were able to envisage Africans
living freely and happily without European interference. Strike
off the fetters which European slavers had placed on them, and
the result was a vision of noble savages living in pastoral freedom
and innocence (see fig. 3). In sonnet 5 of Southey's "Poems concerning the Slave Trade," a slave's rebelliousness is inspired by

> the intolerable thought
> Of every past delight; his native grove,
> Friendship's best joys, and liberty and love
> For ever lost.[9]

Similarly, in "Africa Delivered; or, The Slave Trade Abolished"
(1809), James Grahame writes:

FIG. 3 A typical Edenic African scene, with a slave ship approaching. James Montgomery, James Grahame, and E. Benger, *Poems on
the Abolition of the Slave Trade*, 1809.

In that fair land of hill, and dale, and stream,
The simple tribes from age to age had heard
No hostile voice

—until the arrival of the European slave traders, who introduced to an Edenic Africa those characteristic products of civilization: avarice, treachery, rapine, murder, warfare, and slavery.[10]

Abolitionist portrayals of Africans as perhaps noble but also innocent or "simple" savages were patronizing and unintentionally derogatory. Nevertheless, portrayals of Africans between 1800 and the 1830s were often both more positive and more openminded than those of later years. In saying so, I am slightly extending the period of relative objectivity noted by Katherine George, who argues that accounts of Africa from Herodotus to about 1700 tend to be highly prejudicial but that with the Enlightenment arose new standards of objectivity.[11] Ironically, the expansion of the slave trade itself from the 1600s on meant that Europeans had to develop more accurate knowledge of Africans— both those Africans with whom they did business and those who became their commodities. Many factors contributed to what George sees as a golden age of accuracy and lack of prejudice in writing about Africa; among these were the satiric tradition of the noble savage, turned to effective popular use by Aphra Behn in *Oroonoko; or, the Royal Slave* (1688) and later by many abolitionists; the Enlightenment belief that all people should be treated equally under the law; the growth of the abolitionist movement; and the exploration of the Niger River by Mungo Park and others, starting in the late 1700s. This period of relative objectivity did not end in 1800 but continued well into the nineteenth century, as evidenced by the abolitionist poetry of Southey and Grahame and by such works of social observation as Thomas Bowdich's *Mission from Cape Coast Castle to Ashantee* (1819). Bowdich condemned the Ashanti practice of ritual human sacrifice, but he did not treat that aspect of their culture as representative of the whole, nor did he allow it to interfere with his appreciation for other Ashanti customs, arts, and institutions.[12]

The abolition of slavery in all British territories did not eliminate concern about slavery elsewhere, but the British began to see themselves less and less as perpetrators of the slave trade and more and more as the potential saviors of the African. The blame for slavery could now be displaced onto others—onto Americans, for example. Blame was increasingly displaced onto Africans themselves for maintaining the slave trade as a chief form of economic exchange. This shifting of the burden of guilt is already evident in the Niger Expedition of 1841, "the first step toward a general 'forward policy' in West Africa."[13] Thomas Fowell Buxton, leader of the British antislavery movement after Wilberforce, recognized that the emancipation legislation of 1833 would not eliminate slavery from non-British parts of the world. He therefore proposed to attack slavery at its source, planning the Niger Expedition as a first step toward the introduction of Christianity and "legitimate commerce" to west Africa. In *The African Slave Trade and Its Remedy* (1840), Buxton portrays Africa as a land "teeming with inhabitants who admire, and are desirous of possessing our manufactures."[14] In the past, Africans had learned to trade in human lives; in the future, they must learn to produce something other than slaves. The British would teach them to be both religious and industrious.

Although Buxton repudiated empire building, the Niger Expedition aimed to establish bases from which European values could be spread throughout Africa. Buxton's portrayal of Africa is almost wholly negative: "Bound in the chains of the grossest ignorance, [Africa] is a prey to the most savage superstition. Christianity has made but feeble inroads on this kingdom of darkness" (*A*, pp. 10–11). In a chapter entitled "Superstitions and Cruelties of the Africans," Buxton anticipates many later writers who also seek to show the necessity for increased intervention in Africa: he extracts the most grisly descriptions of such customs as human sacrifice from the writings of Bowdich and others and offers these as the essence of African culture. Buxton's "dark catalogue of crime" combines slavery and savagery; both are seen as disrupting Africa's chances for civilization and salvation (*A*, p. 270). "Such atrocious deeds, as have been detailed in the foregoing pages, keep the African population in a state of callous barbarity, which can only be effectually counteracted by Christian civilisation" (*A* p. 244).

The Niger Expedition ended in disaster when most of its European participants were laid low by malaria, forty-one of them dying. For at least a decade, its failure supported arguments that Europeans should stay out of central Africa; the harsh facts of disease and death themselves contributed to the darkening of the Dark Continent. In his essay on the Niger Expedition (1848), Charles Dickens attacked the aims of philanthropists like Buxton and decried Africa as a continent not fit for civilization—one best left in the dark.

> The history of this Expedition is the history of the Past [rather than the future] in reference to the heated visions of philanthropists for the railroad Christianisation of Africa, and the abolition of the Slave Trade. . . . Between the civilized European and the barbarous African there is a great gulf set. . . . To change the customs even of civilised . . . men . . . is . . . a most difficult and slow proceeding; but to do this by ignorant and savage races, is a work which, like the progressive changes of the globe itself, requires a stretch of years that dazzles in the looking at.[15]

In *Bleak House*, Dickens' placement of Mrs. Jellyby's Borrioboola-Gha mission on the banks of the Niger suggests its utter and absurd futility, like that of the Niger Expedition. In his occasional rantings against "natives," "Sambos," and "ignoble savages," Dickens also vents his hostility toward evangelical philanthropy. He regarded missionaries as "perfect nuisances who leave every place worse than they find it." "Believe it, African Civilisation, Church of England Missionary, and all other Missionary Societies!" he writes. "The work at home must be completed thoroughly, or there is no hope abroad."[16] This was also Thomas Carlyle's attitude in "The Nigger Question" (1849) and again in his response to the rebellion in Jamaica in 1865. According to both Carlyle and Dickens, abolitionist and missionary activities were distractions from more appropriate concerns about poverty and mis-government at home.

As the Governor Eyre Controversy of 1865 showed, many Victorians (including Carlyle and Dickens) sympathized with the poor at home but not with the exploited abroad. Thus, a sizable portion of the Victorian public sided with the South during the American Civil War. Slavery, however, remained an important issue from the 1840s to the end of the century. Slavery is central, for example, to an 1847 novel by Sarah Lee Wallis (whose first husband was Thomas Bowdich), *The African Wanderers*, in which "from one end of Africa to the other we find traces of that horrible traffic." Some of Wallis's "natives" are restless and hostile because they are cannibals "who file their teeth" and lust after human flesh, but more are restless and hostile because their normally pacific lives have been disrupted by the slave trade. When *Uncle Tom's Cabin* appeared in 1852, moreover, it sold more copies in England than in America.[17] One of Harriet Beecher Stowe's most ardent English admirers, Elizabeth Barrett Browning, also contributed to the abolitionist cause with her poems "The Runaway Slave at Pilgrim's Point" and "A Curse for a Nation." Following the Civil War, slavery seemed largely confined to Africa; along with such staples of sensationalist journalism as human sacrifice and cannibalism, slavery looked more and more like a direct extension of African savagery.

After abolishing slavery on their own ground, the British turned to the seemingly humane work of abolishing slavery—and all "savage customs"—on African ground. By the time of the Berlin Conference of 1884, which is often taken as the start of the "scramble for Africa," the British tended to see Africa as a center of evil, a part of the world possessed by a demonic "darkness" or barbarism, represented above all by slavery and cannibalism, which it was their duty to exorcise. The writers most responsible for promoting this point of view—and for maintaining the crusade against the slave trade even after both Britain and the United States were well out of it—were the explorers and missionaries, with Buxton's disciple David Livingstone in the lead.

2

The so-called opening up of Africa by the great Victorian explorers commenced in the late 1850s, facilitated by quinine as a
prophylactic against malaria. Earlier explorers had excited public
interest, but the search for the sources of the White Nile—initi-
ated by Richard Burton and John Speke in 1856 and followed up
by the expeditions of Speke and James Grant, Samuel White
Baker, Livingstone, and Henry Stanley—raised British interest to
a new level. As headline, best-selling reading, the "penetration"
of Africa provided a narrative fascination that has been likened
to excitement about space exploration today.[18] When Alec
MacKenzie, the hero of William Somerset Maugham's *Explorer*
(1907), begins "to read the marvellous records of African exploration," his "blood tingled at the magic of those pages." Inspired
by the journals of Burton, Livingstone, and Stanley, MacKenzie
becomes an explorer who struggles mightily against savagery and
the internal slave trade (not to mention European villainy) and
who thus contributes mightily to imperial expansion. Maugham
offers a fictional hagiography of all the great explorers of Africa,
"men who've built up the empire piece by piece" and whose chief
aim has been to add "another fair jewel to her crown." If the
connection between exploration and empire building was not always evident to MacKenzie's originals, it is paramount for
Maugham: "Success rewarded [MacKenzie's] long efforts. . . . The
slavers were driven out of a territory larger than the United Kingdom, treaties were signed with chiefs who had hitherto been independent . . . and only one step remained, that the government
should . . . annex the conquered district to the empire."[19]

The books that the explorers wrote took the Victorian reading
public by storm. In the first few months after its publication in
1857, Livingstone's *Missionary Travels* sold seventy thousand copies
and made its author wealthy and so famous that he had to avoid
situations where he might be mobbed by admirers. If Livingstone
was already a national hero in the late 1850s, he was a national
saint by the time of his last African journey in 1872. The obverse

side of the myth of the Dark Continent was that of the Promethean and, at least in Livingstone's case, saintly bestower of light (see fig. 4). Even Dickens, with his dislike of evangelical types, made an exception of Livingstone, calling him one of those who "carry into desert places the water of life."[20] Livingstone's apotheosis was complete in 1872 when Stanley, with his great journalistic scoop, published his first bestseller, *How I Found Livingstone*. Stanley's other books were also bestsellers: *In Darkest Africa*, for example, sold one hundred and fifty thousand copies in English, was frequently translated, and, according to one reviewer, "has been read more universally and with deeper interest than any

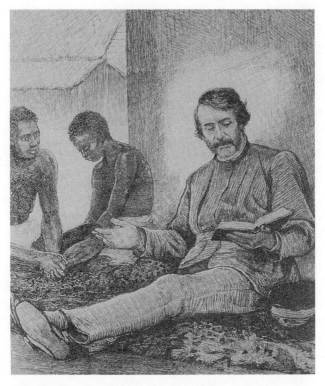

FIG. 4 Livingstone as a saint, carrying the light of Christianity into the Dark Continent. William Garden Blaikie, *The Personal Life of David Livingstone*, 1880.

other publication of" 1890.[21] Still another best-seller was Baker's *Albert N'yanza* of 1866; many others were widely read, including Burton's *Lake Regions of Central Africa* (1861), Speke's *Discovery of the Source of the Nile* (1864), Joseph Thomson's *To the Central African Lakes and Back* (1881), and so on. Although these titles do not figure in standard histories of Victorian literature, such accounts of African exploration exerted an incalculable influence on British culture and the course of modern history. It would be difficult to find a clearer example of the Foucauldian concept of discourse as power or as "a violence that we do to things."[22]

The great explorers' writings are nonfictional quest romances in which the hero-authors struggle through enchanted or bedeviled lands toward a goal, ostensibly the discovery of the Nile's sources or the conversion of the cannibals. But that goal also turns out to include sheer survival and the return home, to the regions of light. These humble but heroic authors move from adventure to adventure against a dark, infernal backdrop where there are no other characters of equal stature—only bewitched or demonic savages. Although they sometimes individualize their portraits of Africans, explorers usually portray them as amusing or dangerous obstacles or as objects of curiosity, while missionaries usually portray Africans as weak, pitiable, inferior mortals who need to be shown the light. Center stage is occupied not by Africa or Africans but by a Livingstone or a Stanley, a Baker or a Burton—Victorian Saint Georges battling the armies of the night. Kurtz's career in devilry suggests that, on at least some occasions or in some ways, it was a losing battle.

Livingstone offers a striking example of how humanitarian aims could contribute to imperialist encroachment. Deeply influenced by Buxton, Livingstone also advocated the "opening up" of Africa by "commerce and Christianity." He had more respect for Africans than most explorers and missionaries, though he still viewed them as "children" and "savages." Occasionally he even expressed doubt that a European presence in Africa would be beneficial, but he also believed that the African was "benighted" and that the European was the bearer of the "light" of civilization and true religion. He held that Africa would be without hope of "raising itself" unless there was "contact with superior races by commerce." Africans were "inured to bloodshed and murder, and care[d] for no god except being bewitched"; without "commerce and Christianity," "the prospects for these dark regions are not bright." Tim Jeal writes of this most humanitarian of explorers that "with his missionary aims and his almost messianic passion for exporting British values [Livingstone] seemed to his successors to have provided the moral basis for massive imperial expansion."[23]

Economic and political motives are, of course, easier to detect in Livingstone's doppelgänger, Stanley. The purpose behind his work in the Congo for King Leopold II of Belgium was not far removed from the aims of the Eldorado Exploring Expedition in *Heart of Darkness*: "To tear treasure out of the bowels of the land was their desire, with no more moral purpose at the back of it than there is in burglars breaking into a safe" (*HD*, p. 31). But that sort of blatant economic motive was not what impelled Livingstone and the horde of missionaries who imitated him. The melodrama of Africa called for intervention by a higher moral power, and the Victorians increasingly saw themselves—again, with Livingstone in the lead—as the highest moral power among nations. The success of the British antislavery movement, after all, seemed to prove that Britain was more virtuous than its rivals for empire. For Livingstone, as for other missionaries and abolitionists, the African was a creature to be pitied, to be saved from slavery, and also to be saved from his own "darkness," his "savagery." At least Livingstone believed that the African could be rescued from "darkness"—that he could be Christianized and perhaps civilized. This attitude was, of course, necessary for any missionary activity. At the same time, missionaries were strongly tempted to exaggerate "savagery" and "darkness" in order to rationalize their presence in Africa, to explain the frustrations they experienced in making converts, and to win support from mission societies at home.[24]

Typical missionary attitudes are suggested by such titles as *Daybreak in the Dark Continent*, by Wilson S. Naylor, and *Dawn in the Dark Continent; or, Africa and Its Missions*, by James Stewart. Typical, too, are these assertions from *By the Equator's Snowy Peak* (1913), May Crawford's autobiography about missionary life in Kenya: "With the coming of the British," she says, "dawned a somewhat brighter" day for Kenya. It is only "somewhat brighter" because of the great backwardness of the natives, not because of any failing by the British. "Loving darkness rather than light," she continues, the "natives" "resent all that makes for progress."[25] Perhaps what the Kenyans resented was the British intrusion into their country, but this Crawford could not see. I have read of no instances where cannibals put missionaries into pots and cooked them, but Africans did sometimes kill, capture, or drive missionaries away from their lands, thus fueling arguments for armed intervention and imperialist annexation.[26] In Anthony Hope's novel *The God in the Car* (1895), Lord Semingham is asked how his great scheme for investing in central Africa is faring. "Everything's going on very well," he replies. "They've killed a missionary." This may be "regrettable in itself," Semingham smiles, "but [it's] the first step towards empire."[27]

The missionary idea that Africa could be redeemed for civilization was more than some explorers were willing to grant. Burton believed that the African was "unimprovable":

He is inferior to the active-minded and objective . . . Europeans, and to the . . . subjective and reflective Asiatic. He partakes largely of the worst characteristics of the lower Oriental types—stagnation of mind, indolence of body, moral deficiency, superstition, and childish passion.[28]

Burton goes to some trouble to undermine the missionary point of view. He declares that "these wild African fetissists [*sic*] are [not] easily converted to a 'purer creed.' . . . Their faith is a web woven with threads of iron." At the same time, Burton agrees with the missionaries when he depicts fetishism as witchcraft and devil worship, Kurtz's "unspeakable rites." "A prey to base passions and melancholy godless fears, the Fetissist . . . peoples with malevolent beings the invisible world, and animates material nature with evil influences. The rites of his dark and deadly superstition" are entirely nefarious, as almost all Victorian writers claimed.[29] In their books and essays on the Dark Continent, the Victorians demote all central African kings to "chiefs" and all African priests (with the exception of Muslims) to "witch doctors" (see fig. 5).

Even if Africans are doomed by their "negro instincts" always to remain "savage," Burton still has a role in mind for them in the work of civilization. Like Carlyle, Burton argues both that abolitionist philanthropy is mistaken and that primitive peoples need civilized masters. His argument is explicitly imperialist:

> I unhesitatingly assert—and all unprejudiced travellers will agree with me—that the world still wants the black hand. Enormous tropical regions yet await the clearing and draining operations by the lower races, which will fit them to become the dwelling-places of civilized man.[30]

Other explorers agreed with Burton. Though a hero in the late stages of the antislavery crusade, Baker believed that "the African . . . will assuredly relapse into an idle and savage state, unless specially governed and forced by industry."[31]

Burton was a marginal aristocrat and Baker came from a well-to-do family of shipowners and West Indian planters. Their racist view of Africans as a natural laboring class, suited only for performing the dirty work of civilization, expresses a nostalgia for lost authority and for a pliable, completely subordinate proletariat that is one of the central fantasies of imperialism. For opposite reasons, that fantasy also appealed to explorers from working-class backgrounds like Livingstone and Stanley: their subordinate status at home was reversed in Africa. Livingstone the factory boy could be Livingstone the great white leader and teacher in Africa, and Stanley the pauper orphan could be Stanley the great pioneer and field marshal, blazing the trail for civilization.

That Africans were suited only for manual labor is an idea often repeated in fiction. In Henry Merriman's *With Edged Tools* (1894), for example, African porters "hired themselves out like animals, and as the beasts of the field they did their work—patiently, without intelligence. . . . Such is the African." The com-

FIG. 5 A typical portrayal of African religion as idol or devil worship. Herbert Ward, *Five Years with the Congo Cannibals*,
1890.

parison with British labor is made explicit when the narrator adds:
"If any hold that men are not created so dense and unambitious
as has just been represented, let him look nearer home in our
own merchant service. The able-bodied seaman goes to sea all his
life, but he never gets any nearer navigating the ship—and he a
white man." The English protagonists are shocked to discover
that the Africans who work for their villainous half-breed partner
are his slaves, to whom he pays no wages. Slavery by the 1890s
was patently a violation of "one of Heaven's laws."[32] But when

the English offer the Africans the choice between freedom and continuing in slavery, most of them choose slavery. Merriman implies that Africans are not suited for freedom, though he leaves cloudy the issue of whether they can ever be elevated to freedom or are genetically doomed to a life no higher than that of beasts of burden.

Racism often functions as a displaced or surrogate class system, growing more extreme as the domestic class alignments it reflects are threatened or erode. As a rationalization for the domination of "inferior" peoples, imperialist discourse is inevitably racist; it treats class and race terminology as covertly interchangeable or at least analogous. Both a hierarchy of classes and a hierachy of races exist; both are the results of evolution or of the laws of nature; both are simpler than but similar to species; and both are developing but are also, at any given moment, fixed, inevitable, not subject to political manipulation. Varieties of liberalism and socialism might view social class as more or less subject to political reform, and in that way the hierarchy of classes never seemed so absolute as the hierarchy of races. Further, while the "social im-perialism" of Joseph Chamberlain offered itself as an alternative to socialism, the spectacle of the domination of "inferior races" abroad also served to allay anxieties about both democratization and economic decline at home.

As in South Africa, the "conquered races" of the empire were often treated as a new proletariat—a proletariat much less distinct from slaves than the working class at home. Of course, the desire for and, in many places, creation of a new, subordinate underclass contradicted the abolitionist stance that all the explorers took. Nevertheless, it influenced all relations between Victorians and Africans, appearing, for example, in the forced labor system of King Leopold's Congo which Stanley helped establish or again in so small an item as Sir Harry Johnston's design for the first post-age stamp of British Central Africa (fig. 6). The Africans who flank the shield and the motto Light in Darkness hold a spade and a pickax—the implements, no doubt, to build the future *white* civ-ilization of Africa.[33]

Fig. 6 Sir Harry H. Johnston's design for the first postage stamp of British Central Africa. Roland Oliver, *Sir Harry H. Johnston and the Scramble for Africa*, courtesy of the Royal Geographical Society.

3

The racist views held by Burton and Baker were at least as close to the science of their day as the somewhat less negative views of the missionaries. As a member of James Hunt's Anthropological Society, Burton was a scientist of sorts. Hunt had founded his group in 1863, after breaking with the Ethnological Society on the issue of whether the Negro race formed a distinct species.[34] Hunt believed that it did; the Darwinians, in contrast, held that the races of mankind had a common origin and therefore supported ideas of the unity of human nature. But Darwinism was only relatively more advanced than Hunt's racism. The development of physical anthropology and of "ethnology" as disciplines concerned with differences between races was reinforced from the 1860s on by Darwinism and social Darwinism; these "sciences" strengthened the stereotypes voiced by explorers and missionaries. Evolutionary anthropology often suggested that Africans, if not nonhuman or a different species, were such an inferior "breed" that they might be impervious to "higher influences."

Just as concerted investigations of race and evolution were beginning, so were investigations of prehistory and of the anthropoid apes. Some of the results can be seen in Charles Darwin's *Descent of Man* (1872) and earlier in Thomas Henry Huxley's *Man's Place in Nature* (1863). Huxley's essay involves a refutation of the idea that Africans, Australians, or other primitive peoples are the "missing link" or evolutionary stage between the anthropoid apes and civilized (white) mankind. But Huxley repeatedly cites evidence that suggests the proximity between the African and the chimpanzee and gorilla, including the story of an African tribe who believe that the great apes were once their next of kin. Into the middle of his otherwise logical argument, moreover, he inserts a wholly gratuitous note on "African cannibalism in the sixteenth century," drawn from a Portuguese account and illustrated with a grisly woodcut depicting a "human butcher shop" (fig. 7).[35]

FIG. 7 "The human butcher shop." Thomas Henry Huxley, *Man's Place in Nature*, 1863.

When an astute, scientific observer such as Huxley indulges in fantasies about cannibalism, something is at work on a level deeper than mere caprice. As Dorothy Hammond and Alta Jablow note, cannibalism was not an important theme in British writing about Africa before mid-century. But "in the imperial period writers were far more addicted to tales of cannibalism than . . . Africans ever were to cannibalism." Typical of the more sensational treatments of anthropophagy is Winwood Reade, who in *Savage Africa* (1863) writes that "the mob of Dahomey are *man-eaters*, they have cannibal minds; they have been accustomed to feed on murder." Reade nonetheless describes his flirtations with "cannibal" maidens, and in a capricious chapter on "The Philosophy of Cannibalism," he distinguishes between ritual cannibalism, which was practiced by some west African societies, and another (mythical) sort which is "simply an act of *gourmandise*." "A cannibal is not necessarily ferocious. He eats his fellow-creatures, not because he hates them, but because he likes them."[36] The more that Europeans dominated Africans, the more "savage" Africans came to seem; cannibalism represented the nadir of savagery, more extreme even than slavery (which, of course, a number of "civilized" nations practiced through much of the nineteenth century).

Evolutionary thought seems almost calculated to legitimize imperialism. The theory that man evolved through distinct social stages—from savagery to barbarism to civilization—led to a self-congratulatory anthropology that actively promoted belief in the inferiority—indeed, the bestiality—of the African. In *The Origin of Civilisation* (1870), John Lubbock argues not just that contemporary "savages" represent the starting point of social evolution but that they are below that starting point. The original primitives from whom Europeans evolved contained the seeds of progress; modern savages had not progressed, according to Lubbock, and hence must be lower on the evolutionary scale than the ancestors of the Europeans. All the more reason, of course, to place them under imperial guardianship and to treat them as nothing more than potential labor.[37] The connection between theories of race and social class appears in George Romanes' *Mental Evolution in Man* (1889):

When we come to consider the case of savages, and through
them the case of pre-historic man, we shall find that, in the
great interval which lies between such grades of mental evolution and our own, we are brought far on the way towards
bridging the psychological distance which separates the gorilla
from the gentleman.[38]

Presumably, everyone is a link somewhere in this late Victorian
version of the great chain of being: if gentlemen are at the farthest
remove from our anthropoid ancestors, the working class is not
so far removed, and "savages" are even closer.

In her examination of the "scientific" codification of racist dog-
mas, Stepan writes:

By the 1850s, the shift from the earlier ethnographic, mono-
genist, historical and philosophical tradition to a more conservative, anthropological, and polygenist approach . . . had advanced quite far in Britain. . . . Races were now seen as forming
a natural but static chain of excellence.[39]

By the end of the century, eugenicists and social Darwinists were
offering "scientific" justifications for genocide as well as for imperialism. The two were inseparable, but whereas imperialism
could be lavishly praised in public, open support for the liqui-
dation of "inferior" races was another matter. In *Social Evolution*
(1894), Benjamin Kidd argued that, try as they might to be humane, the British would inevitably kill off the "weaker" races in
"the struggle for existence":

The Anglo-Saxon has exterminated the less developed peoples
with which he has come into competition . . . through the op-
eration of laws not less deadly [than war] and even more certain in their result. The weaker races disappear before the
stronger through the effects of mere contact . . . The Anglo-
Saxon, driven by forces inherent in his own civilisation, comes
to develop the natural resources of the land, and the consequences appear to be inevitable. The same history is repeating

itself in South Africa. In the words [of] a leading colonist of that country, "the natives must go; or they must work as laboriously to develop the land as we are prepared to do."[40]

Similarly, in *National Life from the Standpoint of Science* (1901), the eugenicist Karl Pearson goes beyond the vision of the black African with spade or pickax performing the groundwork for white civilization in the tropics: "No strong and permanent civilization can be built upon slave labour, [and] an inferior race doing menial labour for a superior race can give no stable community." The solution? Where the abolitionists sought to liberate the slaves, Pearson's "science" seeks to eliminate them or at least push them out of the path of civilization:

> We shall never have a healthy social state in South Africa until the white man replaces the dark in the fields and the mines, and the Kaffir is pushed back towards the equator. The nation organized for the struggle [of existence] must be a *homogeneous* whole, not a mixture of superior and inferior races.[41]

Darwin himself speculated about the causes of the apparently inevitable extinction of primitive races in the encounter with "higher" ones. Genocide decimated the American Indians, Tasmanians, Maoris, and Australians, but Darwin believed that they would have withered on the vine anyway—the less fit races vanishing as the more fit advanced. The Africans did not dwindle away as Europeans encroached on their territory, despite the slave trade; this seemed to some observers proof of their hardiness, their fitness. But to some this apparent fitness only showed the Africans' inferiority in a different light—they were made of coarser stuff from that of the sensitive and poetic Maoris, for example. Darwin is comparatively cautious in his speculations about race. Nevertheless, throughout *The Descent of Man* he emphasizes the distance between "savage" and "civilized" peoples, contrasting "savages" who practice infanticide to types of moral and intellectual excellence like John Howard, the eighteenth-century prison reformer, and Shakespeare. In the last paragraph, he declares that he would rather be related to a baboon than to "a savage who delights to torture his enemies, offers up bloody sacrifices without remorse, treats his wives like slaves, knows no decency, and is haunted by the grossest superstitions."[42] In general, Darwinism lent scientific status to the view that there were higher and lower races, progressive and nonprogressive ones, and that the lower races ought to be governed by—or even completely supplanted by—civilized, progressive races like the British.

There is much irony in the merger of racist and evolutionary theories in Victorian anthropology, which was, in certain respects, the first scientific anthropology. For the Victorians, the distance between primitive and civilized peoples seemed immense, perhaps unbridgeable. But through another sharp transvaluation, anthropology in the modern era has shifted from evolutionism to cultural relativism. First in the work of Franz Boas, and then more generally after World War I, the morally judgmental and racist anthropology of the Victorians gave way to a new version of "objectivity" or even of what might be called scientific primitivism.[43] What Claude Lévi-Strauss has to say in *Tristes Tropiques* about the religious attitudes of "primitives" is exemplary of the transvaluation that anthropology has undergone since its nineteenth-century inception as the study of racial differences and a form of scientific rationalization for empire. Their beliefs are not "superstitions," he declares, but rather "preferences . . . denoting a kind of wisdom [acceptance of individual and ecological limits, reverence for nature] which savage races practised spontaneously and the rejection of which, by the modern world, is the real madness."[44]

4

While the antislavery crusade inspired much poetry before 1833, Victorian poets wrote little about Africa except for patriotic verses on topics such as General Charles Gordon's last stand at Khartoum. Alfred, Lord Tennyson's "Timbuctoo" is perhaps an exception, but it was written in 1829 for a Cambridge poetry contest, and it offers a Romantic account of how the visionary city of Fable has been "darkened" by "keen Discovery" (a paradoxical application of "darken" similar to Marlow's). More typical of later Victorian attitudes is William Makepeace Thackeray's "Timbuctoo," written for the same contest that Tennyson's poem won. Thackeray produced a parody of abolitionist propaganda:

> Desolate Afric! thou art lovely yet!!
> One heart yet beats which ne'er shall thee forget.
> What though thy maidens are a blackish brown,
> Does virtue dwell in whiter breasts alone?
> Oh no, oh no, oh no, oh no, oh no!
> It shall not, must not, cannot, e'er be so.
> The day shall come when Albion's self shall feel
> Stern Afric's wrath, and writhe 'neath Afric's steel.[45]

Other far-flung parts of the world inspired the Victorian muse— Edward FitzGerald's *Rubáiyát of Omar Khayyám* and Edwin Arnold's *Light of Asia* come to mind—but Victorian imaginative discourse about Africa tended toward the vaguely discredited forms of the gothic romance and the boys' adventure story. For the most part, fiction writers imitated the explorers, producing quest romances with gothic overtones in which the heroic white penetration of the Dark Continent is the central theme. H. Rider Haggard's stories fit this pattern, and so—with ironic differences—does *Heart of Darkness*.

Explorers themselves sometimes wrote adventure novels. Baker's *Cast Up by the Sea* (1866) and Stanley's *My Kalulu: Prince, King, and Slave* (1889) are both tales addressed to boys, and both carry abolitionist themes into Africa well after the emancipation of slaves in most other parts of the world (Cuba ended slavery in 1886, Brazil in 1888). "I had in view," writes Stanley, "that I might be able to describe more vividly in such a book as this than in any other way the evils of the slave trade in Africa."[46] The story traces an Arab slaving caravan to Lake Tanganyika; when the Arabs are attacked by the blacks whom they've come to enslave, the only survivors—a few Arab boys—are enslaved instead. Later they are rescued from slavery by Prince Kalulu, who himself escaped from slavery in an earlier episode. But Kalulu and the Arab boys are once more captured by slave-trading blacks, "the Wazavila assassins and midnight robbers," whose attacks on innocent villages provide what Stanley calls "a true picture" of the horrors of the slave trade. Even the Arab slavers are morally superior to the "fiendish" Wazavila. After many scrapes, Kalulu and the Arab boys reach Zanzibar and freedom, well experienced in the horrors of both slavery and the Dark Continent. Stanley's moral is plain: the internal slave trade will cease only when European forces squelch slave-trading tribes like the Wazavila and harness the African to the wheel of—to use Buxton's phrase—"legitimate commerce."

In 1888 the great Scottish explorer of Kenya, Joseph Thomson, published an ostensibly adult novel. The protagonist of *Ulu: An African Romance* is a disgruntled Scotsman named Gilmour (partly modeled on Thomson himself), who escapes from corrupt civilization to the Kenyan highlands. Gilmour accepts as his fiancée a fourteen-year-old African girl, Ulu, whom he proceeds (inconsistently, given his rejection of civilization) to try to civilize before marrying. This African Pygmalion story seems daring for the first fifty pages—a direct assault on Victorian stereotypes of race and empire. But the hero never marries or even civilizes Ulu; instead, he realizes the terrible mistake he has made when he meets the blond, blue-eyed daughter of the local missionary. Ulu then becomes an object of patronizing, cloying concern for the white lovers. Gilmour acknowledges "the impossibility of making Ulu other than she is, an out-and-out little savage, childlike and simple, and lovable in many ways, perhaps, but utterly incapable of assimilating any of the higher thoughts and aspirations of the civilized life." While Gilmour's Pygmalion scheme collapses, the story falls into a stereotypic adventure pattern. The ferocious Masais attack and capture Ulu and the missionary's daughter. "What had [Kate] to expect from these licentious, bloodthirsty savages, the indulgence of whose brutal passions was their sole rule in life?"[47] Fortunately, the Masais have never seen anything so beautiful as Kate; they proceed to worship her as a goddess. Gilmour rescues Kate, and Ulu conveniently sacrifices herself so that the intrepid white couple, who were of course meant for each other all along, can live happily ever after. (It's tempting to correlate this wishful fantasy of love and extermination with the "scientific" rationalizations of genocide mentioned earlier: progress and fulfillment are the domain of Europeans even on an individual level. Nevertheless, Thomson was one of the more liberal defenders of Africans and African rights among the great explorers.) Thomson's story is ludicrously inconsistent, but it is also remarkable for suggesting that the European invasion of Africa might corrupt the innocent savages without civilizing them and for even broaching the possibility of intermarriage. White/black unions were not uncommon in reality: the history of the Griqua and other racially mixed peoples in South Africa testifies to the contrary. But intermarriage was unheard of in fiction.

Except for the stress on love and marriage, there is little to distinguish Thomson's adult novel from the whole subgenre of boys' adventure tales to which Stanley's and Baker's stories belong. An adolescent quality pervades most imperialist literature, as it does much fascist culture in the 1920s and 1930s. Africa was a setting where British boys could become men but also where British men could behave like boys with impunity, as do Haggard's heroes. Africa was a great testing—or teething—ground for moral growth and moral regression; the two processes were often indistinguishable. And since imperialism always entailed violence and exploitation and therefore never could bear much scrutiny, propagandists found it easier to leave it to boys to "play up, play up, and play the game" than to more mature, thoughtful types. Much imperialist discourse was thus directed at a specifically adolescent audience, the future rulers of the world. In the works of Haggard, Captain Frederick Marryat, Mayne Reid, G. A. Henty, W. H. G. Kingston, Gordon Stables, Robert Louis Stevenson, and many others through Rudyard Kipling, Britain turned youthful as it turned outward.

In *Black Ivory: A Tale of Adventure among the Slavers of East Africa* (1873), another boys' novelist, R. M. Ballantyne, emulated Livingstone in seeking to expose "the horrible traffic in human beings"

(see fig. 8). "Exaggeration has easily been avoided," Ballantyne
assures us, "because—as Dr. Livingstone says in regard to the
slave-trade—'exaggeration is impossible.' " Ballantyne wishes both
to expose the atrocities of the slave trade and to expose anti-
Negro stereotypes. Ballantyne writes that his character Chief
Kambira has "nothing of our *nursery* savage . . . [he] does not roar,
or glare, or chatter, or devour his food in its blood."⁴⁸ This is all
to the good, but Ballantyne is inconsistent. His sympathetic Africans are so mainly as melodrama victims; otherwise he portrays
their customs as laughably childish. And he has only praise for
British antislavery squadrons patrolling the coasts and for Britishers intruding inland in east Africa to stop the slave trade.⁴⁹

More interesting than *Black Ivory* is Sir Harry Johnston's *History
of a Slave* (1889), which takes the form of an autobiographical slave
narrative. Himself an explorer and an artist (see fig. 6), Johnston
attacks slavery as an extension of savagery. The atrocities which
his slave narrator depicts are more grisly than anything in Ballantyne's work; most grisly of all are the slow tortures practiced
by the Executioner of Zinder under the Tree of Death. But if the
slave's life under various Muslim masters is violent and cruel, his
life before slavery was just as bloody and even more irrational.
Thus the narrator recounts his earliest memory: "When . . . the
men of our town killed someone and roasted his flesh for a feast
. . . the bones . . . were laid round about the base of [a] tree. The
first thing I remember clearly was playing with [a] skull."⁵⁰ Johnston's exposé of the atrocities of the slave trade is preceded by an
exposé of the alleged atrocities of tribal savagery—no pastoral
innocence here. The solution to the slave trade entails more than
persuading Muslim sheikhs to set black Africans free; it also entails abolishing tribal savagery, and the only way to do this lies
through imperialist annexation, the fulfillment of Britain's "civilizing mission."

Other post–Civil War fictions about Africa also attack the slave
trade as part of a larger pattern of violence and savagery. In *The
Congo Rovers: A Story of the Slave Squadron* (1885) by the American
William Lancaster, the hero is captured by slave-trading natives
and, in a chapter entitled "A Fiendish Ceremonial," narrowly es-

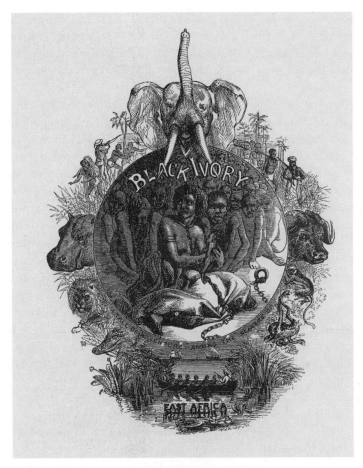

FIG. 8 Frontispiece Robert M. Ballantyne, *Black Ivory: A Tale of Adventure among the Slavers of East Africa*, 1873.

capes being sacrificially murdered. Such a work exhibits all the stereotypes about the Dark Continent that were to be exploited by another popular American writer, Edgar Rice Burroughs, in the Tarzan books. In novels not about slavery, moreover, stress still falls on the violence and irrationality of tribal customs. The publication dates of Haggard's *King Solomon's Mines* (1885) and John

Buchan's *Prester John* (1910) span the period of the main imperialist "scramble for Africa," and in both novels "civilization" is juxtaposed to "savagery" in ways that call for the elimination of the latter. For Haggard and Buchan too, the Dark Continent must be made light.

But Haggard and Buchan also give new life to the Romantic figure of the noble savage—Haggard through his magnificent Zulu warriors, Umbopa and Umslopagass, and Buchan through his black antihero, John Laputa, also from Zulu country. Haggard sees clearly the destruction of Zulu society brought about by the encroachment of whites (*King Solomon's Mines* appeared six years after the Zulu War of 1879); he can also praise primitive customs, contrasting them favorably with civilized ones. He nevertheless maintains a sharp division between the savage and the civilized; his white heroes penetrate the darkness as representatives of vastly higher levels of social evolution. Like aristocrats in Renaissance pastoral, they cleave to their own kind and return to the light. Their friendship with Umbopa cannot hold them in Kukuanaland, and only one other relationship threatens to do so. The romance between Captain John Good and the beautiful Foulata is nipped in the bud when, like Ulu, she is killed near the end of the story. The narrator, Allan Quatermain, concludes:

> I am bound to say that, looking at the thing from the point of view of an oldish man of the world, I consider her removal was a fortunate occurrence, since, otherwise, complications would have been sure to ensue. The poor creature was no ordinary native girl, but a person of great, I had almost said stately, beauty, and of considerable refinement of mind. But no amount of beauty or refinement could have made an entanglement between Good and herself a desirable occurrence; for, as she herself put it, "Can the sun mate with the darkness, or the white with the black?"[51]

Buchan depicts a revolutionary conspiracy led by John Laputa, the self-proclaimed heir of Prester John. To the narrator, Davie Crawfurd, Laputa is a noble but also satanic savage; Davie finds him intensely attractive, but the attraction is charged with a deeply racist and erotic antipathy. Buchan portrays the conspiracy in terms of gothic romance, as a nightmare from which Davie struggles to awake. "You know the [kind of] nightmare when you are pursued by some awful terror," Davie says. "Last night I . . . looked into the heart of darkness, and the sight . . . terrified me."[52] But this "heart of darkness" is not within Davie's psyche; instead, it is Africa and the murderous savagery of Laputa. Haggard can entertain the thought of a free society of noble savages so long as it is distant and mythical; so can Buchan in *A Lodge in the Wilderness*. But in *Prester John*, the idea of independence for Africans is a source only of terror. Laputa must be destroyed, the nightmare dispelled.

Even at its most positive, the romance genre renders the hero's quest as a journey to an underworld, a harrowing of hell; the myth of the Dark Continent fits this pattern perfectly. Conrad dealt with these mythic dimensions in a more conscious way than other writers, producing a quest romance that foreshadows the atrocity literature of the Congo Reform Association—works such as Arthur Conan Doyle's *Crime of the Congo* and Mark Twain's *King Leopold's Soliloquy*, to name two examples by other prominent novelists.[53] By combining the romance and exposé forms, Conrad creates a brilliantly ironic structure in which the diabolic Kurtz demonstrates how the Dark Continent grew dark. For Conrad, the ultimate atrocity is not some form of tribal savagery; it is Kurtz's regression. Kurtz has become "tropenkollered" or "maddened by the tropics"; he has "gone native."[54] In one sense, going native was universal, because in Africa—or in any foreign setting—every traveler must to some extent adopt the customs of the country, eat its food, learn its language, and so on. But Kurtz does something worse—he betrays the ideals of the civilization that he is supposedly importing from Europe. Conrad does not debunk the myth of the Dark Continent: Africa is the location of his hell on earth. But at the center of that hell is Kurtz, the would-be civilizer, the embodiment of Europe's highest and noblest values, radiating darkness.

By universalizing darkness, Conrad passes judgment on imperialism. Marlow looks more favorably upon British than upon Belgian, German, or French imperialism. In the red parts of the map, at least, "one knows that some real work is done" (*HD*, p. 10). But Marlow can also say that

> the conquest of the earth, which mostly means the taking it away from those who have a different complexion or slightly flatter noses than ourselves, is not a pretty thing when you look into it too much. What redeems [conquest] is the idea only. An idea at the back of it; not a sentimental pretence but an idea; and an unselfish belief in the idea—something you can set up, and bow down before, and offer a sacrifice to . . . (*HD*, p. 7)

The modern version of idol worship, it appears, is idea worship. Conrad suggests the universality of darkness by suggesting the universality of fetishism. If the natives in their darkness set Kurtz up as an idol, the European "pilgrims" or traders worship ivory, money, power, reputation. Kurtz joins the natives in their "unspeakable rites," worshiping his own unrestrained power and lust. Marlow himself assumes the pose of an idol, sitting on ship deck with folded legs and outward palms like a Buddha. And Kurtz's Intended is perhaps the greatest fetishist of all, idolizing her image of her fiancé—a fetishism which Marlow refuses to disrupt, as he has earlier disrupted Kurtz's diabolic ceremonies. Marlow's lie leaves Kurtz's Intended shrouded in the protective darkness of her illusions, her idol worship.

Ian Watt identifies nine possible models for Kurtz—the very number suggests the commonness of going native. Stanley is among these models, and so is Charles Stokes, "the renegade missionary," who abandoned the Church Missionary Society, took a native wife, and led a wild career as a slave trader and gun runner.[55] Stokes was not particular about either his stock-in-trade or his customers: he sold guns to Germans working against the British in east Africa and also to French Catholic converts in Buganda, waging a small-scale religious war against the Protestant converts of Stokes' former colleagues. He was finally arrested and executed without trial in the Congo for selling guns to Arab slavers; his demise added to the scandal back in Britain about King Leopold's empire. Stokes' case of backsliding was no doubt extreme, but not unusual. "I have been increasingly struck," wrote Johnston in 1897, "with the rapidity with which such members of the white race as are not of the best class, can throw over the restraints of civilisation and develop into savages of unbridled lust and abominable cruelty."[56] That was another way in which "savages" and the working class sometimes appeared similar. But Kurtz is of "the best class," not a "lower" one: going native could happen to anyone. It could even happen to entire societies. In Charles Reade's novel *A Simpleton* (1873), for example, the Boers have "degenerated into white savages"; the British hero finds that Kaffir "savages" are "socially superior" to them, a typical assertion well before the Boer War of 1899–1902.[57]

Missionaries were perhaps especially susceptible to going native; they frequently expressed fears about regressing, about being converted to heathenism instead of converting the heathen. According to J. S. Moffat, a missionary had to be "deeply imbued with God's spirit in order to have strength to stand against the deadening and corrupting influence around him. . . . I am like a man looking forward to getting back to the sweet air and bright sunshine after being in a coal-mine." Another missionary, S. T. Pruen, believed that merely witnessing heathen customs could be dangerous: "Can a man touch pitch, and not be himself defiled?"[58] The Victorians found strong temptations in Africa, as their frequent references to the allegedly promiscuous sexual customs of Africans show. Burton's prurient anthropology is a notable example; also typical is the sensuousness that Haggard attributes to Foulata and Thomson to Ulu (fig. 9). Never far from their civilized surfaces, the potential for being "defiled"—for "going native" or becoming "tropenkollered"—led Europeans again and again to displace their own "savage" impulses onto Africans. Just as the social class fantasies of the Victorians (*Oliver Twist*, for example) often express the fear of falling into the abyss of poverty, so the myth of the Dark Continent contains the submerged fear of falling out of the light, down the long coal chute of social and

FIG. 9   Henry Stanley resisting temptation. J. W. Buel, *Heroes of the Dark Continent*, 1898.

moral regression. In both cases, the fear of backsliding has a powerful sexual dimension. If, as Freud argued, civilization is based on the repression of instincts and if the demands of repression become excessive, then civilization itself is liable to break down.

Dominique Mannoni has raised the question of the extent to which Europeans "project upon . . . colonial peoples the obscurities of their own unconscious—obscurities they would rather not penetrate." In European writings about Africa, Mannoni says, the savage . . . is identified in the unconscious with a certain image of the instincts. . . . And civilized man is painfully divided between the desire to "correct" the "errors" of the savages and the desire to identify himself with them in his search for some lost paradise (a desire which at once casts doubt upon the merit of the very civilization he is trying to transmit to them).[59]

Kurtz is a product of this painful division. But not even Marlow sees Kurtz's going native as a step toward the recovery of a lost paradise; it is instead a fall into hell, into the abyss of his own darkness. For modern Europeans—Lévi-Strauss again comes to mind—as for the Romantics, the association of primitive life with paradise has once more become possible.[60] But for the Victorians, that association was taboo; they repressed it so much that the African landscapes they explored and exploited were painted again and again with the same tarbrush image of pandemonium. But as they penetrated the heart of darkness only to discover lust and depravity, cannibalism and devil worship, they always also discovered, as the central figure in the shadows, a Stanley, a Stokes, or a Kurtz—an astonished white face staring back.

Nothing points more uncannily to the processes of projection and displacement of guilt for the slave trade, guilt for empire, guilt for one's own savage and shadowy impulses than those moments when white man confronts white man in the depths of the jungle. The archetypal event is Stanley's discovery of Livingstone; the famous scene of "Dr. Livingstone, I presume?" suggests a narcissistic doubling, a repetition or mirroring. The solipsistic repression of whatever is nonself or alien characterizes all forms of cultural and political domination (see fig. 10). In analogous fashion, Haggard's Britishers in *King Solomon's Mines* discover a black race living among the ruins of a great white civilization. When Karl Mauch discovered the ruins of Zimbabwe in 1871, no European was prepared to believe that they had been constructed by Africans. So arose the theory that they were the ruins of King Solomon's Golden Ophir—the work of a higher, fairer race—a myth which archaeologists only began to controvert in 1906; hence, "King Solomon's Mines."[61] Haggard repeats this myth in

FIG. 10 "Dr. Livingstone, I presume?" Stanley, *How I Found Livingstone*, 1872.

other stories. In *She*, Ayesha is a beautiful white demigoddess ruling over a brown-skinned race; and in *Allan Quatermain*, the white explorers discover a mysterious white race in the heart of darkness. So the Dark Continent turned into a mirror, on one level reflecting what the Victorians wanted to see—heroic and saintly self-images—but on another, casting the ghostly shadows of guilt and regression.

5

The myth of the Dark Continent was thus a Victorian invention. As part of a larger discourse about empire, it was shaped by political and economic pressures and also by a psychology of blaming the victim through which Europeans projected many of their own darkest impulses onto Africans. The product of the transition—or transvaluation—from abolitionism to imperialism, the myth of the Dark Continent defined slavery as the offspring of tribal savagery and portrayed white explorers and missionaries as the leaders of a Christian crusade that would vanquish the forces of darkness. The first abolitionists had placed blame for the slave trade mainly on Europeans, but, by mid-century, that blame had largely been displaced onto Africans. When the taint of slavery fused with sensational reports about cannibalism, witchcraft, and apparently shameless sexual customs, Victorian Africa emerged draped in that pall of darkness that the Victorians themselves accepted as reality.

The invasion of preindustrial, largely preliterate societies by the representatives of literate ones with industrialized communications, weapons, and transportation techniques meant a deluge of ruling discourse on one side and what appeared to be total acquiescence and silence on the other. As Frantz Fanon declares, "A man who has a language . . . possesses the world expressed and implied by that language. . . . Mastery of language affords remarkable power."[62] Victorian imperialism both created and was in part created by a growing monopoly on discourse. Unless they became virtually "mimic men," in V. S. Naipaul's phrase, Africans were stripped of articulation: the Bible might be translated into numerous African languages, but the colonizers rarely translated in the other direction, even when they learned Wolof or Zulu. African customs and beliefs were condemned as superstitions, their social organizations were despised and demolished, their land, belongings, and labor often appropriated as ruthlessly as they had been through the slave trade.

But the ethnocentric discourse of domination was not met with silence. Though it has not been easy to recover, modern historians have begun piecing together how Africans responded to their Victorian savior-invaders.[63] The wars of resistance fought by Zulu, Ashanti, Matabele, Ethiopian, Bugandan, and Sudanese peoples have offered perhaps the best evidence. The writings of literate nineteenth-century Africans like the Liberian Edward Blyden, pioneer of the négritude movement, have also been important. Still other responses can be found in the modern independence movements and the writings of nationalists like Fanon, Kwame Nkrumah, Jomo Kenyatta, and Steve Biko. But the legacy of the myth of the Dark Continent and, more generally, of imperialism has been massive and impossible to evade, as stereotypic treatments of Africa by today's mass media continue to demonstrate. The work of liberation from racism and the politics of domination is far from over. Discourse—that most subtle yet also inescapable form of power—in its imperial guise persists, for example, in the most recent assumptions about the antithesis between "primitive" or "backward" and "civilized" or "advanced" societies, about the cultural and historical differences between Afro-Americans and white Americans, and about the legitimacy of the white apartheid regime in South Africa. In this regard, what Nkrumah said in 1965 about the special impact of the American mass media on the African situation is still relevant:

> The cinema stories of fabulous Hollywood are loaded. One has only to listen to the cheers of an African audience as Hollywood's heroes slaughter red Indians or Asiatics to understand the effectiveness of this weapon. For, in the developing continents, where the colonialist heritage has left a vast majority still illiterate, even the smallest child gets the message. . . . And along with murder and the Wild West goes an incessant barrage of anti-socialist propaganda, in which the trade union man, the revolutionary, or the man of dark skin is generally cast as the villain, while the policeman, the gum-shoe, the Federal agent—in a word, the CIA-type spy—is ever the hero. Here, truly, is the ideological under-belly of those political murders which so often use local people as their instruments.[64]

The spirit of Tarzan and Tabu Dick lives on in Western culture, though often reduced to the level of sophisticated buffoonery, as in Saul Bellow's *Henderson, the Rain King*. In criticizing recent American and European failures to imagine Africa without prejudice, Chinua Achebe notes the continuing "desire—one might indeed say the need—in Western psychology to set Africa up as a foil to Europe, a place of negations at once remote and vaguely familiar in comparison with which Europe's own state of spiritual grace will be manifest." As Achebe points out, whether they come from

Victorian or modern England, the America of Grover Cleveland or that of Ronald Reagan, "travellers with closed minds can tell us little except about themselves."[65]

Notes

1. Joseph Conrad, *Heart of Darkness* (New York, 1963), p. 8; all further references to this work, abbreviated *HD*, will be included in the text. Philip D. Curtin writes that "the image of 'darkest Africa,' either as an expression of geographical ignorance, or as one of cultural arrogance, was a nineteenth-century invention" (*The Image of Africa: British Ideas and Action, 1780–1850* [Madison, Wis., 1964], p. 9). See also Dorothy Hammond and Alta Jablow, *The Africa That Never Was: Four Centuries of British Writing about Africa* (New York, 1970), esp. pp. 49–113.

2. Edward W. Said, "Secular Criticism," *The World, the Text, and the Critic* (Cambridge, Mass., 1983), p. 9, and "The World, the Text, and the Critic," ibid., p. 53; Michel Foucault, "Nietzsche, Genealogy, History," *Language; Counter-Memory, Practice: Selected Essays and Interviews*, ed. Donald F. Bouchard, trans. Bouchard and Sherry Simon (Ithaca, N.Y., 1977), p. 148. See also Said, *Orientalism* (New York, 1978).

3. See Eric Williams, *Capitalism and Slavery* (Chapel Hill, N.C., 1944); Williams' theory has been often criticized but not his general thesis of some sort of correlation between abolitionism and industrialization. See Roger T. Anstey, "Capitalism and Slavery: A Critique," *Economic History Review* 21 (Aug. 1968): 307–20; cf. David Brion Davis, *The Problem of Slavery in the Age of Revolution, 1770–1823* (Ithaca, N.Y., 1975), pp. 346–52. Other accounts include Michael Craton, *Sinews of Empire: A Short History of British Slavery* (Garden City, N.Y., 1974), and Howard Temperley, *British Antislavery, 1833–1870* (London, 1972).

4. See Ralph A. Austen and Woodruff D. Smith, "Images of Africa and British Slave-Trade Abolition: The Transition to an Imperialist Ideology, 1787–1807," *African Historical Studies* 2, no. 1 (1969): 69–83. The classic work on motives for expansion is Ronald Robinson, John Gallagher, and Alice Denney, *Africa and the Victorians: The Climax of Imperialism in the Dark Continent* (New York, 1961).

5. Nancy Stepan, *The Idea of Race in Science: Great Britain, 1800–1960* (Hamden, Conn., 1982), p. 1. See also Christine Bolt, *Victorian Attitudes to Race* (Toronto, 1971).

6. William Blake, "The Little Black Boy," *The Poetry and Prose of William Blake*, ed. David V. Erdman (Garden City, N.Y., 1970), p. 9.

7. Robert Southey, "To Horror," *Poetical Works*, 10 vols. (London, 1837–1838), 2: 129.

8. See Eva Beatrice Dykes, *The Negro in English Romantic Thought* (Washington, D.C., 1942), and Wylie Sypher, *Guinea's Captive Kings: British Anti-Slavery Literature of the Eighteenth Century* (Chapel Hill, N.C., 1942).

9. Southey, "Poems Concerning the Slave Trade," in *Poetical Works*, 2: 57.

10. James Grahame, "Africa Delivered; or, the Slave Trade Abolished," in James Montgomery, James Grahame, and E. Benger, *Poems on the Abolition of the Slave Trade* (1809; Freeport, N.Y., 1971), p. 58.

11. See Katherine George, "The Civilized West Looks at Primitive Africa, 1400–1800," *Isis* 49 (Mar. 1958): 62–72. Winthrop D. Jordan reaches a similar conclusion; see *White over Black: American Attitudes toward the Negro, 1550–1812* (Chapel Hill, N.C., 1968), pp. 269–311. See also Curtin, *The Image of Africa*, p. 9.

12. See Thomas Edward Bowdich, *Mission from Cape Coast Castle to Ashantee* (1819; London, 1966). Curtin calls Bowdich one of a group of "enlightened travellers" between 1795 and the 1820s and calls his book "a glowing description of Ashanti society" (*The Image of Africa*, pp. 211, 169).

13. Curtin, *The Image of Africa*, p. 298. The Niger Expedition was "no mere exploring expedition [but] the first step toward a general 'forward policy' in West Africa, reversing the established doctrine of minimum commitments" (p. 298).

14. Thomas Fowell Buxton, *The African Slave Trade and Its Remedy* (1840; London, 1967), p. 342; all further references to this work, abbreviated *A*, will be included in the text. See also John Gallagher, "Fowell Buxton and the New African Policy, 1838–1842," *Cambridge Historical Journal* 10, no. 1 (1950): 36–58.

15. Charles Dickens, "The Niger Expedition," *Works*, 20 vols. (New York, 1903), 18:64.

16. Dickens, quoted in Donald H. Simpson, "Charles Dickens and the Empire,"*Library Notes of the Royal Commonwealth Society*, n.s. 162 (June 1970): 15; Dickens, "The Niger Expedition," p. 63. See also Dickens, "The Noble Savage," *Household Words*, 11 June 1853, pp. 337–39.

17. Mrs. R. Lee [Sarah Wallis], *The African Wanderers: or, The Adventures of Carlos and Antonio* (London, 1847), pp. 230, 126; and see Curtin, *The Image of Africa*, p. 328.

18. The best general account is Alan Moorehead, *The White Nile*, rev.

ed. (New York, 1971); Moorehead likens the great Victorian explorers to astronauts. See also Robert I. Rotberg, ed., *Africa and Its Explorers: Motives, Methods, and Impact* (Cambridge, Mass., 1970).

19. William Somerset Maugham, *The Explorer* (New York, 1909), pp. 45, 175–76. See also Joseph Conrad, "Geography and Some Explorers," *Last Essays* (Freeport, N.Y., 1970), p. 14.

20. Dickens, quoted in Simpson, "Charles Dickens and Empire," p. 15. For Livingstone, see Tim Jeal, *Livingstone* (New York, 1973).

21. M. E. Chamberlain, *The Scramble for Africa*, Seminar Studies in History (London, 1974), p. 28.

22. Foucault, "The Discourse on Language," *The Archaeology of Knowledge*, trans. A. M. Sheridan Smith (New York, 1972), p. 229.

23. David Livingstone, quoted in Jeal, *Livingstone*, pp. 146, 124; Jeal, *Livingstone*, p. 4.

24. See Philip D. Curtin and Paul Bohanan, *Africa and Africans* (Garden City, N.Y., 1971), p. 8.

25. May Crawford, *By the Equator's Snowy Peak: A Record of Medical Missionary Work and Travel in British East Africa* (London, 1913), pp. 29, 56. I am indebted to Carolyn Redouty for calling my attention to these citations.

26. On missionary attitudes, see H. A. C. Cairns, *Prelude to Imperialism: British Reactions to Central African Society, 1840–1890* (London, 1965), and Geoffrey Moorhouse, *The Missionaries* (Philadelphia, 1973).

27. Anthony Hope Hawkins [Anthony Hope], *The God in the Car* (1895; New York, 1896), p. 19.

28. Richard F. Burton, *The Lake Regions of Central Africa*, 2 vols. (1861; New York, 1961), 2:326.

29. Ibid., 2:347–48.

30. Burton, *Two Trips to Gorilla Land and the Cataracts of the Congo*, 2 vols. (1876; New York, 1967), 2:311.

31. Samuel White Baker, *The Albert N'yanza, Great Basin of the Nile, and Exploration of the Nile Sources*, 2 vols. (1866; London, 1962), 1:211.

32. Hugh Stowell Scott [Henry S. Merriman], *With Edged Tools* (1894; London, 1909), pp. 321–22.

33. The stamp design is reproduced in Roland Oliver, *Sir Harry Johnston and the Scramble for Africa* (London, 1957). On racism and class, see Robert Ross, ed., *Racism and Colonialism: Essays on Ideology and Social Structure* (The Hague, 1982); Frantz Fanon, *The Wretched of the Earth*, trans. Constance Farrington (New York, 1963); and Douglas A. Lorimer, *Colour, Class, and the Victorians: A Study of English Attitudes toward the Negro in the Mid-Nineteenth Century* (Leicester, 1978).

34. See Ronald Rainger, "Race, Politics, and Science: The Anthro-

pological Society of London in the 1860s," *Victorian Studies* 22 (Autumn 1978): 51–70.

35. Thomas Henry Huxley, *Man's Place in Nature* (Ann Arbor, Mich., 1959), pp. 58, 69–70; Huxley acknowledges that the "human butcher shop" is "irrelevant" to his argument. Stepan notes that in the nineteenth century, "textbook after textbook compared the Negro to the ape" (*The Idea of Race in Science*, p. 18).

36. Hammond and Jablow, *The Africa That Never Was*, p. 94; Winwood Reade, *Savage Africa; Being the Narrative of a Tour in Equatorial, Southwestern, and Northwestern Africa* (New York, 1864), pp. 54, 136.

37. See Sir John Lubbock, *The Origin of Civilization and the Primitive Condition of Man: Mental and Social Condition of Savages* (1870; London, 1912), pp. 1–2.

38. George John Romanes, *Mental Evolution in Man: Origin of Human Faculty* (New York, 1889), p. 439.

39. Stepan, *The Idea of Race in Science*, pp. 45, 46.

40. Benjamin Kidd, *Social Evolution* (New York, 1894), p. 46.

41. Karl Pearson, *National Life from the Standpoint of Science* (London, 1901), pp. 47–48.

42. Charles Darwin, *The Descent of Man and Selection in Relation to Sex*, 2d ed. (New York, 1874), p. 613; see esp. chap. 7, "On the Races of Man," pp. 162–202. On the question of racial extinction, see also Charles Wentworth Dilke, *Greater Britain: A Record of Travel in English-Speaking Countries during 1866 and 1867* (New York, 1869), pp. 90–100, 221, 250, and 273.

43. See George Stocking, Jr.: "Once the 'one grand scheme' of evolutionism was rejected, the multiplicity of *cultures* which took the place of the cultural *stages* of savagery, barbarism, and civilization were no more easily brought within one standard of evaluation than they were within one system of explanation" (*Race, Culture, and Evolution: Essays in the History of Anthropology* [New York, 1968], p. 229).

44. Claude Lévi-Strauss, *Tristes Tropiques*, trans. John and Doreen Weightman (New York, 1974), p. 123.

45. William Makepeace Thackeray, "Timbuctoo," *Works*, Oxford ed., 17 vols. (London, 1908), 1:2.

46. Henry M. Stanley, *My Kalulu: Prince, King, and Slave* (London, 1889), p. viii.

47. Joseph Thomson and E. Harriet-Smith, *Ulu: An African Romance*, 3 vols. (London, 1888), 2:18–19, 65–66.

48. R. M. Ballantyne, *Black Ivory: A Tale of Adventure among the Slavers of East Africa* (1873; Chicago, 1969), pp. iv, iii, 169.

49. In Ballantyne's best-seller of 1858, one of the three shipwrecked British boys says: "We've got an island all to ourselves. We'll take possession of it in the name of the King; we'll go and enter the service of its black inhabitants. Of course we'll rise, naturally, to the top of affairs. White men always do in savage countries" (*The Coral Island* [London, n.d.], p. 22). Ballantyne expresses the sentiment of total racial and cultural superiority that pervades boys' fiction about "savage countries" even when, as in *Black Ivory*, the target is the slave trade.

50. Sir Harry H. Johnston, *The History of a Slave* (London, 1889), p. 6.

51. H. Rider Haggard, *King Solomon's Mines* (Harmondsworth, 1965), p. 241.

52. John Buchan, *Prester John* (New York, 1910), pp. 211, 148.

53. See S. J. Cookey, *Britain and the Congo Question, 1885–1913* (London, 1968); see also my "*Heart of Darkness*: Anti-Imperialism, Racism, or Impressionism?" *Criticism* 27 (1985): 363–85.

54. "Tropenkollered" was the term used by the Dutch naval officer Captain Otto Lütken, quoted in Ian Watt, *Conrad in the Nineteenth Century* (Berkeley and Los Angeles, 1979), p. 145.

55. Ibid., pp. 141–46. On Stokes, see also Moorhouse, *The Missionaries*, p. 196.

56. Johnston, *British Central Africa: An Attempt to Give Some Account of a Portion of the Territories under British Influence North of the Zambezi*, 3d ed. (London, 1906), p. 68.

57. Charles Reade, *A Simpleton: A Story of the Day* (London, 1873), pp. 250–51.

58. J. S. Moffat and S. T. Pruen, quoted in Cairns, *Prelude to Imperialism*, p. 68.

59. [Dominique] O. Mannoni, *Prospero and Caliban: The Psychology of Colonization*, trans. Pamela Powesland (London, 1956), pp. 19–21.

60. See Lévi-Strauss, *Tristes Tropiques*; see also Stanley Diamond, *In Search of the Primitive* (New Brunswick, N.J., 1974), and Eric R. Wolf, *Europe and the People without History* (Berkeley and Los Angeles, 1982).

61. See Karl Peters, *King Solomon's Golden Ophir: A Research into the Most Ancient Gold Production in History* (1899; New York, 1969); this work is one example of the speculation about the Zimbabwe ruins that underlies Haggard's stories. The first scientific work demonstrating that the ruins had been built by Africans was David Randall-MacIver, *Mediaeval Rhodesia* (London, 1906). As late as the 1960s, works published in Rhodesia and South Africa were still insisting that the original builders were non-African.

62. Frantz Fanon, *Black Skin, White Masks*, trans. Charles Lam Markmann (New York 1967), p. 18.

63. For nineteenth-century African responses to the European invasion, see Philip D. Curtin ed., *Africa and the West: Intellectual Responses to European Culture* (Madison, Wis., 1972); Robert I. Rotberg and Ali A. Mazrui, eds., *Protest and Power in Black Africa* (New York, 1970); and Terence O. Ranger, ed., *Aspects of Central African History* (Evanston, Ill., 1968).

64. Kwame Nkrumah, *Neo-Colonialism: The Last Stage of Imperialism* (London, 1965), p. 246.

65. Chinua Achebe, "An Image of Africa," *Research in African Literatures* 9 (Spring 1978): 2, 12. See also Ezekiel Mphahlele, *The African Image* (New York, 1962).

From *The Crime of the Congo*

ARTHUR CONAN DOYLE

◆ ◆ ◆

How the Congo Free State Came to Be Founded

In the earlier years of his reign King Leopold of Belgium began to display that interest in Central Africa which for a long time was ascribed to nobility and philanthropy, until the contrast between such motives, and the actual unscrupulous commercialism, became too glaring to be sustained. As far back as the year 1876 he called a conference of humanitarians and travellers, who met at Brussels for the purpose of debating various plans by which the Dark Continent might be opened up. From this conference sprang the so-called International African Association, which, in spite of its name, was almost entirely a Belgian body, with the Belgian King as President. Its professed object was the exploration of the country and the founding of stations which should be rest-houses for travellers and centres of civilization.

On the return of Stanley from his great journey in 1878, he was met at Marseilles by a representative from the King of Belgium, who enrolled the famous traveller as an agent for his Association. The immediate task given to Stanley was to open up the Congo for trade, and to make such terms with the natives as would enable stations to be built and depôts established. In 1879 Stanley was at work with characteristic energy. His own intentions were admirable. "We shall require but mere contact," he wrote, "to satisfy the natives that our intentions are pure and honourable, seeking their own good, materially and socially, more than our own interests. We go to spread what blessings arise from amiable and just intercourse with people who have been strangers to them." Stanley was a hard man, but he was no hypocrite. What he said he undoubtedly meant. It is worth remarking, in view of the accounts of the laziness or stupidity of the natives given by King Leopold's apologists in order to justify their conduct towards them, that Stanley had the very highest opinion of their industry and commercial ability. The following extracts from his writings set this matter beyond all doubt:

"Bolobo is a great centre for the ivory and camwood powder trade, principally because its people are so enterprising."

Of Irebu—"a Venice of the Congo"—he says:

"These people were really acquainted with many lands and tribes on the Upper Congo. From Stanley Pool to Upoto, a distance of 6,000 miles, they knew every landing-place on the river banks. All the ups and downs of savage life, all the profits and losses derived from barter, all the diplomatic arts used by tactful savages, were as well known to them as the Roman alphabet to us. . . . No wonder that all this commercial knowledge had left its traces on their faces; indeed, it is the same as in your own cities in Europe. Know you not the military man among you, the lawyer and the merchant, the banker, the artist, or the poet? It is the same in Africa, MORE ESPECIALLY ON THE CONGO, WHERE THE PEOPLE ARE SO DEVOTED TO TRADE."

"During the few days of our mutual intercourse they gave us a high idea of their qualities—industry, after their own style, not being the least conspicuous."

"As in the old time, Umangi, from the right bank, and Mpa, from the left bank, despatched their representatives with ivory tusks, large and small, goats and sheep, and vegetable food, clamorously demanding that we should buy from them. Such urgent entreaties, accompanied with blandishments to purchase their stock, were difficult to resist."

"I speak of eager native traders following us for miles for the smallest piece of cloth. I mention that after travelling many miles to obtain cloth for ivory and redwood powder, the despairing natives asked: 'Well, what is it you do want? Tell us, and we will get it for you.' "

Speaking of English scepticism as to King Leopold's intentions, he says:

"Though they understand the satisfaction of a sentiment when applied to England, they are slow to understand that it may be a sentiment that induced King Leopold II. to father this International Association. He is a dreamer, like his *confrères* in the work, because the sentiment is applied to the neglected millions of the Dark Continent. They cannot appreciate rightly, because there are no dividends attaching to it, this ardent, vivifying and expansive sentiment, which seeks to extend civilizing influences among the dark races, and to brighten up with the glow of civilization the dark places of sad-browed Africa."

One cannot let these extracts pass without noting that Bolobo, the first place named by Stanley, has sunk in population from 40,000 to 7,000; that Irebu, called by Stanley the populous Venice of the Congo, had in 1903 a population of fifty; that the natives who used to follow Stanley, beseeching him to trade, now, according to Consul Casement, fly into the bush at the approach of a steamer, and that the unselfish sentiment of King Leopold II. has developed into dividends of 300 per cent. per annum. Such is the difference between Stanley's anticipation and the actual fulfilment.

Untroubled, however, with any vision as to the destructive effects of his own work, Stanley laboured hard among the native chiefs, and returned to his employer with no less than 450 alleged treaties which transferred land to the Association. We have no record of the exact payment made in order to obtain these treaties, but we have the terms of a similar transaction carried out by a Belgian officer in 1883 at Palabala. In this case the payment made to the Chief consisted of "one coat of red cloth with gold facings, one red cap, one white tunic, one piece of white baft, one piece of red points, one box of liqueurs, four demijohns of rum, two boxes of gin, 128 bottles of gin, twenty red handkerchiefs, forty singlets and forty old cotton caps." It is clear that in making such treaties the Chief thought that he was giving permission for the establishment of a station. The idea that he was actually bartering away the land was never even in his mind, for it was held by a communal tenure for the whole tribe, and it was not his to barter. And yet it is on the strength of such treaties as these that twenty millions of people have been expropriated, and the whole wealth and land of the country proclaimed to belong, not to the inhabitants, but to the State—that is, to King Leopold.

With this sheaf of treaties in his portfolio the King of the Belgians now approached the Powers with high sentiments of humanitarianism, and with a definite request that the State which he was forming should receive some recognized status among the nations. Was he at that time consciously hypocritical? Did he already foresee how widely his future actions would differ from his present professions? It is a problem which will interest the historian of the future, who may have more materials than we upon which to form a judgment. On the one hand, there was a furtive secrecy about the evolution of his plans and the despatch of his expeditions which should have no place in a philanthropic enterprise. On the other hand, there are limits to human powers of deception, and it is almost inconceivable that a man who was acting a part could so completely deceive the whole civilized world. It is more probable, as it seems to me, that his ambitious mind discerned that it was possible for him to acquire a field of action which his small kingdom could not give, in mixing himself with the affairs of Africa. He chose the obvious path, that of a civilizing and elevating mission, taking the line of least resistance without any definite idea whither it might lead him. Once faced with the facts, his astute brain perceived the great material possibilities of the country; his early dreams faded away to be replaced by unscrupulous cupidity, and step by step he was led downward until he, the man of holy aspirations in 1885, stands now in 1909 with such a cloud of terrible direct personal responsibility resting upon him as no man in modern European history has had to bear.

It is, indeed, ludicrous, with our knowledge of the outcome, to read the declarations of the King and of his representatives at that time. They were actually forming the strictest of commercial monopolies—an organization which was destined to crush out all general private trade in a country as large as the whole of Europe with Russia omitted. That was the admitted outcome of their enterprise. Now listen to M. Beernaert, the Belgian Premier, speaking in the year 1885:

> "The State, of which our King will be the Sovereign, will be a sort of international Colony. There will be no monopolies, no privileges. . . . Quite the contrary: absolute freedom of commerce, freedom of property, freedom of navigation."

Here, too, are the words of Baron Lambermont, the Belgian Plenipotentiary at the Berlin Conference:

> "The temptation to impose abusive taxes will find its corrective, if need be, in the freedom of commerce. . . . No doubt exists as to the strict and literal meaning of the term 'in commercial matters.' It means . . . the unlimited right for every one to buy and to sell."

THE QUESTION OF HUMANITY is so pressing that it obscures that of the broken pledges about trade, but on the latter alone there is ample reason to say that every condition upon which this State was founded has been openly and notoriously violated, and that, therefore, its title-deeds are vitiated from the beginning.

At the time the professions of the King made the whole world his enthusiastic allies. The United States was the first to hasten to give formal recognition to the new State. May it be the first, also, to realize the truth and to take public steps to retract what it has done. The churches and the Chambers of Commerce of Great Britain were all for Leopold, the one attracted by the prospect of pushing their missions into the heart of Africa, the others delighted at the offer of an open market for their produce. At the Congress of Berlin, which was called to regulate the situation, the nations vied with each other in furthering the plans of the King of the Belgians and in extolling his high aims. The Congo Free State was created amid general rejoicings. The veteran Bismarck, as credulous as the others, pronounced its baptismal blessing. "The New Congo State is called upon," said he, "to become one of the chief promoters of the work" (of civilization) "which we have in view, and I pray for its prosperous development and for the fulfilment of the noble aspirations of its illustrious founder." Such was the birth of the Congo Free State. Had the nations gathered round been able to perceive its future, the betrayal of religion and civilization of which it would be guilty, the immense series of crimes which it would perpetrate throughout Central Africa, the lowering of the prestige of all the white races, they would surely have strangled the monster in its cradle.

It is not necessary to record in this statement the whole of the provisions of the Berlin Congress. Two only will suffice, as they are at the same time the most important and the most flagrantly abused. The first of these (which forms the fifth article of the agreement) proclaims that "No Power which exercises sovereign rights in the said regions shall be allowed to grant therein either monopoly or privilege of any kind in commercial matters." No words could be clearer than that, but the Belgian representatives, conscious that such a clause must disarm all opposition, went out of their way to accentuate it. "No privileged situation can be created in this respect," they said. "The way remains open without any restriction to free competition in the sphere of commerce." It would be interesting now to send a British or German trading expedition up the Congo in search of that free competition which has been so explicitly promised, and to see how it would fare between the monopolist Government and the monopolist companies who have divided the land between them. We have travelled some distance since Prince Bismarck at the last sitting of the Conference declared that the result was "to secure to the commerce of all nations free access to the centre of the African Continent."

More important, however, is Article VI., both on account of the issues at stake, and because the signatories of the treaty bound themselves solemnly, "in the name of Almighty God," to watch over its enforcement. It ran: "All the Powers exercising sovereign rights or influence in these territories pledge themselves to watch over the preservation of the native populations and the improvement of their moral and material conditions of existence, and to work together for the suppression of slavery and of the slave trade." That was the pledge of the united nations of Europe. It is a disgrace to each of them, including ourselves, the way in which they have fulfilled that oath. Before their eyes, as I shall show in the sequel, they have had enacted one long, horrible tragedy, vouched for by priests and missionaries, traders, travellers and consuls, all corroborated, but in no way reformed, by a Belgian commission of inquiry. They have seen these unhappy people, who were their wards, robbed of all they possessed, debauched, degraded, mutilated, tortured, murdered, all on such a scale as has never, to my knowledge, occurred before in the whole course of history, and now, after all these years, with all the facts notorious, we are still at the stage of polite diplomatic expostulations. It is no answer to say that France and Germany have shown even less regard for the pledge they took at Berlin. An individual does not condone the fact that he has broken his word by pointing out that his neighbour has done the same.

The Development of the Congo State

Having received his mandate from the civilized world King Leopold proceeded to organize the Government of the new State,
which was in theory to be independent of Belgium, although
ruled by the same individual. In Europe, King Leopold was a
constitutional monarch; in Africa, an absolute autocrat. There
were chosen three ministers for the new State—for foreign affairs,
for finances and for internal affairs; but it cannot be too clearly
understood that they and their successors, up to 1908, were nom-
inated by the King, paid by the King, answerable only to the King,
and, in all ways, simply so many upper clerks in his employ. The
workings of one policy and of one brain, as capable as it is sinister,
are to be traced in every fresh development. If the ministers were
ever meant to be a screen, it is a screen which is absolutely trans-
parent. The origin of everything is the King—always the King.
M. van Ectvelde, one of the three head agents, put the matter
into a single sentence: "C'est à votre majesté qu'appartient l'État."
They were simply stewards, who managed the estate with a very
alert and observant owner at their back.

One of the early acts was enough to make observers a little
thoughtful. It was the announcement of the right to issue laws
by arbitrary decrees without publishing them in Europe. There
should be secret laws, which could, at any instant, be altered. The
Bulletin Officiel announced that "Tous les Actes du Gouvernement
qu'il y a intérêt à rendre publics seront insérés au *Bulletin Officiel*."
Already it is clear that something was in the wind which might
shock the rather leathery conscience of a European Concert.
Meanwhile, the organization of the State went forward. A
Governor-General was elected, who should live at Boma, which
was made the capital. Under him were fifteen District Commis-
saries, who should govern so many districts into which the whole
country was divided. The only portion which was at that time at
all developed was the semi-civilized Lower Congo at the mouth
of the river. There lay the white population. The upper reaches
of the stream and of its great tributaries were known only to a

few devoted missionaries and enterprising explorers. Grenfell and
Bentley, of the Missions, with von Wissman, the German, and
the ever-energetic Stanley, were the pioneers who, during the few
years which followed, opened up the great hinterland which was
to be the scene of such atrocious events.

But the work of the explorer had soon to be supplemented
and extended by the soldier. Whilst the Belgians had been entering the Congo land from the west, the slave-dealing Arabs had
penetrated from the east, passing down the river as far as Stanley
Falls. There could be no compromise between such opposite
forces, though some attempt was made to find one by electing
the Arab leader as Free State Governor. There followed a long
scrambling campaign, carried on for many years between the Arab
slavers on the one side and the Congo forces upon the other—
the latter consisting largely of cannibal tribes—men of the Stone
Age, armed with the weapons of the nineteenth century. The
suppression of the slave trade is a good cause, but the means by
which it was effected, and the use of Barbarians who ate in the
evening those whom they had slain during the day, are as bad as
the evil itself. Yet there is no denying the energy and ability
of the Congo leaders, especially of Baron Dhanis. By the year 1894
the Belgian expeditions had been pushed as far as Lake Tanganyika, the Arab strongholds had fallen, and Dhanis was able to
report to Brussels that the campaign was at an end, and that
slave-raiding was no more. The new State could claim that they
had saved a part of the natives from slavery. How they proceeded
to impose upon all of them a yoke, compared to which the old
slavery was merciful, will be shown in these pages. From the time
of the fall of the Arab power the Congo Free State was only
called upon to use military force in the case of mutinies of its
own black troops, and of occasional risings of its own tormented
"citizens." Master of its own house, it could settle down to exploit
the country which it had won.

In the meantime the internal policy of the State showed a
tendency to take an unusual and sinister course. I have already
expressed my opinion that King Leopold was not guilty of conscious hypocrisy in the beginning, that his intentions were

vaguely philanthropic, and that it was only by degrees that he sank to the depths which will be shown. This view is borne out by some of the earlier edicts of the State. In 1886, a long pronouncement upon native lands ended by the words: "All acts or agreements are forbidden which tend to the expulsion of natives from the territory they occupy, or to deprive them, directly or indirectly, of their liberty or their means of existence." Such are the words of 1886. Before the end of 1887, an Act had been published, though not immediately put into force, which had the exactly opposite effect. By this Act all lands which were not actually occupied by natives were proclaimed to be the property of the State. Consider for a moment what this meant! No land in such a country is actually occupied by natives save the actual site of their villages, and the scanty fields of grain or manioc which surround them. Everywhere beyond these tiny patches extend the plains and forests which have been the ancestral wandering-places of the natives, and which contain the rubber, the camwood, the copal, the ivory, and the skins which are the sole objects of their commerce. At a single stroke of a pen in Brussels everything was taken from them, not only the country, but the produce of the country. How could they trade when the State had taken from them everything which they had to offer? How could the foreign merchant do business when the State had seized everything and could sell it for itself direct in Europe? Thus, within two years of the establishment of the State by the Treaty of Berlin, it had with one hand seized the whole patrimony of those natives for whose "moral and material advantage" it had been so solicitous, and with the other hand it had torn up that clause in the treaty by which monopolies were forbidden, and equal trade rights guaranteed to all. How blind were the Powers not to see what sort of a creature they had made, and how short-sighted not to take urgent steps in those early days to make it retrace its steps and find once more the path of loyalty and justice! A firm word, a stern act at that time in the presence of this flagrant breach of international agreement, would have saved all Central Africa from the horror which has come upon it, would have screened Belgium from a lasting disgrace, and would have spared Europe a question which has already, as it seems to me, lowered the moral standing of all the nations, and the end of which is not yet.

Having obtained possession of the land and its products, the next step was to obtain labour by which these products could be safely garnered. The first definite move in this direction was taken in the year 1888, when, with that odious hypocrisy which has been the last touch in so many of these transactions, an Act was produced which was described in the *Bulletin Officiel* as being for the "Special protection of the black." It is evident that the real protection of the black in matters of trade was to offer him such pay as would induce him to do a day's work, and to let him choose his own employment, as is done with the Kaffirs of South Africa, or any other native population. This Act had a very different end. It allowed blacks to be bound over in terms of seven years' service to their masters in a manner which was in truth indistinguishable from slavery. As the negotiations were usually carried on with the capita, or headman, the unfortunate servant was transferred with small profit to himself, and little knowledge of the conditions of his servitude. Under the same system the State also enlisted its employees, including the recruits for its small army. This army was supplemented by a wild militia, consisting of various barbarous tribes, many of them cannibals, and all of them capable of any excess of cruelty or outrage. A German, August Boshart, in his "Zehn Jahre Afrikanischen Lebens," has given us a clear idea of how these tribes are recruited, and of the precise meaning of the attractive word "libéré" when applied to a State servant. "Some District Commissary," he says, "receives instructions to furnish a certain number of men in a given time. He puts himself in communication with the chiefs, and invites them to a palaver at his residence. These chiefs, as a rule, already have an inkling of what is coming, and, if made wise by experience, make a virtue of necessity and present themselves. In that case the negotiations run their course easily enough; each chief promises to supply a certain number of slaves, and receives presents in return. It may happen, however, that one or another pays no heed to the friendly invitation, in which case war is declared, his villages are burned down, perhaps some of his people are shot, and his stores or gardens are plundered. In this way the wild king is soon tamed, and he sues for peace, which, of course, is granted on condition of his supplying double the number of slaves. These men are entered in the State books as 'libérés.' To prevent their running away, they are put in irons and sent, on the first opportunity, to one of the military camps, where their irons are taken off and they are drafted into the army. The District Commissary is paid £2 sterling for every serviceable recruit."

Having taken the country and secured labour for exploiting it in the way described, King Leopold proceeded to take further steps for its development, all of them exceedingly well devised for the object in view. The great impediment to the navigation of the Congo had lain in the continuous rapids which made the river impassable from Stanley Pool for three hundred miles down to Boma at the mouth. A company was now formed to find the capital by which a railway should be built between these two points. The construction was begun in 1888, and was completed in 1898, after many financial vicissitudes, forming a work which deserves high credit as a piece of ingenious engineering and of sustained energy. Other commercial companies, of which more will be said hereafter, were formed in order to exploit large districts of the country which the State was not yet strong enough to handle. By this arrangement the companies found the capital for exploring, station building, etc., while the State—that is, the King—retained a certain portion, usually half of the company's shares. The plan itself is not necessarily a vicious one; indeed, it closely resembles that under which the Chartered Company of Rhodesia grants mining and other leases. The scandal arose from the methods by which these companies proceeded to carry out their ends—those methods being the same as were used by the State, on whose pattern these smaller organizations were moulded.

In the meantime King Leopold, feeling the weakness of his personal position in face of the great enterprise which lay before him in Africa, endeavoured more and more to draw Belgium, as a State, into the matter. Already the Congo State was largely the outcome of Belgian work and of Belgian money, but, theoretically, there was no connection between the two countries. Now the Belgian Parliament was won over to advancing ten million francs for the use of the Congo, and thus a direct connection sprang up which has eventually led to annexation. At the time of this loan King Leopold let it be known that he had left the Congo Free State in his will to Belgium. In this document appear the words, "A young and spacious State, directed from Brussels, has pacifically appeared in the sunlight, thanks to the benevolent support of the Powers that have welcomed its appearance. Some Belgians administer it, while others, each day more numerous, there increase their wealth." So he flashed the gold before the eyes of his European subjects. Verily, if King Leopold deceived other Powers, he reserved the most dangerous of all his deceits for his own country. The day on which they turned from their own honest, healthy development to follow the Congo lure, and to administer without any previous colonial experience a country more than sixty times their own size, will prove to have been a dark day in Belgian history.

The Berlin Conference of 1885 marks the first International session upon the affairs of the Congo. The second was the Brussels Conference of 1889–90. It is amazing to find that after these years of experience the Powers were still ready to accept King Leopold's professions at their face value. It is true that none of the more sinister developments had been conspicuous, but the legislation of the State with regard to labour and trade was already such as to suggest the turn which affairs would take in future if not curbed by a strong hand. One Power, and one only, Holland, had the sagacity to appreciate the true situation, and the independence to show its dissatisfaction. The outcome of the sittings was various philanthropic resolutions intended to strengthen the new State in dealing with that slave trade it was destined to re-introduce in its most odious form. We are too near to these events, and they are too painfully intimate, to permit us to see humour in them; but the historian of the future, when he reads that the object of the European Concert was "to protect effectually the aboriginal inhabitants of Africa," may find it difficult to suppress a smile. This was the last European assembly to deal with the affairs of the Congo. May the next be for the purpose of taking steps to truly carry out those high ends which have been forever spoken of and never reduced to practice.

The most important practical outcome of the Brussels Conference was that the Powers united to free the new State from those free port promises which it had made in 1885, and to permit it in future to levy ten per cent. upon imports. The Act was hung up for two years owing to the opposition of Holland, but the fact of its adoption by the other Powers, and the renewed mandate given to King Leopold, strengthened the position of the new State to such an extent that it found no difficulty in securing a further loan from Belgium of twenty-five millions of francs, upon condition that, after ten years, Belgium should have the option of taking over the Congo lands as a colony.

If in the years which immediately succeeded the Brussels Conference—from 1890 to 1894—a bird's-eye view could be taken of the enormous river which, with its tributaries, forms a great twisted fan radiating over the whole centre of Africa, one would mark in all directions symptoms of European activity. At the Lower Congo one would see crowds of natives, impressed for the service and guarded by black soldiers, working at the railway. At Boma and at Leopoldville, the two termini of the projected line, cities are rising, with stations, wharves, and public buildings. In the extreme southeast one would see an expedition under Stairs exploring and annexing the great district of Katanga, which abuts upon Northern Rhodesia. In the furthest northeast and along the whole eastern border, small military expeditions would be disclosed, fighting against rebellious blacks or Arab raiders. Then, along all the lines of the rivers, posts were being formed and stations established—some by the State and some by the various concessionnaire companies for the development of their commerce.

In the meantime, the State was tightening its grip upon the land with its products, and was working up the system which was destined to produce such grim results in the near future. The independent traders were discouraged and stamped out, Belgian, as well as Dutch, English and French. Some of the loudest protests against the new order may be taken from Belgian sources. Everywhere, in flagrant disregard of the Treaty of Berlin, the State proclaimed itself to be the sole landlord and the sole trader. In some cases it worked its own so-called property, in other cases it leased it. Even those who had striven to help King Leopold in the earlier stages of his enterprise were thrown overboard. Major Parminter, himself engaged in trade upon the Congo, sums up the situation in 1892 as follows: "To sum up, the application of the new decrees of the Government signifies this: that the State considers as its private property the whole of the Congo Basin, excepting the sites of the natives' villages and gardens. It decrees that all the products of this immense region are its private property, and it monopolizes the trade in them. As regards the primitive proprietors, the native tribes, they are dispossessed by a simple circular; permission is graciously granted to them to collect such products, but only on condition that they bring them for sale to the State for whatever the latter may be pleased to give them. As regards alien traders, they are prohibited in all this territory from trading with the natives."

Everywhere there were stern orders—to the natives on the one hand, that they had no right to gather the products of their own forests; to independent traders on the other hand, that they were liable to punishment if they bought anything from the natives. In January, 1892, District Commissary Baert wrote: "The natives of the district of Ubangi-Welle are not authorized to gather rubber. It has been notified to them that they can only receive permission to do so on condition that they gather the produce for the exclusive benefit of the State." Captain Le Marinel, a little later, is even more explicit: "I have decided," he says, "to enforce rigorously the rights of the State over its domain, and, in consequence, cannot allow the natives to convert to their own profit, or to sell to others, any part of the rubber or ivory forming the fruits of the domain. Traders who purchase, or attempt to purchase, such fruits of this domain from the natives—which fruits the State only authorizes the natives to gather subject to the condition that they are brought to it—render themselves, in my opinion, guilty of receiving stolen goods, and I shall denounce them to the judicial authorities, so that proceedings may be taken against them." This last edict was in the Bangala district, but it was followed at once by another from the more settled Equateur district, which shows that the strict adoption of the system was universal. In May, 1892, Lieutenant Lemaire proclaims: "Considering that no concession has been granted to gather rubber in the domains of the State within this district, (1) natives can only gather rubber on condition of selling the same to the State; (2) any person or persons or vessels having in his or their possession, or on board, more than one kilogramme of rubber will have a *procès-verbal* drawn up against him, or them, or it; and the ship can be confiscated without prejudice to any subsequent proceedings."

The sight of these insignificant officials and captains, who are often non-commissioned officers of the Belgian army, issuing proclamations which were in distinct contradiction to the expressed will of all the great Powers of the world, might at the time have seemed ludicrous; but the history of the next seventeen years was to prove that a small malignant force, driven on by greed, may prove to be more powerful than a vague general philanthropy, strong only in good intentions and platitudes. During these years—from 1890 to 1895—whatever indignation might be felt among traders over the restrictions placed upon them, the only news received by the general public from the Congo Free State concerned the founding of new stations, and the idea prevailed that King Leopold's enterprise was indeed working out upon the humanitarian lines which had been originally planned. Then, for the first time, incidents occurred which gave some glimpse of the violence and anarchy which really prevailed.

The first of these, so far as Great Britain is concerned, lay in the treatment of natives from Sierra Leone, Lagos, and other British Settlements, who had been engaged by the Belgians to come to Congoland and help in railway construction and other work. Coming from the settled order of such a colony as Sierra Leone or Lagos, these natives complained loudly when they found themselves working side by side with impressed Congolese, and under the discipline of the armed sentinels of the Force Publique. They were discontented and the discontent was met by corporal punishment. The matter grew to the dimensions of a scandal.

In answer to a question asked in the House of Commons on March 12th, 1896, Mr. Chamberlain, as Secretary of State for the Colonies, stated that complaints had been received of these British subjects having been employed without their consent as soldiers, and of their having been cruelly flogged, and, in some cases, shot; and he added: "They were engaged with the knowledge of Her Majesty's representatives, and every possible precaution was taken in their interests; but, in consequence of the complaints received, the recruitment of labourers for the Congo has been prohibited."

This refusal of the recruitment of labourers by Great Britain was the first public and national sign of disapproval of Congolese methods. A few years later, a more pointed one was given, when the Italian War Ministry refused to allow their officers to serve with the Congo forces.

Early in 1895 occurred the Stokes affair, which moved public opinion deeply, both in this country and in Germany. Charles Henry Stokes was an Englishman by birth, but he resided in German East Africa, was the recipient of a German Decoration for his services on behalf of German colonization, and formed his trading caravans from a German base, with East African natives as his porters. He had led such a caravan over the Congo State border, when he was arrested by Captain Lothaire, an officer in command of some Congolese troops. The unfortunate Stokes may well have thought himself safe as the subject of one great power and the agent of another, but he was tried instantly in a most informal manner upon a charge of selling guns to the natives, was condemned, and was hanged on the following morning. When Captain Lothaire reported his proceedings to his superiors they signified their approbation by promoting him to the high rank of Commissaire-Général.

The news of this tragedy excited as much indignation in Berlin as in London. Faced with the facts, the representatives of the Free State in Brussels—that is, the agents of the King—were compelled to admit the complete illegality of the whole incident, and could only fall back upon the excuse that Lothaire's action was *bona-fide*, and free from personal motive. This is by no means certain, for as Baron von Marschall pointed out to the acting British Ambassador at Berlin, Stokes was known to be a successful trader in ivory, exporting it by the east route, and so depriving the officers of the Congo Government of a ten per cent. commission, which would be received by them if it were exported by the west route. "This was the reason," the report continued, quoting the German Statesman's words, "that he had been done away with, and not on account of an alleged sale of arms to Arabs, his death being, in fact, not an act of justice, but one of commercial protection, neither more nor less."

This was one reading of the situation. Whether it was a true one or not, there could be no two opinions as to the illegality of the proceedings. Under pressure from England, Lothaire was tried at Boma and acquitted. He was again, under the same pressure, tried at Brussels, when the Prosecuting Counsel thought it consistent with his duty to plead for an acquittal and the proceedings became a fiasco. There the matter was allowed to remain. A Blue Book of 188 pages is the last monument to Charles Henry Stokes, and his executioner returned to high office in the Congo Free State, where his name soon recurred in the accounts of the violent and high-handed proceedings which make up the history of that country. He was appointed Director of the Antwerp Society for the Commerce of the Congo—an appointment for which King Leopold must have been responsible—and he managed the affairs of that company until he was implicated in the Mongalla massacres, of which more will be said hereafter.

It has been necessary to describe the case of Stokes, because it is historical, but nothing is further from my intention than to address national *amour propre* in the matter. It was a mere accident that Stokes was an Englishman, and the outrage remains the same had he been a citizen of any State. The cause I plead is too broad, and also too lofty, to be supported by any narrower appeals than those which may be addressed to all humanity. I will proceed to describe a case which occurred a few years later to show that men of other nationalities suffered as well as the English. Stokes, the Englishman, was killed, and his death, it was said by some Congolese apologists, was due to his not having, after his summary trial, announced that he would lodge an immediate appeal to the higher court at Boma. Rabinck, the Austrian, the victim of similar proceedings, did appeal to the higher court at Boma, and it is interesting to see what advantage he gained by doing so.

Rabinck was, as I have said, an Austrian from Olmutz, a man of a gentle and lovable nature, popular with all who knew him, and remarkable, as several have testified, for his just and kindly treatment of the natives. He had, for some years, traded with the people of Katanga, which is the southeastern portion of the Congo State where it abuts upon British Central Africa. The natives were at the time in arms against the Belgians, but Rabinck had acquired such influence among them that he was still able to carry on his trade in ivory and rubber for which he held a permit from the Katanga Company.

Shortly after receiving this permit, for which he had paid a considerable sum, certain changes were made in the company by which the State secured a controlling influence in it. A new manager, Major Weyns, appeared, who represented the new régime, superseding M. Lévêque, who had sold the permits in the name of the original company. Major Weyns was zealous that the whole trade of the country should belong to the Concessionnaire Company, which was practically the Government, according to the usual, but internationally illegal, habit of the State. To secure this trade, the first step was evidently to destroy so well-known and successful a private trader as M. Rabinck. In spite of his permits, therefore, a charge was trumped up against him of having traded illegally in rubber—an offence which, even if he had no permit, was an impossibility in the face of that complete freedom of trade which was guaranteed by the Treaty of Berlin. The young Austrian could not bring himself to believe that the matter was serious. His letters are extant, showing that he regarded the matter as so preposterous that he could not feel any fears upon the subject. He was soon to be undeceived, and his eyes were opened too late to the character of the men and the organization with which he was dealing. Major Weyns sat in court-martial upon him. The offence with which he was charged, dealing illegally in rubber, was one which could only be punished by a maximum imprisonment of a month. This would not serve the purpose in view. Major Weyns within forty minutes tried the case, condemned the prisoner, and sentenced him to a year's imprisonment. There was an attempt to excuse this monstrous sentence afterward by the assertion that the crime punished was that of selling guns to the natives, but as a matter of fact there was at the time no mention of anything of the sort, as is proved by the existing minutes of the trial. Rabinck naturally appealed against such a sentence. He would have been wiser had he submitted to it in the nearest guard-house. In that case he might possibly have escaped with his life. In the other, he was doomed. "He will go," said an official, "on such a nice little voyage that he will act like this no more, and others will take example from it." The voyage in question was the two thousand miles which separated Katanga from the Appeal Court at Boma. He was to travel all this way under the sole escort of black soldiers, who had their own instructions. The unfortunate man felt that he could never reach his destination alive. "Rumours have it," he wrote to his relatives, "that Europeans who have been taken are poisoned, so if I disappear without further news you may guess what has become of me." Nothing more was heard from him save two agonized letters, begging officials to speed him on his way. He died, as he had foreseen, on the trip down the Congo, and was hurriedly buried in a wayside station when two hours more would have brought the body to Leopoldville. If it is possible to add a darker shadow to the black business it lies in the fact that the apologists of the state endeavoured to make the world believe that their victim's death was due to his own habit of taking morphia. The fact is denied by four creditable witnesses, who knew him well, but most of all is it denied by the activity and energy which had made him one of the leading traders of Central Africa—too good a trader to be allowed open competition with King Leopold's huge commercial monopoly. As a last and almost inconceivable touch, the whole of the dead man's caravans and outfits, amounting to some £15,000, were seized by those who had driven him to his death, and by the last reports neither his relatives nor his creditors have received any portion of this large sum. Consider the whole story and say if it is an exaggeration to state that Gustav Maria Rabinck was robbed and murdered by the Congo Free State.

Having shown in these two examples the way in which the Congo Free State has dared to treat the citizens of European States who have traded within her borders, I will now proceed to detail, in chronological order, some account of the dark story of that State's relations to the subject races, for whose moral and material advantage we and other European Powers have answered. For every case I chronicle there are a hundred which are known, but which cannot here be dealt with. For every one known, there are ten thousand, the story of which never came to Europe. Consider how vast is the country, and how few the missionaries or consuls who alone would report such matters. Consider also that every official of the Congo State is sworn neither at the time nor *afterward* to reveal any matter that may have come to his knowledge. Consider, lastly, that the missionary or consul acts as a deterrent, and that it is in the huge stretch of country where neither are to be found that the agent has his own unfettered way. With all these considerations, is it not clear that all the terrible facts which we know are but the mere margin of that welter of violence and injustice which the Jesuit, Father Vermeersch, has summed up in the two words, "Immeasurable Misery!"

Joseph Conrad's First Cruise in the *Nellie*

G. F. W. HOPE

◆　◆　◆

I ARRANGED A CRUISE in the *Nellie* for Joseph Conrad who had just arrived from Australia, where he had been for about two years in command of the *Otago*, owned by Simpson & Co. of Adelaide. He was at the time waiting for his passport into Russia to visit with his Uncle. As he had nothing to do for a few days, I asked him to come down to spend a few days with me, and as he hadn't seen my boat, to undertake a cruise in her with two other friends of mine. I thought this would be a good opportunity to introduce Conrad to Keen and Mears. The *Nellie* had accommodation for four—two in the main cabin and two in the ladies' cabin. She had a lead keel. This made one feel safe in her as she had a small beam for her length.

My friend Mears had sailed two voyages in the *Duke of Sutherland* as an apprentice with Captain Louttit. The *Duke of Sutherland* was the first British full-rigged ship that Conrad had sailed in, so that there would be three out of the four of us who had sailed in "The Old Duke," though at different times. As Keen and Mears couldn't join us till the Saturday afternoon, I arranged to make a start on Friday with Conrad and to spend the night at Hole Haven, going on to the Medway on the Saturday so as to get up to Chatham the Saturday evening to pick up Keen and Mears at the "Bull Inn" (immortalized by Dickens in *The Pickwick Papers*) about 7 o'clock for dinner. Conrad therefore came down to my house on the Thursday evening, much to the delight of the children with whom he was an immense favourite, as also with Mrs. Hope.

The next day we went aboard the *Nellie*, taking with us a cold leg of lamb and the usual bottle of mint sauce (we always started our cruises with a leg of lamb), some bottles of Reffel's Beer and sundry small stores and our suit-cases. We pulled aboard about 10 o'clock, stowed our gear and then proceeded to explain to Conrad how the ropes went, although he had had some experience in his youth at managing a small vessel. But things are rove differently in every craft one enters, whether they are large or small. However, he had never been in a yawl before, so, having explained the main ropes and how they led, we took the sail covers off the mainsail and foresail, [and] hoisted them along with the mizzen and jib. I then offered the tiller to Conrad, but he said he would rather I took her clear of the yachts which had moorings near to us. Still I insisted that he take the tiller, even just for a minute, while I went forward to let go the moorings. This he was glad to do. It was nearly high water and the tide began to ebb in our "bight" at Greenhithe, half an hour before it was high water out in the river.

We had a wonderful day to begin our trip. The wind was South West, it looked to last, and there was enough of it without setting the topsail.

Conrad thought the *Nellie* was a nice little craft, easy to handle, except that she wasn't good at "going about." She had too straight a stern—otherwise she was splendid. When we got down to the Lower Hope reach, we saw the Thames Sand Company's dredger busy at work loading a barge at the West Blythe buoy. We passed several sailing ships and steamers as we made our way down to Hole Haven. When we got near the Haven I told Conrad I would take the foresail in and to keep her well down to the sea wall so as not to run any risk of touching the spit as we approached the creek. We had a fair wind in, so I lowered the main sail and took in the mizzen. We then ran up above the jetty, and let go the anchor just inside of the eel schoots. We then stowed the sails and brought forth the lamb.

After dinner we went ashore to the "Lobster Smack" Inn. This was a favourite resort of mine. The house was beautifully kept, the beds spotlessly clean and the cooking excellent but plain. There were some old nautical pictures on the walls, evidently drawn by a sailorman and very old. They were not much to look at as works of art, but they were correct in every detail. In the parlour we found the Chief-Officer of the Coast Guard, also Captain S. of the *Secret*, a man I had learned to know very well. I introduced Conrad to them and we all gathered round to have a yarn. Captain S. told us that when he was Second Mate with his father, who was captain of an East Indiaman, they were carrying pilgrims from India to the Red Sea. With a head wind there was always trouble with the pilgrims, as every time they put the ship round, the pilgrims wanted to know where the EAST was because their prayers were always said facing Mecca. So they kept running aft to the compass to see how her head was. Finally the "Old Man" told his son to chalk a compass on the main deck, and to make the EAST of the compass very large and definite. This plan when worked out seemed to satisfy them, and they gave no more trouble.

Just then Mr. Beckwith (the Landlord) came in and told us he had had a bother with a young policeman who had come to relieve their regular man when he was away. He said this fellow called him up about eleven o'clock the night before and made rather a din for that time of the night. Beckwith stuck his head out of the little inn window and asked what the fellow wanted. The reply was that he couldn't get over the ferry to South Benfleet. This puzzled old Beckwith, and [he] asked him further questions. The fellow told him he had had some bother to awaken the ferryman, and when he did come down to his boat, he was very slow in getting her off. When about halfway over he said to him: "Now then old Kruger, shake a leg there!" At that Kruger stopped rowing altogether and said, "Who are you calling 'old Kruger'? I shan't fetch you over at all, and the tide will serve for you to walk across the stepping stones when it comes to be one o'clock in the morning." At that, he turned his boat round and pulled back to Benfleet. At his wit's end, the fellow then called after him, "*Mr. Smith*, I'll give you a shilling if you will come back and take me across." The answer came back, "Don't call me Mister, nor yet 'Old Kruger'! I wouldn't take you over if you offered me *five* shillings! Go back to Beckwith and ask him to give you a bed, or if he won't, go to the wall to the Coast Guard's Watch shed and good luck to you all the same!" When he at last got to my inn I said: "The best thing is to do as Smith told you—go to the coast guard on duty and ask him to let you stop in their hut till the tide is low enough for you to walk easily over." This was the end of the yarn. Beckwith then turned to us, and looking at Conrad, said, "You see Gentlemen what a little incivility may cost you. If he had not tried to play the clown with old Smith, the ferryman, then he would have brought him across alright, although he is a rum old bugger if you rub him up the wrong way."

We then all had a drink, and invited Beckwith to join his glass with ours. Conrad then told a tale (which I had heard before) of when he was a youngster about eighteen. He joined up with a party of four men—an Englishman, an American, a Spaniard, in a little lateen rigged vessel smuggling arms for Don Carlos's party, when the Spaniards were trying to get up a revolution. They ran two cargoes, but when running the third, a Spanish Revenue Cruiser hove in sight and chased them until they finally had to run their lateener ashore on the rocks, only just escaping with their lives. (Conrad made a very good tale of this in after years, called *The Arrow of Gold*.)

When this yarn was finished the Coast Guard Officer took over as we filled up our glasses again. It seems that before he was in the Coast Guard, he was in a ship where the liberty men were mustered for going ashore, and among them was a Petty Officer who was heartily disliked by all hands. Where they had to go ashore, they found the place thick with mud nearly up to their knees so that the liberty men got the boat's crew to carry them ashore on their backs. This meant they would be spared taking off their highly polished black boots and rolling their pants up to the knees. Now, when this unpleasant Petty Officer was being carried ashore, the man who had him on his back said: "I feel so queer all of a sudden that I think I shall faint! Yes, I feel as though I should fall in a minute or two." With that, he turned right over into the thick mud, not only dropping the Petty Officer in the stuff, but he himself turning over on top of him, squashing him well down into the mud. You can imagine the mess the Petty Officer now found himself in! Naturally, he couldn't say anything to the man (shamming sick) but he said quite a lot to the other men looking on, who, of course, were jarring their slats laughing at him. They all knew it was done on purpose to serve the Petty Officer out.

It was then my turn at a yarn, and I told the company a tale told to me by a late Sergeant of Marines. This Sergeant said one day, when his ship was in harbour, and the Commander and some of the Officers were going ashore, the Commander said to his servant (a Private in the Marines), "You can give my cabin a good clean out while I'm ashore." So as soon as the commander had left his cabin, the Marine started work, starting first to brush the Commander's full dress uniform which was a magnificent affair. Suddenly he held back his brush, and wondered how he should look in so fine a garment. Then and there he proceeded to put on the whole uniform, cocked hat and even buckled on the dress sword. Just as he was engaged in admiring himself in the glass, the door opened and in stepped the Commander who had altered his mind about going ashore. He sized up the situation calmly, and said, "Oh, I see, *Commander* Jones, it is a good thing I returned to ship in time to introduce you to my brother officers! Please follow me onto the quarter deck." So the poor Marine had to go up with the Commander and be introduced to each of the Officers (of course they knew it was only Private Jones) but they, realizing the joke, pretended not to know and each one shook hands with Jones. When this farce was over—it was seriously carried through—the Commander sent Jones below, uniform and all. Conrad thought this yarn very choice.

Another yarn this same Marine told me concerned a crusty old ship's surgeon. One day a sailor said he wanted to see the Doctor at once. When brought to the Doctor, he was asked his trouble. The man replied: "Well Sir, I can't exactly tell but I think it is something wrong with my bowels." "*Bowels!*" said the doctor. "I never heard of an A. B. having bowels! What you mean is *guts!* Only Commissioned Officers have what you name 'bowels'!"

We now felt it time to be moving, so we broke up the party saying Goodnight to them all, Captain S. going aboard *Secret*, and we to the *Nellie*. I exclaimed to Conrad when we got aboard what a good landlord old Beckwith was. He would never let a man have too much beer. Many of the men working on the sea-wall used to spend their evenings in the Bar Parlour of "The Lobster Smack," and if one of them seemed to be getting lively, Beckwith used to say, "Now then, Billy, you have had quite enough grog: you can have more tomorrow but not a drop more today." And strange to say, those words were quite enough for them. Very few rows took place in the house.

Beckwith told me once that he had a nasty row with the crew of one of the Dutch eel schoots. They entered the Bull half drunk and began trouble. Beckwith ordered them out of the house, but they wouldn't go so he took one big man by the shoulders to put him out, whereon the rest of the crew turned on old Beckwith. It developed into a general row with all concerned, as the Englishmen took Beckwith's side, helping to turn out the Dutchmen. There was a free fight, even on the pavement; but the Dutchmen were beaten in the end.

Next morning, Conrad thought he should like to go for a walk along the sea wall to see something of the island. I took him to the part of the wall where the men were at work. These walls have to [be] kept a certain height to keep back the tide. They are continually falling into disrepair, and for this reason, a Commission exists, made up of the owners of the land, who from time to time inspect the condition the wall, and that all repairs are done properly. The walls must be kept up to a standard height, as they gradually keep sinking down as the dykes do in Holland. The workmen dig clay from the land side of the wall and take it in wheelbarrows up planks to the top of the wall, then dump it down. One man rams it into place and then replaces the Kentish rag stones. Some years after the time I am writing about, one November in 1902 I think it was, the tide flooded two-thirds of Canvey Island and began to come through the wall near Beckwith's house. But it didn't do any serious damage. Yet at the time, all the east coast was flooded. I remember going up the River Crouch beyond Burnham, and seeing vast field upon field submerged. It ruined a great many farmers who had land adjoining the rivers. Thus, it is most necessary for the workmen to be very accurate with their levels. All this activity interested Conrad very much.

We continued to walk some way along this sea wall, until it was time for the morning papers to arrive. Beckwith's retriever dog used to go out to meet the Postman and bring back the paper in his mouth, depositing it in the Bar Parlour. One of the maids always gave him a biscuit after the delivery. The dog did this routine every day except Sunday. It seemed to realize it was Sunday, but on all other days of the week, it never missed going to meet the Postman and he always had his rewarding biscuit.

After admiring this trick and having a look at the news in the paper (accompanied with a glass of Beckwith's beer), we had an early dinner as we wanted to get under way about one o'clock so as to get the first of the tide out of the creek and make progress to the Jenkin Buoy. We had a few words with Captain S. who was anchored near us in the *Secret*. He told us that he spent a good deal of time in Hole Haven with his young son, who amused himself with sailing toy boats. But he was a smart little fellow and handled the dinghy belonging to his father's boat well.

After dinner we got under way, having shouted Goodbye to Captain S. We then made three or four short tacks out of the creek and then a long one right across the river down towards the Jenkin Buoy. We entered the Swatchway a little above the bobbing buoy. As it was still quite early, no barges were met and as the tide had only just turned at Gravesend we had the Swatch-way all to ourselves. When we got to the Medway end of it, we found the tide running strong out of that river, and as we should have a head wind to beat against us as well, we decided to anchor for an hour or so to allow the tide to slacken. When we got under way again, we had to beat up to Sheerness. We went quite near the men-of-war laying at the buoys; amongst them was H.M.S. *Valorous*, one of the last of the paddle-wheel frigates. She had just come from a foreign station, and had an enormous pennant flying which showed she was about to be paid off.

Conrad was interested to see her at such close quarters. This was the old *Valorous* that Brady used to tell us such yarns about. She was broken up shortly afterwards. I think she was out at the Crimean War, but am not quite certain about that. When we got opposite to the mouth of the Swale, I pointed out to Conrad the place where we should lay when we came out of the Swale from the east end, coming back, as we intended to go down to Margate the next day (Sunday) and put Keen ashore there after which we intended to come back through the Swale from the east end of it. I had never been in that end of it myself, so it would be new to all three of us, because tomorrow, in going to Margate, we should go outside Sheerness by the "Nore" Channel and then into the four-fathom channel to Margate.

We had to beat the whole way to Chatham. Conrad was very interested in what [he] saw, for although he had been several times up and down the Thames, this was the first time he had been up the Medway. I showed him the curious tower built, I believe, by "The Peculiar People." It is on the hills to the left of Chatham Dockyard. Then, at the lower entrance to the Dock-yard, the old *Leonidas* and Upnor Castle. I also pointed out the position of the Dutch fleet under Admiral De Ruyter, when they bombarded Upton Castle and sank two or three of our line of battle ships and then got clean away. We were now getting up to the Sun Pier at Chatham, and as there [was] an empty buoy, I made fast to it and took the dinghy ashore to ask permission. All yachts belonging to any recognised yacht club have the right to moor at the Admiralty buoys (if not in use) but I was not sure about the Ordnance buoys. I therefore always sought permission, sooner or later.

We now stowed the sails and made ready for our two other
friends to join us, Keen and Mears. We decided to put them
together in the main cabin, while we took the after cabin. When
all these arrangements were completed, we locked up the companion hatch and went ashore, leaving the dinghy in charge of
a boy.

As we walked up Chatham High Street towards the "Bull"
where we were to meet Keen and Mears, I pointed out all the
sights of interest, especially those mentioned by Dickens, because
Conrad was an admirer of Dickens. One of these was the "Seven
Travellers Inn" and the Cathedral on the left, also "The Bull Inn."
This is a very nice old place and the grub is always good, served
by English waiters. I took him over the Castle, from the high
walls of which you have a splendid view of the Medway. It can
be seen winding along for miles towards Maidstone. Leaving the
Castle we went along the fields where Pickwick informs us that
Winkle was going to fight the duel with Dr. Slammer of the 97th
Regiment.

When we got back to the "Bull" we found Keen there, but
Mears was coming by train arriving an hour later. About seven
o'clock Mears turned up, so we all dined and had a very good
dinner as usual. After a cup of delicious coffee we went down to
the Sun Pier as I wanted to get my crew aboard and settled down
as soon as possible. It took us half an hour to get to the Pier,
because it takes rather longer escorting people who are new to
the town, owing to the many interesting landmarks to be seen
and explained.

We found the dinghy after a little trouble, as the boy we left
in charge had taken a friend of his out for a row thinking we
should not be down before ten o'clock. But I managed to hail
him on the water and we got aboard in good time. I had prepared
Keen for a very small yacht, so he thought the *Nellie* more roomy
than he expected.

I told them all we should get under way about ten o'clock in
the morning. We played cards till time to turn in. Conrad said

he wanted to have a swim in the morning so I turned them out about seven o'clock. We then went ashore at the opposite side of the river where there is a stretch of waste ground, and as there was no one about at this early hour we all stripped and had a good refreshing swim. Back aboard the *Nellie* I cooked them a big breakfast of ham and eggs, tinned coffee and milk. They did well. When breakfast was over we got the mainsail and mizzen set, also the topsail as there was little wind. Then the jib was set. After casting off the moorings from the buoy and hoisting up the foresail we were off down the river.

At first we didn't make much headway as the flood was still running up, but in about an hour this had ceased and we made better way to get down the river. Again I pointed out Upnor Castle, the Chatham Dockyard and later, the war ships in long reach. Finally we got down to Sheerness where again I pointed out H.M.S. *Valorous*, especially to Mears who knew Brady well. I told him she was one of the ships he served in when he was in the Navy.

We got rather more wind as we passed Nore Lightship. We then went down the inside channel (so-called), passed the Spaniard Buoy and down the four-fathom channel when we came in sight of Whitstable, Herne Bay, with the Reculvers Towers. But here the wind failed us and there didn't seem any chance of reaching Margate. Keen looked at his timetable and there didn't seem much time now to get to Margate. He thought it best not to attempt it, but rather to go ashore at Birchington. I agreed to dodge the *Nellie* "on and off" while Conrad and Mears put Keen ashore in the dinghy. Here the water was very shoal, but we saw with our glasses that the Causeway was a very long one and we hoped it would run out far enough for the dinghy to go alongside, so I bid Goodbye to Keen telling him how sorry I was to be unable to get him to Margate. He was decent about this and off they went. I could see that they had some doubts about landing. Keen made a long jump out of the dinghy and apparently missed the Causeway and went over his knees into the water (they told me this when they returned) so that he had to travel all the way

up to London in wet trousers. It was rather a poor ending to
what otherwise would have been a very enjoyable day.

As soon as Conrad had made fast the dinghy, we steered for
Margate Pier and fetched there about seven o'clock, so after stow-
ing the sails and locking the cabin up, we pulled ashore and then
made the dinghy fast to the Pier. We strolled up the town and
came to a decent looking inn where we went in and had dinner.
Margate was teeming with tourists, mostly from the East End of
London. Back aboard we had further yarns about the old *Duke of
Sutherland*. Curiously enough, a Mr. Bastard was Second Mate when
Conrad was in her. Mears too knew Bastard eight years later.
Bastard afterwards got a job at the Sailors' Home in London and
Conrad often went to see him there. I never knew him as he
wasn't Second Mate when I was in the ship during my first voyage
in her. Alex Louttit was Second when I was Third Mate during
my last voyage in her.

We then turned in. The next morning didn't look too fine. It
was inclined to blow from the North-West. So we went ashore
and had some grub in the middle of the day, having had our
breakfast on board before we started out.

We walked about Margate but didn't think much of the place.
About three o'clock it came on to blow rather hard so we
thought it best to make a start and run up the Swale. The
weather now was thick as well as blowing so we decided to house
the topmast, double-reef the mainsail and reef the foresail, setting
neither the mizzen nor jib. We hove up the anchor and set the
reefed foresail, steering for the Swale. The weather got thicker
and was disagreeable. We made the buoy at the eastern end of
the Swale and nearly ran into a large brigantine at anchor. As
soon as I judged we were about opposite to Faversham Creek, we
let go our anchor and gave her all the chain we could. It then
came on to blow very hard, and although we were some way up
the Swale, we couldn't find shelter and had to stay where we
were.

All night it blew. We found we were just opposite Faversham
Creek. The tide hadn't ebbed a notch. It was kept high by the

beastly wind. A small cutter yacht had also run in for shelter, bringing up near us. One of its crew lost his cap overboard, and two of the hands took their dinghy to pick it up. But it was blowing so damned hard that they could not regain their yacht and so had to go into Faversham Creek for safety. We saw nothing more of them. For the rest of the day we played at dominoes. It was the strongest wind I had met on this coast. When we finally turned in about midnight the wind was still roaring, but it abated during the early hours of the morning.

When the daylight came we were all startled by a most extra-ordinary and weird noise. We all three rushed onto the deck, to find that the chain was rubbing on the bottom of *Nellie*! As the tide had been kept up high by the strong winds of the day before, now it had fallen almost calm. The water had all run out of the Creek, and we found ourselves nearly on a sandbank. We had only just time to heave her off into deeper water. But the morning was splendid with the sun newly up from the horizon. We heard a curlew crying over the marshes—otherwise all was very still after the cruel gale of the day before.

We all took an early breakfast, then shook the reefs out of the main and foresails. Then the mainsail was hoisted, the mizzen set, and the anchor hove up. Once up, up went the jib and foresail and we steered forward on our trip on the Swale. There was a fair wind which suited us as the *Nellie* drew six feet six inches of water aft so that in a narrow creek, as the Swale is, it was difficult to assist her taking the ground. When we got to the bridge a "Huffler" came off to us to get us under the bridge. We paid the "Huffler" as soon as we had cleared it and continued our way to Queenboro'. There are some large timber floats op-posite Queenboro', and a Norwegian barque was discharging baulks of oak. We could see she was Norwegian by her windmill, as all Norwegian vessels are compelled to be fitted with them. These are all fixed in the same position just forward of the mizzen mast. If the vessel leaks the windmill pumps her out. However, they do not improve the appearance of the vessels.

Deciding that we should be better off at Sheerness we hove up the anchor and set forth. I remembered a good hotel near the Pier called the "Fountain." It took us about an hour to get there. We anchored off the Pier in water deep enough to keep afloat at low water. We got the topmast up, stowed the sails, and made her look shipshape once again. After locking up the companion hatch we went ashore and went to the "Fountain" where we ordered dinner. This is the hotel where all the Captains of the men-of-war stay. Everything there is very nice and congenial. After dinner (excellent) we walked around the town of Sheerness but there wasn't much to see there. It is rather pleasant on the Eastern side facing the entrance to the Thames but it is essentially a naval port. After inspecting the sights we went aboard again, as we intended to turn in early so as to arise early for a start for home.

We turned out about four o'clock in the morning and got under way with a slight wind from the South-West, running down with the tide to the Gran Spit Buoy. There we anchored till the tide slackened. About ten o'clock we got under way again for home. We had a head wind all the way and reached Green-hithe about two o'clock. Then we picked up the moorings, stowed the sails, and packed our gear. When *Nellie* was shipshape with the burgee and ensign down, locking up, we went ashore in the dinghy.

I think Conrad and Mears enjoyed the trip very much, but I'm afraid Keen did not as having to return to town in wet trousers was sufficient to dampen any enthusiasm he may have felt at first. The fact is that a man must be very fond of the sea to really enjoy a trip such as we had.

To the End of the Night

ZDZISŁAW NAJDER

❖　❖　❖

ON 24 APRIL 1890, a few days before Conrad returned
to Brussels from Poland, Henry Morton Stanley, the famed
nineteenth-century traveler, delivered a speech in the building of
the Brussels Exchange. He had just arrived in great triumph after
a successful expedition for the relief of Emin Pasha, who had been
cut off by the Mahdist revolt. "What does the greatness of a
monarch consist in?" he asked. "If it is the extent of his territory,
then the Emperor of Russia is the greatest of all. If it is the
splendour and power of military organization then William II
takes first place. But if royal greatness consists in the wisdom and
goodness of a sovereign leading his people with the solicitude of
a shepherd watching over his flock, then the greatest sovereign
is your own."[1]

The Congo Free State, extending over a huge area of nearly
900,000 square miles, was under the direct rule of Leopold II, the
king of Belgium. It officially became a European dependency in
1885, relatively late, following the decision of the Berlin Congress
at which Leopold, the shrewd monarch of a small country, man-

aged to play skillfully against each other the rivalry and jealousy of powerful states. He also knew how to make clever use of slogans about progress, the civilizing mission, and the enlightenment and ennoblement of savages. "To bring civilization to the only part of this globe where it has not yet penetrated, to pierce the darkness which envelops entire populations—is, I dare say, a crusade worthy of this age of progress."[2] Stanley, in King Leopold II's service from 1879 to 1884 as an explorer and administrator on behalf of the Association Internationale pour l'Exploration et la Civilisation en Afrique, last lent his personal authority and propagandistic gift by publishing, among others, a two-volume laudatory report, *The Congo and the Founding of Its Free State: A Story of Work and Exploration.*[3]

The Société Anonyme Belge pour le Commerce du Haut-Congo was established on 10 December 1888. The Society had two objectives: to spread the financial burdens of colonization among a body of shareholders and stimulate the development of the country; and to monopolize trading by the state and build up an administrative network. Although the Congo had huge potential resources, for the time being the Belgian king was sinking enormous capital, almost his entire wealth, into the building of railway stations and roads. Individuals grew rich, but the state itself did not become self-supporting until 1899.[4] Thus, there was a great demand for energetic organizers; Albert Thys (1849–1915) was among the leading ones.

Did Conrad—or rather Conrad Korzeniowski, as he was known at that time—believe in the official phraseology, and, if so, to what extent? The personal passion he displayed later in his private and public attacks on King Leopold II—he treated no other politician with such venom—suggests the existence of some deep-seated grudge. The irony of "An Outpost of Progress," *Heart of Darkness*, and *The Inheritors* is directed mainly at the false pretenses of "civilizing" activity. And in one of his uncle Tadeusz Bobrowski's letters written to the Congo, we find a fragment that immediately brings to mind the problems set out in *Heart of Darkness*, and seems to show that during his conversations at Kazimierówka Korzeniowski himself took in good faith the "missionary" slogans of the colonizers. Bobrowski wrote, "You are probably looking around at people and things as well as at the 'civilizing' (confound it) affair in the machinery of which you are a cog— before you feel able to acquire and express your own opinion. Don't wait however until it all crystallizes into clear sentences, but tell me something of your health and your first impressions."[5] It is therefore quite probable that Korzeniowski sailed south convinced that he would be participating in an enterprise whose justification was not merely financial.

From Tenerife, the first port of call of the *Ville de Maceio*, he wrote to Marguerite Poradowska on 15 May. "My dear little Aunt," he began in the mixture of sentimental banter and melancholia that he probably thought becoming, for "the time being I am reasonably happy, which is all one can expect in this rotten world. It was raining on the day we left Bordeaux. A sad day; not a happy departure; haunting memories; vague regrets; still vaguer hopes. I doubt the future. For indeed—I ask myself—why should one trust it? And also why be sad? A little illusion, many dreams, a rare flash of happiness then disillusionment, a little anger and much pain, and then the end—peace! That is the programme and we shall be seeing this tragicomedy to the finish. One must be resigned."[6] Baines calls these phrases "typically Conradian reflections."[7] Indeed, similar thoughts are often found in Conrad's writings, and by and large they expressed his general attitude toward life; in this particular instance, however, they are most likely written for effect, *pour épater sa chère petite tante.*

The tone of another letter, posted from Freetown in Sierra Leone to Karol Zagórski, is entirely different: it has none of the pompous resignation displayed in the correspondence with Poradowska. Writing to his Polish cousin, Korzeniowski postured as a boisterous *szlachcic*, although the news he was conveying was far from cheerful. Obviously he had not been well briefed by the Society about working conditions in the Congo. "As far as I can make out from my 'lettre d'instruction' I am destined to the command of a steamboat, belonging to M. Delcommune's exploring party, which is being got ready. I like this prospect very much, but I know nothing for certain as everything is supposed

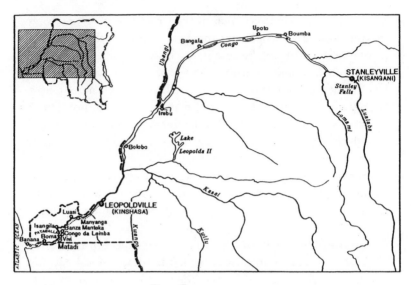

THE CONGO
.... caravan trail

to be kept secret."[8] The fact that he himself had not tried to secure the necessary information may indicate either credulity or the lack of responsibility for which his uncle had reproached him in the past.

One of his fellow passengers on the *Ville de Maceio*, Prosper Harou, was well acquainted with the Central African situation and painted a rather discouraging picture: 60 percent of the employees of the Company resigned their posts before six months were up; others, who could not stand the tropical climate, were quickly sent back to Europe; still others died from various diseases and exhaustion; and only 7 percent completed their three-year contracts, such as the one signed by Korzeniowski. Sending this information to Zagórski, Korzeniowski confessed his feelings of apprehension, but commented with bravado, "Yes! But a Polish *szlachcic* cased in British tar! What a concoction! Nous verrons! In any case I shall console myself by remembering—faithful to our national traditions—that I sought this trouble myself." The motif "you sought this trouble yourself" comes to the forefront of Bobrowski's reply to another letter from Korzeniowski, which had been written on the voyage on 28 May: "Firstly, we must fortify ourselves with patience, secondly with a certain amount of optimism;—which will come more easily to me sitting here in Kazimierówka than they will to you. I cannot even rely too much on your 'youth,' when everything seems rosy, for at Christ's age no room is left for illusions. The only consolation you can find in perfecting your perseverance and your optimism amidst your present struggles with life is in the exclamation of Molière with which you are familiar: 'tu l'as voulu, tu l'as voulu, Georges Dandin.' "[9]

The *Ville de Maceio* called at various ports: Tenerife in the Canary Islands, Dakar, Conakry in French Guinea, Freetown, Grand Bassam on the Ivory Coast, Grand Popo in Dahomey, and Libreville in Gabon. Korzeniowski must have had a lot of time for meditation and correspondence. If we are to accept as autobiographical Marlow's confessions in *Heart of Darkness*, the voyage was a very lonely one, but not because he was not used to the role of a passenger: he had been one on several occasions and for longer periods of time, for example, a year before on his homeward passage.[10] No, he must have felt lonely because he had just spent three months with his family and friends—an unusual experience for him—and possibly also because he met on board the type of people described in later African novels: nouveaux riches, shady speculators, and businessmen without scruples. Near Grand Popo he saw a French man-of-war, *Le Seignelay*, shelling a Negro camp hidden in the jungle;[11] the incident acquired a symbolic significance in *Heart of Darkness*.

On 12 June the *Ville de Maceio* reached Boma, fifty miles upriver from the Congo estuary. The next day Korzeniowski started off in a small steamer for Matadi, thirty miles farther up, the most distant navigable place on the lower reaches of the Congo.[12]

From Boma, on the threshold of the unknown, he sent a long letter to Poradowska, full of sentimental avowals.

As to events—nothing new. As to feelings—nothing new either. And herein lies the misfortune; for if one could get rid of one's heart and memory (and also brain) and then acquire a new set of those things, life would become perfectly amusing. As it is impossible, life is not so; it is desperately sad! For example: one of the things I wanted to forget, unsuccessfully, was the memory of my charming aunt. Of course this is not possible and consequently I remember and am sad. Where are you? How are you? Have you forgotten me? Are you left alone? Are you working? Especially that! Have you found the forgetfulness and peace of creative, absorbing work? So there. I ask myself all that. You have given my life a new interest and a new affection; I am most grateful to you for this. Grateful for all the sweetness, for all the bitterness, of this priceless gift. I am looking now down two avenues cut in a thick and confused mass of dangerous foliage. Where do they lead? You follow one, I the other. They branch out. Will you find a ray of sunlight, however pale, at the end of yours? I hope you do! I wish it for you! For a long time I have not been interested in the end to which my road takes me. I have walked with my head lowered, cursing the stones. Now I am interested in another traveler. This makes me forget the small annoyances on my own road.[13]

The "annoyances" in the literal sense were to begin soon. We know about them from a diary that Korzeniowski kept for the first sixty-seven days of his stay in the Congo. It is the only document of its kind among all Conrad materials. The author confined himself almost exclusively to short, factual notes that enable us to reconstruct with a fair degree of accuracy the various stages of his journey and the changes of his moods. What adds importance to the diary is the fact that it is one of Korzeniowski's earliest known English texts. Here and there are signs of French influence on the vocabulary, and Polish on the syntax, showing that the future writer had not yet completely mastered the English language.

At Matadi, Korzeniowski and Harou were held up for fifteen

days by Joseph-Louis-Hubert Gosse, the manager of the Company's local trading post. Korzeniowski made the following entries in his diary:

> Made the acquaintance of Mr. Roger Casement, which I should consider as a great pleasure under any circumstances and now it becomes a positive piece of luck.
>
> Thinks, speaks well, most intelligent and very sympathetic.
>
> Feel considerably in doubt about the future. Think just now that my life amongst the people (white) around here cannot be very comfortable. Intend avoid acquaintances as much as possible.
>
> Have been myself busy packing ivory in casks. Idiotic employment. Health good up to now. . . . Prominent characteristic of the social life here: people speaking ill of each other.[14]

Many years later he wrote about his having shared a room with Casement "for some three weeks," but the recollection must be inaccurate; Casement left Matadi on 24 June and probably did not return until just before Korzeniowtski's departure.[15] Roger Casement was at that time employed by the Compagnie du Chemin de Fer du Congo as a supervisor of the projected building of a railway line from Matadi to Kinshasa. On several occasions Casement and Korzeniowski made joint expeditions into the nearby villages in search of Negro porters, whose services were acquired by negotiating with the local chiefs.[16] Casement was very well acquainted with the area, having already spent several years in the Congo, once at Matadi as the manager of an American camp for exploratory expeditions directed by General Henry Sanford.

In *Heart of Darkness*, which contains a fairly large, albeit unevenly supplied, measure of autobiographical facts, Conrad presents the construction of the railway line from Matadi as both chaotic and inefficient; he described a line of chained black prisoner-porters and the grove of death where the sick and utterly exhausted black workers were left to die slowly. Confusion, stupidity, and cruelty sum up the fictional picture of that center of civilization. Although Norman Sherry doubts whether Matadi was in fact so horrifying at that time, he quotes an account, published in 1907 but relating to the year 1892, of a high mortality rate among the railroad workers and the fact that blacks were forced to work against their will; he does not explain why the situation in 1890 should have been any different.[17]

But to recreate what Korzeniowski did see and experience during his stay in the Congo, this kind of comparison is not the most important. Even if we establish what he could have seen and what he did actually see, we have to ask more basic questions: In what categories did he perceive it? How did he understand it? Louis Goffin, the Belgian engineer quoted by Sherry, claims that the enforced labor of the sick and terrified Negroes, who were dying at the rate of five a day, was necessary in order to "construct this line of railway, to suppress for ever the far more awful tax of human porterage along this route of the caravans between the Upper and Lower Congo," but he overlooks the fact that the beaten Negroes were interested neither in having a railway line nor in the caravan route for transporting ivory to Europe. Another account cited by Sherry tells of the difficulties involved in finding porters for the construction of that line. An English missionary complained about their lack of subordination and their unwillingness to be moved from their homes.[18] And so once again we are presented with a white man's point of view, which ignores the fact that those porters were hired out by their village chiefs; that they were separated for weeks from their families; that they worked for no or little pay; that they were exposed to disease, mutilation, or death during the long marches with heavy loads; and, finally, that they saw no point in it all. The same situation may be looked at from two entirely opposite points of view: "stupid savages do not want to contribute to progress," or "poor wretches are forced to work till they drop dead."

Korzeniowski never subscribed to the first extreme, but his personal notes reflect an attitude different from that presented in *Heart of Darkness*. Jotting down his immediate impressions in his diary and letters, he seems to have adopted the perspective of a European traveler exposed to discomfort. One may assume that Casement, who was later to become famous for his crusade for humanitarian treatment of the natives in the colonies, told Korzeniowski about the practices of European administrators and traders. But we do not know what Casement's attitude was then and in what categories he saw the problems. After all, he had for many years been one of the cogs in the "civilizing" machinery and, at the time, he was in charge of the construction work on a railway line.

It is evident that Korzeniowski was struck at first by the greed and duplicity of the white bearers of "civilization" eager for quick profits, and by the chaos and stupidity of many of their enterprises. It was only later that he became aware of the outrages perpetrated against the native population and their country.

Matadi was, at that time, an important center of trade, inhabited by well over one hundred Europeans, but, above all, it was a center of communication and transport: the sea routes from the ocean and from Europe crossed the caravan route that led into the rich interior of the Congo. Although Korzeniowski expected to leave Matadi by 19 June, he did not start on his 230-mile-long journey until 28 June.[19] Each day he sketched in his diary the road he had covered, marking the bearings and the profile of the terrain, in the belief that the data might be useful in the future. He was rather liberal in assessing the distance covered, sometimes counting as many as three or even more than four miles per hour, which was of course impossible.

Saturday, 28th June.
     Left Matadi with Mr. Harou and a caravan of 31 men. Parted with Casement in a very friendly manner. Mr. Gosse saw us off as far as the State station. . . .

Sund[ay], 29th.
     Ascent of Pataballa sufficiently fatiguing. Camped at 11h a.m. at Nsoke River. Misquitos [*sic*].

Monday, 30th.

To Congo da Lemba after passing black rocks. Long ascent. Harou giving up. Bother. Camp bad. Water far. Dirty. At night Harou better. . . .

Wednesday, 2nd July.

Started at 5:30 after a sleepless night. Country more open. Gently andulating [*sic*] hill. Road good in perfect order. (District of Lukungu.) Great market at 9:30. Bought eggs and chickens.

Feel not well today. Heavy cold in the head. Arrived at 11 at Banza Manteka. Camped on the market place. Not well enough to call on the missionary. Water scarce and bad. Camp[in]g place dirty. . . .

Thursday, 3rd July.

. . . Met an off[ic]er of the State inspecting; a few minutes afterwards saw at a camp[in]g place the dead body of a Bac-kongo. Shot? Horrid smell. . . . Another range parallel to the first mentioned, with a chain of low foothills running close to it. . . . General tone of landscape gray-yellowish (dry grass), with reddish patches (soil) and clumps of dark-green vegeta-tion scattered sparsely about, mostly in steep gorges between the high mountains or in ravines cutting the plain. Noticed Palma Christi—Oil Palm. Very straight, tall and thick trees in some places. Name not known to me. Villages quite invisi-ble. . . .

Friday, 4th July.

Left camp at 6h a.m. after a very unpleasant night. March-ing across a chain of hills and then in a maze of hills. At 8:15 opened out into an andulating [*sic*] plain. . . . Sharp ascents up very steep hills not very high. The higher mountains recede sharply and show a low hilly country. At 9:30 market place. . . .

Saw another dead body lying by the path in an attitude of meditative repose.

In the evening three women of whom one albino passed our camp. Horrid chalky white with pink blotches. Red eyes.

Red hair. Features very Negroid and ugly. Mosquitos. At night
when the moon rose heard shouts and drumming in distant
villages. Passed a bad night.

Saturday, 5th July.
  . . . Today fell into a muddy puddle. Beastly. The fault of
the man that carried me. After camp[in]g went to a small
stream, bathed and washed clothes. Getting jolly well sick of
this fun. . . .

Sunday, 6th July.
  Started at 5:40. The route at first hilly, then after a sharp
descent traversing a broad plain. At the end of it a large market
place. At 10h sun came out.
  After leaving the market, passed another plain, then walking on the crest of a chain of hills passed 2 villages and at 11h
arrived at Nsona. Village invisible. . . .
  . . . good camp[in]g place. Shady. Water far and not very
good. This night no mosquitos owing to large fires lit all round
our tent. . . .

Monday, 7th July.
  . . . Walking along an andulating [sic] plain towards the In-
kandu market on a hill. Hot, thirsty and tired. At 11h arrived
in the M[ar]ket place. About 200 people. Business brisk. No
water. No camp[in]g place. After remaining for one hour, left
in search of a resting place.
  Row with carriers. No water. At last, about 1½ p.m., camped
on an exposed hillside near a muddy creek. No shade. Tent on
a slope. Sun heavy. Wretched. . . .
  Night miserably cold. No sleep. Mosquitos.

Tuesday, 8th July.
  The country presents a confused wilderness of hills land
slips on their sides showing red. Fine effect of red hill covered
in places by dark-green vegetation.[20]

For people unaccustomed to such physical exertions and to the climate, the journey must have been extremely tiring, although the travelers moved at the rate of a dozen or so miles a day, unburdened, and carried by the porters across bogs and rivers in hammocks. On the morning of 8 July they reached Manyanga, where an Englishman, Reginald Heyn, was manager of a transport base.[21] There the travelers stayed seventeen days. "Both have been sick," wrote Korzeniowski in his diary, "most kindly care taken of us." Sherry suggests, erroneously, that the time taken by the march—almost double the normal time—from Matadi to Kinshasa was not entirely justified and that it was the cause of Korzeniowski's conflict with his superiors.[22] However, Korzeniowski's march was by no means a slow one. If we compare the distances he covered with an official itinerary published a few years later for the benefit of caravans traveling from Matadi to Léopoldville, we see that he on the whole walked faster than the instructions suggested.[23] Besides, he was not making the protracted journey alone. The unscheduled halt in Manyanga had taken place with the knowledge of the Society's official and in the company of another of its employees, Prosper Harou, ill at the time; although a Congo veteran, Harou fared worse than Korzeniowski. Also, the porters had to be changed in Manyanga and there may have been difficulties with finding new ones.

On the afternoon of 25 July the party started off on their way "with plenty of hammock carriers. H. lame and not in very good form. Myself ditto but not lame."

Sunday, 27th.

Left at 8h am. Sent luggage carriers straight on to Luasi and went ourselves round by the Mission of Sutili.

Hospitable reception by Mrs. Comber. All the missio[naries] absent.

The looks of the whole establishment eminently civilized and very refreshing to see after the lots of tumble-down hovels in which the State and Company agents are content to live. . . .

Tuesday, 29th.

Left camp at 7h after a good night's rest. Continuous ascent;

rather easy at first. Crossed wooded ravines and the river Lunzadi by a very decent bridge.

At 9h met Mr Louette escorting a sick agent of the Comp[an]y back to Matadi. . . . Bad news from up the river. All the steamers disabled. One wrecked.

. . . Met ripe pineapple for the first time. On the road today passed a skeleton tied up to a post. Also white man's grave—no name. Heap of stones in the form of a cross.

Health good now.

Wednesday, 30th.

. . . Two hours' sharp walk brought me to Nsona na Nsefe. Market. ½ hour after, Harou arrived very ill with billious [*sic*] attack and fever. Laid him down in Gov[ernmen]t shimbek. Dose of Ipeca [*sic*]. Vomiting bile in enormous quantities. At 11h gave him 1 gramme of quinine and lots of hot tea. Hot fit ending in heavy perspiration. . . . Row with carriers all the way. Harou suffering much through the jerks of the hammock. . . .

Expect lots of bother with carriers tomorrow. Had them all called and made a speech which they did not understand. They promise good behaviour.

Thursday, 31st.

Left at 6h. Sent Harou ahead and followed in ½ hour. Road presents several sharp ascents and a few others easier but rather long. . . . Great difficulty in carrying Harou. Too heavy. Bother. Made two long halts to rest the carriers. . . .

Friday, 1st of August 1890.

Left at 6:30 am after a very indifferently passed night. Cold, heavy mists. . . .

Put up at Gov[ernmen]t shanty.

Row between the carriers and a man stating himself in Gov[ernmen]t employ, about a mat. Blows with sticks raining hard. Stopped it. Chief came with a youth about 13 suffering from gunshot wound in the head. Bullet entered about an inch above the right eyebrow and came out a little inside. The roots of the hair, fairly in the middle of the brow in a line

with the bridge of the nose. Bone not damaged apparently.
Gave him a little glycerine to put on the wound made by the
bullet on coming out. Harou not very well. Mosquitos. Frogs.
Beastly. Glad to see the end of this stupid tramp. Feel rather
seedy. Sun rose red. . . . [24]

It was the dawn of August 2. On that day the caravan arrived
at the port of Kinshasa, the Company's next trade and transport
base. The news about the accidents involving steamers turned out
to be only partly true. The *Florida*, which Korzeniowski was to
command, had been seriously damaged on 18 July but on the
twenty-third she was towed to Kinshasa for repair. The boat was
unfit for sailing but in any case Korzeniowski could not have
assumed command immediately on an unknown river and in
unfamiliar conditions. He was therefore taken the next day on
board the 15-ton river steamer *Roi des Belges*, commanded by a
twenty-five-year-old Dane, Ludvig Rasmus Koch.[25] The *Roi des Belges* was hurrying off to help another steamer, the *Ville de Bruxelles*,
which on 16 July had got stuck on a root near Upoto.[26]

Before his departure from Kinshasa Korzeniowski posted his
sixth letter from the journey to his uncle Tadeusz, who replied:

I see from your last letter that you feel a deep resentment
towards the Belgians for exploiting you so mercilessly. In general there is no love in your heart for the Latin races, but this
time, you must admit, nothing forced you to put yourself into
Belgian hands. You can say to yourself: "Tu l'as voulu, Georges
Dandin"; and if you had paid any attention to my opinion on
the subject when discussing it with me, you would have certainly detected a lack of enthusiasm in me for this project.

As a traditional Polish *szlachcic* I value more the certain and
less glamorous than a more glamorous uncertainty! In the first
place, whatever happened, I ask you most sincerely to calm
down and not to get worked up lest it should affect your liver,
"Ne v[ou]s gâter pas le sang et le foie." Secondly, let me observe
that by breaking your agreement you would expose yourself
to considerable financial loss, and you certainly lay yourself

open to an accusation of irresponsibility which may be harmful to your further career. Unless your health becomes affected you should stick it out; at least that is my opinion.[27]

This is the first sign of Korzeniowski's becoming sufficiently displeased with working conditions in the Congo to consider breaking the contract after less than two months. We may guess that the reason directly responsible for it was not the fact that he had been forced, in spite of poor health, to start immediately on another journey, but his personal conflict with the Company's manager, Camille Delcommune, two years younger than himself. Delcommune, who wanted to leave as soon as possible to go up-river, awaited the new captain with impatience. Norman Sherry rightly points to the probability that the real conversation with Delcommune is reflected in the text and manuscript of *Heart of Darkness*: "My first interview with the manager was curious. He did not ask me to sit down after my twenty-mile walk that morning. . . . He began to speak as soon as he saw me. I had been very long on the road. . . . He paid no attention to my explanations."[28] Knowing Korzeniowski's touchiness we can imagine how sharply he must have reacted at the reproof; or just at being addressed in a discourteous way; or, simply, at the manager's lack of interest in the reasons for the delay or in Korzeniowski's health. A photograph of Delcommune gives the impression of a bully; his "ship-keeper's" approach could antagonize the "Polish *szlachcic* cased in British tar," poisoning their relationship right from the start; moreover Korzeniowski's past experiences and impressions could not dispose him well toward the representative of the Company's highest authority in Africa. Alas, they were destined to spend a considerable time together.

The river steamer bearing the majestic name of *Roi des Belges*, in reality a small, clumsy, and noisy contraption resembling a tin box, packed tightly with passengers and the crew, left Kinshasa on 3 August on her way up the Congo.[29] Korzeniowski, watching Koch, got into the habit of recording in detail all navigation instructions, bearings, landmarks, dangerous spots, and so forth in his diary, whose second part consists almost entirely of notes on and sketches of the river bed. When they reached Bangala (later renamed Nouvelle Anvers) on 19 August, his entries stopped, either because he fell ill or because he heard—or decided himself—that he was not going to command a ship on the Congo.[30]

The notes reveal his total preoccupation, both as a potential commander and as a diarist, with the difficulties of navigation, which required constant concentration. "When about the middle of the open snatch steer right across to clear Ganchu's Point. Pass the point cautiously. Stones. . . . Sandbank always covered in the bight. . . . The landing must be approached cautiously on account of stones and snags. Round P[oin]t U cautiously. When entering the reach keep rather on the outer edge of the current following the right shore. Sandbank on left shore not visible. . . . Leave the island to starb[oard] and follow its inner shore to take the narrow p[assa]ge. Sound[in]gs 9 to 5 feet. . . . This passage is between the m[ai]n land on Port side and 2 islands on starb[oar]d. Where the 1st is[lan]d finishes there is a sandbank. Steering close in to the islands in a s[ou]nd[ing]s 10 to 5 feet—Steer over to M[ai]n shore and back again."[31] And so it goes, page after page. Constant alertness was all the more needed since the boat advanced with exceptional speed.[32] It covered more than a thousand miles in twenty-eight days.

A reader of Korzeniowski's hastily jotted notes, accompanied by drawings relating mainly to the depth of the current, shallows, promontories, snags, islands, and reefs—notes that, apart from the river, concentrate almost exclusively on landmarks such as hilltops or trees discernible from afar, and places supplying timber—may easily recapture the sense of complete isolation from the rest of the world, the oppressive solitude, amidst water and jungle, that must have been experienced by the man in command.

Sherry's assertion that, in spite of *Heart of Darkness*, Korzeniowski's impressions of the journey could not have been "a sense of oppressiveness and isolation" and that the passage up the Congo was "a routine, highly organised venture along a fairly frequented riverway linking quite numerous settlements of trading posts and factories," contrasts strongly with the picture suggested by the established evidence.³³ About two hundred miles above Kinshasa the Congo becomes a huge, elongated lake, interspersed with islands and shoals, with the other bank often invisible. True, the *Roi des Belges* apparently passed six other boats, but what were six small steamers in four weeks' navigation on a river whose banks were mostly hidden by tropical vegetation? In parts, the Congo measures a few miles in width; in others it spreads over ten, twisting and turning before it branches out into yet new creeks, meanders, and bays. It is not even certain whether they actually saw all those ships—at the rate of one every four and a half days. They passed several missions hundreds of miles apart. And as to the villages, Korzeniowski spotted no more than six over a distance of more than five hundred miles. *Heart of Darkness* does not claim to be a dependable traveler's guide, but it does depict the threatening atmosphere of isolation quite convincingly.

In order to support his thesis about the density of population along the upper part of the Congo, Sherry cites statements by Camille's elder brother Alexandre Delcommune and a Belgian missionary, dating from 1888 and the beginning of 1890.³⁴ Those statements, however, lack substance; moreover, they refer mainly to a relatively short stretch—just over one hundred miles—of the river. Both reports appeared in the Brussels *Mouvement Géographique*, which, of course, published only encouragingly optimistic material. Six months after Korzeniowski, a group of traders covered the same route on board the same steamer, and one of them wrote in a letter to Europe: "The country is ruined. Passengers in the steamer *Roi des Belges* have been able to see for themselves that from Bontya, half a day's journey below our factory at Upoto, to Boumba [that is, about two hundred miles along the river] inclusive, there is not an inhabited village left— that is to say four days' steaming through a country formerly so rich, today entirely ruined."³⁵ This impartial document is valuable not only as geographic information but also as testimony to the effects of Belgian colonization. It is fully corroborated by the report submitted to President Benjamin Harrison by African-American historian George Washington Williams, who noted that

"Nothing is so deceptive as estimating a population in a heathen country."[36] A modern historian of colonialism in the Congo basin tersely sums up: "The heavy demand for African labor disrupted traditional productive activities throughout most of the equatorial forest."[37]

On board the river steamer, apart from Koch and Korzeniowski, there was a Belgian mechanic named Gossens, and about twenty-five black crew members (recruited usually from among the Bangalis, who were not averse to cannibalism). The steamer was a wood-burning vessel, and many hands were needed to keep her running. In addition to two canoes the *Roi des Belges* towed two scows for carrying the wood supply that had to be periodically replenished. Woodcutters worked at night felling and chopping trees in places previously selected. There were also four passengers on board—Camille Delcommune and three agents of the Company (Alphonse Keyaerts, E. F. L. Rollin, and Vander Heyden).[38]

Neither the captain nor—most probably—his assistant had much time for contact with other Europeans on board. J. R. Troup, who on that same *Roi des Belges* took part in one of Stanley's expeditions, left the following description of the working routine of then-Captain Shagerström: "He would be at his post on the bridge, shouting his orders, and we would soon be again on our way . . . Shagerström used to take up his quarters [on the upper deck] from the time we started till we pulled up for the night, some ten hours, and would have his breakfast and lunch sent up to him while he was engaged in piloting us through the intricate channels of the mighty Congo! There was no one to share this task with him, to relieve him of his anxieties."[39]

On 1 September 1890 the party reached Stanley Falls (now Kisangani), which was then an important government station and a district administrative center. It was there that the representative of the government of the Congo Free State lived, and a military detachment was stationed under the command of a white second lieutenant; there were many administration buildings and trade agencies, warehouses with ivory, and so forth. Stanley Falls represented a strategic point not only as the last town in the upper part of the river that could be reached by steamers, but chiefly because of its significant role in the long-lasting conflict between the Arabs and the Belgians.[40] The main object of the Arab penetration of West Africa was the slave trade, which the European countries strongly opposed, thereby helping the natives. This help was, however, only temporary, since European exploitation turned out to be more drastic and even more destructive for the blacks than the old form.

In his essay "Geography and Some Explorers" (1923), Conrad recalls, "The subdued thundering mutter of the Stanley Falls hung in the heavy night air of the last navigable reach of the Upper Congo, while no more than ten miles away, in Reshid's camp just above the Falls, the yet unbroken power of the Congo Arabs slumbered uneasily. Their day was over. . . . I said to myself with awe, 'This is the very spot of my boyish boast.' "[41]

In place of romance and adventure he found ruthless competition for trade and power, and an organization bent on making quick, huge profits. In place of primordial vegetation, he found a landscape where the jungle, exploding with succulent foliage, contrasted grotesquely with the angular elements of imported architecture. All those European buildings that were a source of pride to the local whites must have given him the impression of façades incongruously superimposed upon the omnipresent density of tropical nature. Even the small misshapen steamer, oozing smoke and shaking and croaking, could be taken for a symbol of the repellent, albeit profitable, European penetration.

After several days in Stanley Falls, Korzeniowski received the following letter of appointment from Delcommune, dated 6 September:

> Mr. Conrad Korzeniowski,
> Captain.
> I have the honor to ask you to take over the command of the *SS Roi des Belges* as of today, until the recovery of Captain Koch.
> Yours etc.
> Camille Delcommune[42]

As a matter of fact, this nomination constitutes the only basis for Conrad's later claim of having commanded a "steamer." The date of departure has not been established, but it may be inferred from the fact that on 15 September the *Roi des Belges* was halfway down the river, and that she reached Kinshasa on the twenty-fourth; thus she probably left Stanley Falls on the seventh or eighth.[43]

The steamer took aboard Georges Antoine Klein, a twenty-seven-year-old Frenchman suffering from dysentery, who had recently been appointed the Company's commercial agent at Stanley Falls.[44] Klein died during the journey, on 21 September, and was buried at Tchumbiri.[45] His name, later changed to Kurtz, may be found in the manuscript of *Heart of Darkness.*[46] Apart from Klein's presence on board, and his death, there seems to be no reason to suppose that he had much in common with the demonic character in the novel.[47]

It is not known whether or for how long Korzeniowski was in command of the ship on the way to Kinshasa. When the *Roi des Belges* arrived in Bangala on 15 September, Captain Koch was already back in charge.[48] Going downstream with the current, the steamer now moved almost twice as fast. There is nothing to indicate that Korzeniowski was still preparing himself for command in the upper part of the Congo. We know that he had no choice but to remain in the company of a man toward whom he felt a strong—and reciprocated—antipathy.

On his arrival at Kinshasa on 24 September, Korzeniowski found a letter from his uncle Kazimierz's daughter, Maria Bobrowska, who had just married Teodor Tyszka, as well as three letters from Madame Poradowska. Without delay he sent back an affectionate letter to his "Dear Maryleczka," "Indeed, I do not deserve to have a place in your heart—for I am practically a stranger to you—nevertheless the affectionate words you have written are most precious to me. I shall carefully preserve them in my heart." Of his plans he wrote, "I am very busy with all the preparations for a new expedition to the River Kasai. In a few days I shall probably be leaving Kinchassa again for a few months, possibly even for a year or longer."[49]

Unfortunately, until now no one has established what expedition Korzeniowski had in mind—it has been wrongly assumed
to be the expedition up the River Lomami, undertaken several
weeks later by Alexandre Delcommune.[50] The expedition up the
River Kasai would have followed a different route, shorter and
more explored. Korzeniowski might have thought that he would
sail in one of the Company's steamers, of which there were
three.[51] Two days later, as we learn from his extensive letter to
Poradowska, his employers changed their plans:

> No point in deceiving oneself! I definitely regret having
> come here. I regret bitterly. With a man's typical selfishness I
> shall talk about myself. I cannot stop myself. To whom should
> I unburden my heart if not to you? . . .
>
> I find everything repugnant here. Men and things, but es-
> pecially men. And I am repugnant to them, too. From the
> director in Africa, who has taken the trouble of telling a good
> many people of his intense dislike of me, down to the lowest
> mechanic, all have a gift of getting on my nerves; as a result
> I am not as pleasant to them as I might be. The director is a
> common ivory-dealer with sordid instincts who imagines him-
> self a merchant while in fact he is only a kind of African
> shopkeeper. His name is Delcommune. He hates the English,
> and I am of course regarded as one. While he is here I can
> hope for neither promotion nor a raise in salary. Anyhow, he
> told me that promises made in Europe are not binding here
> unless they are in the contract. . . . Anyhow, I cannot expect
> anything since I have no vessel to command. The new boat
> will be finished in June of next year, perhaps. Meanwhile my
> position here is vague, and I am having troubles because of
> that. . . .
>
> To crown the pleasures, my health is far from good. *Keep it
> to yourself*, but the truth is that going up the river I had the
> fever four times in two months, and then at the Falls (its native
> country) I had an attack of dysentery which lasted five days. I
> feel rather weak physically, and a little bit discouraged, and
> upon my word I think I am homesick for the sea and want

to look again on the expanse of that salt water which has so
often cradled me, which has so many times smiled at me in
the sparkling sunshine of a beautiful day, which many times
too has thrown in my face the threat of death, with a whirl
of white foam whipped by the wind under a dark December
sky. I miss all that. But most of all I regret having tied myself
down for three years. True, it is hardly likely that I shall last
them out. Either they will pick some groundless quarrel with
me to send me home (and on my soul I sometimes wish they
would), or another attack of dysentery will send me back to
Europe, if not into the other world, which would at last solve
finally all my troubles![52]

Looking for a way of leaving Africa without breaking his contract, Korzeniowski turned back to the idea, based on false information, that he could command one of the Company's ocean-
going ships.

What was the reason for the conflict with Delcommune and
the other employees of the Société Anonyme? Strangely, neither
Jean-Aubry nor Baines poses this question, and Sherry confines
himself to the already mentioned possibility that the director was
antagonized by Korzeniowski's slow journey from Matadi to Kinshasa. This, however, would not justify the profound and recip-
rocal antipathy affecting the entire staff of the Company. Besides,
Korzeniowski was not the only British employee. It is difficult to
ward off the suspicion that the explanation lay precisely in those
"base instincts" that motivated not only Delcommune but also
the Company itself and practically everything else that Korzeniowski had unexpectedly encountered in Africa. "Unreliable"
persons, and Korzeniowski must have appeared as such to the
speculators, are not admitted to business. In those days the profits
of the trading companies exploiting the Congo amounted to several hundred percent of the invested capital per year. To get some
idea of their methods of work, it is worth noting that agents were
paid high premiums for bringing down the costs of procuring
rubber and ivory; thus, massive deliveries of those commodities
were made compulsory, and punitive expeditions, made up of

members of hostile tribes and cannibals, were launched against noncomplying natives. For the Negroes, however, those enforced deliveries often meant starvation, since they were left with no time to cultivate and harvest their land. Bribery, as well as the disposal of unreliable witnesses, served to conceal those practices.[53]

Ending his letter of 26 September to Madame Poradowska, Korzeniowski wrote, "I am leaving in an hour by canoe for Bamou, to select wood and have it cut for the construction of the local station. I shall remain in the forest camp for 2 or 3 weeks, unless ill. It suits me, rather." Bamou is a village on the French side of the Congo, about thirty miles down the river from Kinshasa. We do not know how long he stayed there, but it is certain that he fell ill. On 19 October he wrote from Kinshasa to Bobrowski that he was unwell and intended to return to Europe. His uncle commented, "I found your handwriting so greatly changed—which I ascribe to the weakening and exhausting effect of fever and dysentery—that I have since then given myself over to far from happy thoughts! I made no secret from you that I was absolutely against your African plans."[54]

On 24 October 1890, four days after Korzeniowski dispatched his letter to Kazimierówka, Captain Duhst, a Dane in the service of the Congo Free State, himself ill at the time and carried in a hammock, made the following entry in his diary: "Camped in a negro town, which is called Fumemba [a day and a half's walk from Kinshasa]. I am in company with an English Captain Conrad from the Kinshassa Company: he is continually sick with dysentery and fever." And again on 27 October: "Marched from 6 morning until 9, when we ate breakfast. We are just on the spot where Lieutenant Puttervelle died and I was ill with fever. Here the ways part, and I took leave of Captain Conrad, who is going to Manyanga and Isangila, and from there to Vivi." By 10 November Duhst was already at Boma, and there he mentioned Korzeniowski for the last time: "Have not seen Captain Conrad since I left him in Manyanga."[55] Sherry writes, "It is possible that Conrad stayed at Manyanga to recuperate, as he did on the upward journey. There can be no doubt at all that Conrad's illness was at its most severe during this last journey over the caravan trail."[56] And he follows with a recollection of Conrad's wife: "I had heard from several of his friends how nearly he had died from dysentery while being carried to the coast when he left the Congo."[57]

And so the expedition came to an end. We know quite well how it began: the initial negotiations and preparations, the bravura and despondency on the passage to Africa, the exhausting march upstream along the great river. Gradually, as Korzeniowski penetrates deeper and deeper into the interior, getting closer to the core of affairs, scented with rubber and gleaming with ivory, he vanishes from sight. The image becomes confused, blurred, obscure. There is something symbolic when a wanderer recedes into the dark regions of our ignorance about his movements and thoughts, simultaneously nearing the end of his dismal experiences and of his own strength.

We hardly know anything about his life during the last months of the year 1890. He was at Kinshasa at the time that the great exploratory expedition of Alexandre Delcommune was starting on its way aboard the *Ville de Bruxelles* and the already repaired *Florida*.[58] He had seen, before his own expedition to Bamou, the members of the Delcommune expedition, whom he was later to describe so caustically in *Heart of Darkness*.[59] November is shrouded in obscurity. Of December all we know is that on the fourth he was at Matadi.[60] We do not know when and on what boat he returned to Europe. Toward the end of January he appeared in Brussels; on 1 February he was in London.[61] His letters contain no mention of his recent experiences. Apparently he just wanted to forget.

Notes

1. Speech of 24 April 1890, G. Martelli, *Leopold to Lumumba: A History of the Belgian Congo, 1877–1960* (London, 1962), p. 124.

2. Speech by King Leopold II at the African Geographic Conference in Brussels, September 1876. Cited in Jocelyn Baines, *Joseph Conrad: A Critical Biography* (London, 1960), p. 107.

3. *The Congo and the Founding of Its Free State: A story of Work and Exploration*, vols. 1 and 2 (London, 1885).

4. Ruth M. Slade, *English-Speaking Missions in the Congo Independent State* (1878–1908) (Brussels, 1959), p. 238; *The Times* (London), 16 January 1899.

5. Tadeusz Bobrowski to Konrad Korzeniowski, 24 June 1890, in reply to a letter from Tenerife, 15 May 1890, in Zdzisław Najder, ed., *Conrad's Polish Background: Letters to and from Polish Friends*, trans. Halina Carroll (London, 1964), pp. 128–29 (henceforth abbreviated *CPB*).

6. René Rapin, ed., *Lettres de Joseph Conrad à Marguerite Poradowska* (Geneva, 1966), p. 66.

7. Baines, *Joseph Conrad*, p. 111.

8. Korzeniowski to Karol Zagórski, 22 May 1890, *CPB*, p. 211.

9. Bobrowski to Korzeniowski, 22 July 1890, in reply to letter of 28 May, posted from Libreville probably on 9 June, *CPB*, p. 130. The 28 May letter contains the information about Korzeniowski's three-year contract.

10. *Heart of Darkness* (London, 1946) p. 61; see Norman Sherry, *Conrad's Western World* (Cambridge, 1971), p. 25.

11. Korzeniowski to Kazimierz Waliszewski, 16 December 1903, *CPB*, p. 242.

12. Conrad, *Congo Diary and Other Uncollected Pieces*, ed. Zdzisław Najder (Garden City, N.Y., 1978), p. 7 (henceforth abbreviated *CDAUP*). If the date on the letter to Poradowska (see note 13) is correct, Korzeniowski arrived at Boma in the evening. Libreville is about 550 sea miles away from Boma, and the steamer would need at least three days to cover the distance.

13. Rapin, *Lettres*, p. 67. Korzeniowski says that he began writing the letter in Libreville on 10 June as the ship was leaving the port, in order to have it ready for posting in Boma.

14. *CDAUP*, p. 7.

15. Korzeniowski to J. Quinn, 24 May 1916, in Frederick R. Karl and Laurence Davies, eds., *The Collected Letters of Joseph Conrad*, 6 vols. to date (Cambridge, 1983–   ), 5: 596.

16. Brian Inglis, *Roger Casement* (London, 1973), p. 31.

17. Norman Sherry, *Conrad's Western World* (Cambridge, 1971), pp. 32–33 (henceforth abbreviated *CWW*). I consider anachronistic Sherry's remark about the improbability, from the point of view of hygiene, of the existence of the "grove of death."

18. Ibid., pp. 36–37.

19. Korzeniowski to Marguerite Poradowska, 18 June 1890, in Rapin, *Lettres*, pp. 68–69. The only explanation may be the fact that he was held up by Gosse, a Belgian ex-officer who died six months later (G. Jean-Aubry, *Vie de Conrad* [Paris, 1947], p. 158.)

20. *CDAUP*, pp. 7–11.

21. Jean-Aubry, *Vie de Conrad*, pp. 7–11.

22. *CWW*, pp. 45–47.

23. *Carte des routes de portage dans la région des chutes du Congo*, dressée par le lieutenant Louis, chef de bureau à l'Etat du Congo, n.p., n.d. [1894?].

24. *CDAUP*, pp. 12–15.

25. *CWW*, pp. 56 and 399–401. The *Roi des Belges* was assembled in Leopoldville in 1887 (ibid., p. 57).

26. Ibid., p. 50 (from *Mouvement Géographique*, 2 November 1890).

27. Bobrowski to Korzeniowski, 9 November 1890, reply to letter of 3 August, received on 6 November via London, *CPB*, p. 133. Previous letters reached Bobrowski from Tenerife, Libreville, Banana (at the estuary of the Congo), Matadi, and Manyanga; only the reply to the second of these letters has survived.

28. *Heart of Darkness*, pp. 73–75; *CWW*, pp. 45–46. In the manuscript the conversation is reported in the form of a dialogue.

29. Contrary to Jean-Aubry's statement (*Vie de Conrad*, p. 161) and Sherry's doubts (*CWW*, p. 40) based on a notice in *Mouvement Géographique*, Conrad's diary proves unquestionably that the ship left on 3 August. This date appears on the first page of Part 2, and the date 4 August refers to the second day of the journey.

30. I have established the place where the diary stops on the basis of a detailed map; about his illness, Korzeniowski wrote to Poradowska on 26 September 1890 (Rapin, *Lettres*, p. 69).

31. *CDAUP*, pp. 22–24, 37.

32. *CWW*, p. 49.

33. Ibid., pp. 51 and 61. Sherry's suggestion that the impressions Conrad wanted to evoke in the readers of *Heart of Darkness* correspond with his impression of the Congo (p. 61) is unfounded, and paying the Negroes their "wages" in copper wire, as described in the story, is no less grotesque for having been in reality a common practice.

34. Ibid., p. 51.

35. Edmund D. Morel, *King Leopold's Rule in Africa* (London, 1904), p. 39.

36. George Washington Williams, "A Report upon the Congo-State and Country to the President of the Republic of the United States of

America," reprinted in Robert Kimbrough, ed., *Heart of Darkness*, Norton Critical (3d) Edition (New York, 1988), p. 93.

37. Samuel H. Nelson, *Colonialism in the Congo Basin* (Athens, Ohio, 1994), p. 100. See also William J. Samarin, *Black Man's Burden: African Colonial Labor on the Congo and Ubangi Rivers, 1880–1900* (Boulder, Colo.: 1989), pp. 47–48 and 120.

38. *CWW*, pp. 56 and 59–60. Wood was not cut every day, as the author assumes; inferring from Korzeniowski's diary, it seems to have been cut approximately every two or three days.

39. J. R. Troup, *With Stanley's Rear Column* (London, 1890), p. 125, quoted in Sherry, *Western World*, p. 58.

40. *CWW*, pp. 64–69.

41. Conrad, *Last Essays*, p. 17.

42. Jean-Aubry, *Vie de Conrad*, p. 164.

43. Table of shipping reprinted from *Mouvement Géographique* in *CWW*, p. 377.

44. *CWW*, pp. 73–74.

45. Ibid., p. 77.

46. John Dozier Gordan, *Joseph Conrad: The Making of a Novelist* (Cambridge, Mass., 1940), p. 37.

47. There has been much speculation about the origin of Kurtz. Jean-Aubry, with his habitual naïveté, linked Kurtz with the real Klein; Jerry Allen found him reminiscent of Major E. M. Barttelot, a British member of Stanley's 1888–1890 expedition; Sherry points at the analogies between Kurtz and a leading agent of the Société du Haut Congo, A. E. C. Hodister. In *King Leopold's Ghost* (Boston, 1998, p. 137), Adam Hochschild adds one Léon Rom, a ruthless commissioner in Matadi district. These sources seem quite possible, but they are not indispensable. The model for Kurtz was supplied on the one hand by literary and philosophical tradition, on the other by the behavior of a great many Europeans in Africa. In the end, as a character with his own specific life history, Kurtz is the author's own creation.

48. Otto Lütken, "Joseph Conrad in the Congo," *The London Mercury* 22, no. 127 (1930): 40–43. The author, a Danish captain who also served in the Congo, relies on a diary kept by another Dane, Captain Duhst, who lay ill at Bangala and was visited by Koch. The latter never mentioned that someone else had taken over command of the *Roi des Belges*. Duhst's entry is dated 17 September 1890; since the *Roi des Belges* reached Bangala on the fifteenth and left on the sixteenth, one may assume that

Koch visited his countryman on the sixteenth and Duhst made the entry the following day.

49. Korzeniowski to Maria Bobrowska, 24 September 1890, *CPB*, pp. 212–213.

50. Jean-Aubry, *Vie de Conrad*, pp. 167–168; Baines, *Joseph Conrad*, p. 118; *CWW*, pp. 73–76. Distinguishing these two expeditions explodes the theory of a sharp contrast in mood between Korzeniowski's letters of 24 and 26 September.

51. *CWW*, p. 376.

52. Korzeniowski to Poradowska, 26 September 1890, in Rapin, *Lettres*, pp. 70–72.

53. Morel, *King Leopold's Rule*; Morel, *Red Rubber* (Manchester, 1906); the Casement Report, released in 1904 by the British government as "Correspondence and Report from His Majesty's Consul at Boma Respecting the Administration of the Independent State of the Congo"; also Neal Ascherson, *The King Incorporated: Leopold II in the Age of Trusts* (London, 1963), esp. pp. 195–203, 241–260. Morel tends to exaggerate in his generalizations, but his books contain a great deal of documentary material.

54. Bobrowski to Korzeniowski, 27 December 1890, *CPB*, p. 134, reply to letter of 19 October, received on 24 December.

55. Lütken, "Conrad in the Congo," p. 41. Manyanga lies on both banks of the Congo, seventy-five miles as the crow flies from Matadi. In order to get to Isangila and Vivi one had to cross over to the right bank. Isangila lies about twenty miles from Vivi, the first "capital" of the Congo Free State. Vivi lies on the west bank, opposite Matadi. Duhst's last entry is not very clear, for it would appear from it that after parting on 27 October, he and Korzeniowski met once again at Manyanga. Eugène-Jean-Baptiste-Guillaume Puttevils, whose name Duhst misspells, died on 17 June 1889 and was buried at Nsona na Nsefe. See *Biographie Coloniale Belge* (Brussels, 1951), 3:719–720.

56. *CWW*, p. 88.

57. Jessie Conrad, *Joseph Conrad and His Circle* (London, 1935), p. 13.

58. *Mouvement Géographique*, 3 May 1891.

59. *CWW*, p. 85.

60. Ibid., p. 87.

61. Korzeniowski to Poradowska, [1 February 1891], in Rapin, *Lettres*, p. 77; and Poradowska to Korzeniowski, 4 February 1891, ibid., p. 210.

The Typescript of
"The Heart of Darkness"

MARION MICHAEL AND WILKES BERRY

◆   ◆   ◆

C ONRAD BEGAN WRITING the story first called "The
Heart of Darkness" in mid-December 1898 and finished the
first draft, represented by the fragmentary holograph, in early
February 1899.[1] In addition to the holograph, now located at Yale,
another pre-publication state of "The Heart of Darkness" exists,
a fragmentary typescript which was among the items in the William T. H. Howe Collection purchased by Dr. Albert A. Berg in
1940.[2] A study of this typescript provides the textual scholar with
information that is vital to his understanding of the stages in the
early history of the transmission of the story and thus ultimately
to his establishing an authoritative text. Further, a comparison of
the readings of the typescript, reflecting internal revisions in both
accidentals and substantives, against the readings of the holograph
and the serial printing in *Blackwood's Edinburgh Magazine* allows one
to gauge Conrad's evolving thoughts about the rendering of an
idea and to realize the great care which Conrad gave to finding
the right words, in the right order, to suit his artistic purposes.

By early January 1899, Conrad had written ninety pages of

"The Heart of Darkness," this much of the holograph making up Part I of the printed story. By this time, Jessie Conrad had begun to prepare a typescript for the story's scheduled publication in *Blackwood's*. On 9 January 1899, Conrad wrote to David Meldrum, William Blackwood's literary agent in London:

> I send you pp. 1 to 35 typed of *The Heart of Darkness* and from 35 (typed) it goes on to p. 58 of Manuscript.
>   pp 58 to 90
> which is all written up to yesterday. I am awfully sorry to send the pencil *MS* but my wife is not well enough to go on and I want you to have the first half of the story at once. May I ask you to have *The Whole* typed out on my acc/t in at least 2 copies. One for Mr McClure and one for *Maga*. The type *from the MS* should be corrected by me before going to printers so you perhaps will let me have that portion for that purpose as soon as ready.[3]

To this letter Conrad added the postscript, "Where MS. illegible let them leave blank spaces I can fill up when correcting." Meldrum, following Conrad's request, had his typist prepare two copies of the Jessie Conrad typescript and of pages fifty-eight to ninety of the holograph, one copy of which was given to Robert McClure who was to secure the American copyright for the story.[4] Concerned about copyright and about having the first installment of "The Heart of Darkness" appear in the February issue of *Blackwood's*, Meldrum, on 11 January 1899, sent one of the fair copies of the Jessie Conrad typescript directly to Edinburgh. He then sent Conrad a typed copy of pages fifty-eight to ninety of the holograph for revision, urging Conrad to send the revised copy to William Blackwood "at once."[5] By 13 January 1899 Conrad had completed the revision of this portion of the typescript and had sent it directly to Edinburgh.[6] Conrad's correspondence with Blackwood shows that a revised typescript used as setting copy for Parts II and III of the serial printing once existed.[7] However, the only typescript which has survived is that which Jessie Conrad prepared. Located in the Berg Collection of the New York Public Library, it is identified as the typescript to which Conrad referred in his letter to Meldrum of 9 January 1899 by the notation on page 35, "to p. 58 of MS fourth line."[8]

The fragmentary typescript of "The Heart of Darkness" consists of thirty-four sheets. Except for one passage, the type is double-spaced throughout. The notation "pages 2 and 3" is superinscribed in ink over the typed "2" of the second sheet, resulting in the pagination running from 1 to 35. On the verso of page 18 appears a passage which Jessie Conrad abandoned after typing only thirteen words, probably because she neglected to double-space the lines. A second abandoned start appears on the verso of page 33. It contains seventy-five words of text; and except for the repetition of the word "of" in the phrase "suggestion of of sedentary desk life," the omission of the letter "d" from the word "mentioned," and the misspelling of "first" as "furst," there is no evidence that shows why she abandoned the passage in order to retype it. Important in the demonstration of the kind of editorial control which Conrad exercised in the preparation of the typescript is the fact that at another point Jessie Conrad apparently typed holograph passages out of sequence, making it necessary for Conrad to cut the typed copy into three parts, labeling the margins of the parts "page 5 top," "page 5 middle," and "page 5 bottom." The three sections were then glued in sequence to a single sheet. Similar cutting and gluing occurred on page 6 and page 25. In all three instances, a full understanding of what is occurring at this point in the preparation of the typescript is made impossible by the fact that the passages are glued over typed copy which cannot be examined without damage being done to the typescript. The sections glued onto page 5 and page 25 are typed copy containing extensive handwritten revisions. However, the section on page 6 is entirely handwritten, and a comparison of it against the holograph reading provides an immediate illustration of the complexities in the relationship between the typescript and the holograph. The holograph passage is Conrad's explanation of what an episode means to Marlow. Initially Conrad wrote:

to him the meaning of an episode was not inside like a kernel
but outside in the unseen, enveloping the tale which brought
it out only as a glow brings out a haze, in the likeness of one
of these misty halos that now and then are made visible by
the spectral illumination of moonshine. (11)

He then cancelled "brought it out only" and interlined "could
bring it out" above the cancellation. In the typescript, after the
word "kernel," Conrad transcribed the remainder of the passage
onto a small sheet of paper which he glued to the bottom of
page 6. In making the transcription, he restored the first holograph reading "brought it out only" and made other revisions in
substantives and in accidentals creating the typescript reading:

to him the meaning of an episode was not inside like a kernel
but outside, enveloping the tale which brought it out only as
a glow brings out a haze, in the likeness of one of these misty
halos that, sometimes, are made visible by the spectral illumination of moonshine. (6)

Conrad revised the typescript throughout in pencil and in ink.
Most of the revisions are in ink; and, as our evidence will show,
they occurred subsequent to those made in pencil. Many of these
revisions are Conrad's corrections of misspellings, most of which
derive from inaccurate typing. Conrad made ninety-one corrections of misspellings by superinscribing letters over typed copy,
by cancelling the misspelling and interlining the correction above
the cancellation, by cancelling single letters, and by writing in
corrections between or above typed letters. Conrad failed to correct typescript misspellings in thirteen instances: "adminstration,"
"euthusiastic," "preceeded," "ammount," "interresting," "dim-
mensions," "flanel," "contemptously," "rythmically," "uncongeinal," "unfamilar," "alse" (for "else"), and "apalling." All thirteen misspellings were corrected in the serial printing. In two
instances in the preparation of the typescript, Jessie Conrad silently corrected holograph misspellings: "lenght" and "abandon-
ned"; and she corrected the reading "the clink keep time" to "the

clink kept time." In two other instances, she altered holograph spellings, "upwards" to "upward" and "legionnaries" to "legion-aries," the typed spellings providing the serial readings.

In addition to the revision of misspellings, Conrad extensively revised the typed punctuation. The specific kinds of handwritten revisions in accidentals range widely: commas, dashes, apostro-phes, quotation marks, and parentheses added to the typed punctuation; hyphens added to compound words ("custom-house," "God-forsaken," "barrack-like," etc.); periods changed to exclamation marks; lower case letters raised to capitals; and cap-itals changed to lower case. Where existing holograph pages cor-respond to the typescript, collation reveals that in many instances the revisions represent Conrad's restoration of holograph acci-dentals that Jessie Conrad failed to type or typed inaccurately. For example, corresponding pages of holograph and typescript show that without exception Jessie Conrad typed the holograph exclamation mark as a period, leading one to the conclusion that probably all eleven instances of the alteration of the typescript period to an exclamation mark are restorations of holograph readings.[9] In addition, collation of holograph and typescript pages shows that Conrad in several instances revised accurately typed holograph accidentals, sometimes combining these with substan-tive revisions, to change sentence structure.

In all, Conrad revised accidentals 370 times in the thirty-four pages of typescript, nearly half of these revisions being the addi-tion of commas. Among the variety of reasons for Conrad's add-ing commas are to set off parenthetical expressions such as ap-positional phrases, adverbial phrases, and conversational idioms such as vocatives and interjections; to separate independent clauses joined by a coordinate conjunction; and to separate co-ordinate elements such as verbs or adjectives in a series. A con-sistent effect of these additions is to provide a sentence cadence in keeping with the narrative mode of the story, Marlow remi-niscing to four friends. For example, in the following passage the commas after " 'em," "legionaries," "build," "hundred," and "two" are handwritten additions to typed copy. As revised, the passage reveals Conrad's skillful and intelligent use of pointing to produce natural speech rhythms, thus providing a conversational, or even colloquial, style appropriate to Marlow's narration:

> Imagine the feelings of a commander of a fine what d'ye call 'em, trireme in the Mediterranean, ordered suddenly to the north; run overland across the Gauls in a hurry; put in charge of one of these craft the legionaries, a wonderful lot of handy men they must've been too, used to build, apparently by the hundred, in a month or two, if we may believe what we read. (7)[10]

One other aspect of Conrad's revision of accidentals must be mentioned. The type face on both the comma key and the semi-colon key was broken, resulting in the tail of the comma and semicolon printing very dimly on the page, the comma appearing to be a period, the semicolon appearing to be a colon. In several instances, but not all, Conrad completed these accidentals, especially commas, by partially tracing over them in pencil or in ink. That he did not do a thorough job of completing them becomes an important consideration for anyone who studies the typescript using photocopy. In all of these instances, a close examination of the Berg typescript reveals the faint remnant of a tail on both the typed comma and semicolon.

Revisions in substantives also appear throughout the typescript and represent restoration, cancellation, and alteration or expansion of narrative elements. These revisions reach out into many areas of concern for both the textual and the literary critic.

As he was later to do with Meldrum's typist, Conrad evidently asked his wife, where she could not decipher the holograph, to leave blank spaces in the typescript which he in proofing would fill in. In the typescript the words "trireme" (7), "recrudescence" (26), and "splay" (32) are handwritten additions in the spaces which Jessie Conrad provided. All three reproduce holograph readings, the spelling "trireme" being a correction of the holograph misspelling "trirereme" (12). However, at several points, because of faulty typing or the inability to decipher a word, Jessie Conrad created in the typescript new substantives which changed

Conrad's meaning. As examples, she typed the holograph readings "greyish whitish specks" (36A) as "greenish whitish specks" (22), "swung her up lazily" (38) as "swung her up easily" (24), and "rags were wound round their loins" (46) as "rugs were wound round their loin" (27). In the holograph the natives sickened and "became inefficient" (50); in the typescript they sickened "because inefficient" (30). Similarly, the holograph description of the river banks "rotting into mud" (40) becomes in the typescript the more conventional "rolling into mud" (24); and the description of the coast which lay near the French steamer as having a "featureless" and "monotonous grimness" (36A) becomes "featureless" and "monstrous grimness" (22). In all of these instances, Conrad revised the typescript to agree with the holograph, thus in the latter three examples removing inefficiency as a cause of the natives' sickness and restoring his image of decay and the rhetorical balance between "featureless" and "monotonous grimness."

Critical to one's understanding of the authority of the typescript substantives are the facts that Conrad at several points did not detect his wife's inadvertent collaboration and that faulty typing led him in two instances to make substantive revisions that he otherwise would not have made. In the holograph Marlow "lived in a tent in the yard" (54); in the typescript Jessie Conrad silently moved him to only slightly better quarters, "a hut in the yard" (33). While, in keeping with the scene of prevailing stillness, the ensign of the French man-of-war "drooped limp like a rag" in the holograph (38), in the typescript it illogically "dropped" (24). At yet another point Jessie Conrad typed the holograph description of the natives at the Central Station "lost, in uncongenial strangeness" (50) as "lost, in uncongeinal strangers" (30). Although he failed to see the misspelling, Conrad revised "strangers" to "surroundings," thus losing the more poignant and, we would argue, textually sound holograph reading. Finally, on these matters, the typewriter which Jessie Conrad used was evidently not equipped with any kind of margin release; and because she could not accurately judge line spacing, she frequently omitted letters from words typed at the end of a line or failed to type a hyphen for end-line word division. Throughout the typescript Conrad has filled in missing letters of words and has added hyphenation for word division consistent with holograph readings. However, the inability to judge line length caused Jessie Conrad to type the holograph reading "I told him I expected to see soon" (43) as "I to him I expected to see soon" (26) the "ld" of "told" being omitted at the end of the typed line. In revising the typescript, Conrad cancelled the "to" at the end of the line and interlined "said to" above it, giving the reading "I said to him I expected to see soon," a change which he probably would not have made but for the faulty typing. All of these changes in substantives which came about in the process of the preparation of the typescript, along with others not cited for the purpose of illustration, became the printed readings.

Apart from these considerations of corruption that came about in the process of transmission are the typescript revisions which reflect Conrad's evolving thoughts about the artistic effect of "The Heart of Darkness." Cancellations in the typescript involve single words or phrases within a sentence and at times lengthy passages, resulting in a somewhat quicker pace for the narrative. Conrad expanded narrative detail by interlining additional words above typed copy. For instance, the typed copy reads, "The sea-reach of the Thames stretched before us like an interminable waterway" (1). By interlining above the words "like" and "an," Conrad expanded the sentence to read "before us like the beginning of an interminable waterway." In addition, he capitalized the "s" of "sea-reach." In some instances, expansions reflect Conrad's emphasizing the oral frame of the narrative by providing reminders of an audience for Marlow's story. The typed reading "I had returned to London . . ." is expanded to "I had then, as your [*sic*] remember, just returned to London . . ." (11). Conrad also revised the typescript to emphasize the bond of friendship among the five persons aboard the *Nellie*. The typed phrase "tolerant of each other's yarns" is expanded to "tolerant of each other's yarns—and even convictions" (2–3). Similarly, Conrad substituted new readings for the typed readings by cancelling words in the typed copy and writing in the new word above the cancellation or by tracing over the type. Thus typed references to the sea as the "master"

(6) of a seaman's existence and to "nature itself" (24) are revised to the more conventional "mistress" and to "nature herself," and a somewhat contradictory reference to "luminious [sic] void" becomes "luminous space" (1). Several revisions in the typescript represent Conrad's sharpening the ironic thrust of Marlow's narration; for example, he altered Marlow's reference to himself as "Something like an agent something like a lower sort of apostle" to "Something like an emissary of light, something like a lower sort of apostle" (21).

Further, an examination of the following typescript passage illustrates for the purposes of this discussion Conrad's impressive ability in the act of revision to refine imagistic shape and to direct narrative focus. In the interests of accuracy we have rendered the passage in the first instance, except for corrective strikeovers, exactly as Jessie Conrad typed it. Therefore, our discussion of Conrad's revisions must necessarily go beyond our immediate point. In type the passage reads as follows:

> We looked at the venerable stream not in
> the vivid flush of the day that passes but in the pacific yet
> august light of its immortal past. And indeed nothing is easier
> for a man who as the phrase went, follows the sea" in reveren
> and affection to evoke the great spirit of the past when lookin
> looking at the lower reaches of the Thames. (4)

Working upon the face of the typed copy, Conrad cancelled the verb "went" and added the verb "goes" above it. Also he completed the dimly typed comma which appeared after "went." He added double quotation marks before "follows," the letters "ce" to complete the word "reverence," and a comma after the word "affection." He made all of these revisions in pencil. Later, evidence indicates, he undertook a second revision of the passage. This time, using ink, he traced over the pencilled "goes," deleted the pencilled comma which had appeared after "went," and added yet another comma. Also, he traced over the pencilled double quotation marks previously added before "follows" and superinscribed an "ed" over the "s" in "follows," changing the tense of the verb. He drew wavy ink lines over "lookin," which was an end-of-line typing error, and traced over a dimly typed "ht" in the word "light." He interlined the verb "has," along with a comma, above the typed "who as." More to the point is the fact that he revised "the day" to "a short day," "passes" to "comes and is gone for ever," and "its immortal past" to "abiding memories." The result is that the revised typescript rendering of the passage is as follows:

> We looked at the venerable stream not in the vivid flush of a short day that comes and is gone for ever but in the pacific yet august light of abiding memories. And indeed nothing is easier for a man who has, as the phrase goes, "followed the sea" in reverence and affection, to evoke the great spirit of the past when looking at the lower reaches of the Thames.

Conrad made a third revision of the passage in the proofs for the serial printing.[11] He revised the phrase "comes and is gone for ever" to "comes and departs for ever," rhetorically balancing the two verbs. He revised the second sentence to read, "And indeed nothing is easier for a man who has, as the phrase goes, 'followed the sea' in reverence and affection, than to evoke the great spirit of the past upon the lower reaches of the Thames."[12] The passage as finally revised provides a more impressive sense of timelessness than had been provided in the earlier versions, particularly a more impressive sense of the intermingling of time present and time past, a major thematic element of "The Heart of Darkness."

The cumulative effect of the study of the revisions which Conrad made in the typescript in both accidentals and substantives is to reveal the extent of control which he exercised in its preparation and, thus, in relation to the preparation of a critical edition, to establish the authority of the typescript in the history of the transmission of the text of *Heart of Darkness*. In fact, we contend that Conrad supervised the preparation of the typescript to the extent of, at one point, dictating to Jessie Conrad a change from the manuscript reading which describes sailors' yarns as having "an effective simplicity" (11) to the typed reading "a direct simplicity" (6). The revision of accidentals becomes an important key in establishing the textual authority of the typescript. Although, as we have cited, he extensively revised typescript accidentals, his pointing remains light in relation to the extensive house styling which occurred before the serial edition was printed in *Blackwood's*. In fact, over 700 new accidentals separate the serial printing from the thirty-four pages of typescript. It is editorially critical to the establishment of an authoritative text for one to know that the heavy layer of accidentals which the *Blackwood's* editor himself introduced into the text set the precedent for the accidentals of all subsequent printings in both England and America. It is clear from this evidence that, although ultimately multiple copy-texts will be necessary, the fragmentary typescript, with due concern to free it of the corruptions in accidentals and substantives we have cited, becomes one's first and best choice as copy-text for a critical edition of *Heart of Darkness*.

Notes

1. A letter to David Meldrum written on 21 December 1898, published in *Joseph Conrad: Letters to William Blackwood and David S. Meldrum*, ed. William Blackburn (Durham, N.C., 1958), p. 35, provides the first indication of Conrad's being at work on the story. The best indication of the time when he finished it is in a letter to Sir Algernon Methuen written on 7 February 1899, published in G. Jean-Aubry, *Joseph Conrad: Life and Letters* (New York: Doubleday, 1927), I, 267.

2. Carl L. Cannon, *American Book Collectors and Collecting from Colonial Times to the Present* (New York: H. W. Wilson, 1941), pp. 185–86. The Howe bookplate is attached to page 1 of the typescript.

3. *Letters to Blackwood*, pp. 40–41. Conrad's italics.

4. p. 41.

5. Ibid.

6. Ibid., p. 42.

7. Ibid., p. 51.

8. We are grateful to the New York Public Library, the Yale University

Library, and the Trustees of the Conrad Estate for permission to examine and to quote from the holograph and typescript.

9. In some older model typewriters one typed an exclamation mark by first striking the period key, then backspacing to type an apostrophe, which was vertical, above it. The apostrophe on Jessie Conrad's typewriter, however, is a comma, imprinted by raising the carriage and striking the comma key. It is quite likely, therefore, that she was not able to type an exclamation mark.

10. In fact, in this passage textual investigation argues for the restoration to the printed story of the conversational idiom "say" which Jessie Conrad failed to type from the holograph reading "of say a commander" (p. 14).

11. A letter from Meldrum to Blackwood, dated 14 January 1899, refers to Conrad's proof revisions as "Most Excellent!" *Letters to Blackwood*, p. 43.

12. "The Heart of Darkness," *Blackwood's Edinburgh Magazine* 165 (1899): 194.

The Feast, by J*s*ph C*nr*d

MAX BEERBOHM

◆　◆　◆

THE HUT IN which slept the white man was on a clearing
between the forest and the river. Silence, the silence murmurous and unquiet of a tropical night, brooded over the hut
that, baked through by the sun, sweated a vapour beneath the
cynical light of the stars. Mahamo lay rigid and watchful at the
hut's mouth. In his upturned eyes, and along the polished surface
of his lean body black and immobile, the stars were reflected,
creating an illusion of themselves who are illusions.

The roofs of the congested trees, writhing in some kind of
agony private and eternal, made tenebrous and shifty silhouettes
against the sky, like shapes cut out of black paper by a maniac
who pushes them with his thumb this way and that, irritably, on
a concave surface of blue steel. Resin oozed unseen from the
upper branches to the trunks swathed in creepers that clutched
and interlocked with tendrils venomous, frantic and faint. Down
below, by force of habit, the lush herbage went through the farce
of growth—that farce old and screaming, whose trite end is de-
composition.

Within the hut the form of the white man, corpulent and pale, was covered with a mosquito-net that was itself illusory like everything else, only more so. Flying squadrons of mosquitoes inside its meshes flickered and darted over him, working hard, but keeping silence so as not to excite him from sleep. Cohorts of yellow ants disputed him against cohorts of purple ants, the two kinds slaying one another in thousands. The battle was undecided when suddenly, with no such warning as it gives in some parts of the world, the sun blazed up over the horizon, turning night into day, and the insects vanished back into their camps.

The white man ground his knuckles into the corners of his eyes, emitting that snore final and querulous of a middle-aged man awakened rudely. With a gesture brusque but flaccid he plucked aside the net and peered around. The bales of cotton cloth, the beads, the brass wire, the bottles of rum, had not been spirited away in the night. So far so good. The faithful servant of his employers was now at liberty to care for his own interests. He regarded himself, passing his hands over his skin.

"Hi! Mahamo!" he shouted. "I've been eaten up."

The islander, with one sinuous motion, sprang from the ground, through the mouth of the hut. Then, after a glance, he threw high his hands in thanks to such good and evil spirits as had charge of his concerns. In a tone half of reproach, half of apology, he murmured—

"You white men sometimes say strange things that deceive the heart."

"Reach me that ammonia bottle, d'you hear?" answered the white man. "This is a pretty place you've brought me to!" He took a draught. "Christmas Day, too! Of all the— But I suppose it seems all right to you, you funny blackamoor, to be here on Christmas Day?"

"We are here on the day appointed, Mr. Williams. It is a feast-day of your people?"

Mr. Williams had lain back, with closed eyes, on his mat. Nostalgia was doing duty to him for imagination. He was wafted to a bedroom in Marylebone, where in honour of the Day he lay late dozing, with great contentment; outside, a slush of snow in the street, the sound of church-bells; from below a savour of especial cookery.

"Yes," he said, "it's a feast-day of my people."

"Of mine also," said the islander humbly.

"Is it though? But they'll do business first?"

"They must first do that."

"And they'll bring their ivory with them?"

"Every man will bring ivory," answered the islander, with a smile gleaming and wide.

"How soon'll they be here?"

"Has not the sun risen? They are on their way."

"Well, I hope they'll hurry. The sooner we're off this cursed island of yours the better. Take all those things out," Mr. Williams added, pointing to the merchandise, and arrange them—neatly, mind you!"

In certain circumstances it is right that a man be humoured in trifles. Mahamo, having borne out the merchandise, arranged it very neatly.

While Mr. Williams made his toilet, the sun and the forest, careless of the doings of white and black men alike, waged their warfare implacable and daily. The forest from its inmost depths sent forth perpetually its legions of shadows that fell dead in the instant of exposure to the enemy whose rays heroic and absurd its outposts annihilated. There came from those inilluminable depths the equable rumour of myriads of winged things and crawling things newly roused to the task of killing and being killed. Thence detached itself, little by little, an insidious sound of a drum beaten. This sound drew more near.

Mr. Williams, issuing from the hut, heard it, and stood gaping towards it.

"Is that them?" he asked.

"That is they," the islander murmured, moving away towards the edge of the forest.

Sounds of chanting were a now audible accompaniment to the drum.

"What's that they're singing?" asked Mr. Williams.

"They sing of their business," said Mahamo.

"Oh!" Mr. Williams was slightly shocked. "I'd have thought they'd be singing of their feast."

"It is of their feast they sing."

It has been stated that Mr. Williams was not imaginative. But a few years of life in climates alien and intemperate had disordered his nerves. There was that in the rhythms of the hymn which made bristle his flesh.

Suddenly, when they were very near, the voices ceased, leaving a legacy of silence more sinister than themselves. And now the black spaces between the trees were relieved by bits of white that were the eyeballs and teeth of Mahamo's brethren.

"It was of their feast, it was of you, they sang," said Mahamo.

"Look here," cried Mr. Williams in his voice of a man not to be trifled with. "Look here, if you've—"

He was silenced by sight of what seemed to be a young sapling sprung up from the ground within a yard of him—a young sapling tremulous, with a root of steel. Then a thread-like shadow skimmed the air, and another spear came impinging the ground within an inch of his feet.

As he turned in his flight he saw the goods so neatly arranged at his orders, and there flashed through him, even in the thick of the spears, the thought that he would be a grave loss to his employers. This—for Mr. Williams was, not less than the goods, of a kind easily replaced—was an illusion. It was the last of Mr. Williams' illusions.

Conrad's Impressionism

IAN WATT

◆　　◆　　◆

M IST OR HAZE is a very persistent image in Conrad. It appeared as soon as he began to write: there was an "opaline haze" over the Thames on the morning when he had recalled Almayer; and the original Olmeijer had first come into Conrad's view through the morning mists of Borneo. In *Heart of Darkness* the fugitive nature and indefinite contours of haze are given a special significance by the primary narrator; he warns us that Marlow's tale will be not centered on, but surrounded by, its meaning; and this meaning will be only as fitfully and tenuously visible as a hitherto unnoticed presence of dust particles and water vapor in a space that normally looks dark and void. This in turn reminds us that one of the most characteristic objections to Impressionist painting was that the artist's ostensive "subject" was obscured by his representation of the atmospheric conditions through which it was observed. Claude Monet, for instance, said of the critics who mocked him: "Poor blind idiots. They want to see everything clearly, even through the fog!"[1] For Monet, the fog in a painting, like the narrator's haze, is not an accidental interference which stands between the public and a clear view of the artist's "real" subject: the conditions under which the viewing is done are an essential part of what the pictorial—or the literary—artist sees and therefore tries to convey.

A similar idea, expressed in a similar metaphor, occurs twenty years later in Virginia Woolf's classic characterization of "Modern Fiction" (1919). There she exempts Conrad, together with Hardy, from her objections to traditional novels and those of her Edwardian contemporaries, H. G. Wells, Arnold Bennett, and John Galsworthy.[2] Her basic objection is that if we "look within" ourselves we see "a myriad impressions" quite unrelated to anything that goes on in such fiction; and if we could express "this unknown and uncircumscribed spirit" of life freely, "there would be no plot, no comedy, no tragedy, no love interest or catastrophe in the accepted style, and perhaps not a single button sewn on as the Bond Street tailors would have it." For, Virginia Woolf finally affirms, "Life is not a series of gig lamps symmetrically arranged; life is a luminous halo, a semi-transparent envelope surrounding us from the beginning of consciousness to the end."

The implications of these images of haze and halo for the essential nature of modern fiction are made somewhat clearer by the analogy of French Impressionist painting, and by the history of the word *impressionism*.

As a specifically aesthetic term, "Impressionism" was apparently put into circulation in 1874 by a journalist, Louis Leroy, to ridicule the affronting formlessness of the pictures exhibited at the Salon des Indépendants, and particularly of Claude Monet's painting entitled *Impression: Sunrise*. In one way or another all the main Impresssionists made it their aim to give a pictorial equivalent of the visual sensations of a particular individual at a particular time and place. One early critic suggested that "l'école des yeux" would be a more appropriate designation for them than "Impressionists";[3] what was new was not that earlier painters had been blind to the external world, but that painters were now attempting to give their own personal visual perceptions a more complete expressive autonomy; in the words of Jean Leymarie, what distinguished the French Impressionists was an intuitive "response to visual sensations, devoid of any theoretical princi-ple."[4] It was this aim which, as E. H. Gombrich has said, allots the Impressionist movement a decisive role in the process of art's long transition from trying to portray what all men know to trying to portray what the individual actually sees.[5]

The history of the words "impression" and "impressionism" in English embodies a more general aspect of the long process whereby in every domain of human concerns the priority passed from public systems of belief—what all men know—to private views of reality—what the individual sees. Beginning with the root meaning of "impression"—from *premere*, to "press" in a pri-marily physical sense, as in the "impression" of a printed book—the *Oxford English Dictionary* documents a semantic flow towards meanings whose status is primarily psychological. The meaning of impression as "the effect produced by external force or influ-ence on the senses or mind" was apparently established as early as 1632; and afterwards it proceeded to reflect the process whereby, from Descartes onwards, the concentration of philosophical thought upon epistemological problems gradually focussed atten-tion on individual sensation as the only reliable source of ascer-tainable truth. The most notable single name connected with the process is probably that of David Hume, who opened *A Treatise of Human Nature* (1739–1740) with the ringing assertion, "All the per-ceptions of the human mind resolve themselves into two distinct kinds, which I shall call IMPRESSIONS and IDEAS." He had then attributed greater "force and violence" to impressions, as opposed to ideas, which he defined as merely the "less lively perceptions" which occur when we reflect on our original sense-impressions.[6] It was in protest against this empirical tradition in philosophy that the first English usage of "impressionism" occurred. In 1839 John Rogers, an eccentric word-coiner who entitled his attack on popery *Antipopopriestian*, wrote an ironical panegyric of the two main English prophets of "universal doubt": "All hail to Berkeley who would have no matter, and to Hume who would have no mind; to the Idealism of the former, and to the *Impressionism* of the latter!"[7]

It is appropriate that the word "impressionism" should be connected with Hume, since he played an important part in making the psychology of individual sensation supplant traditional philosophy as the main avenue to truth and value. One incidental result of this in the romantic and post-romantic period was that the religious, imaginative, emotional, and aesthetic orders of being became increasingly private, a trend which in the course of the nineteenth century led both to the Aesthetic movement and to Impressionism. The most influential figure here is Walter Pater. In the famous "Conclusion" to *The Renaissance* (1868–1873), for instance, he speaks of how every person enclosed in "the narrow chamber of the individual mind" can directly experience only "the passage and dissolution of impressions, images, sensations"; these are "unstable, flickering, inconsistent," and the individual mind is therefore condemned to keep "as a solitary prisoner its own dream of a world."

This epistemological solipsism became an important part of the cultural atmosphere of the nineties; but by then the main English usage of the term "impressionism" was in reference to the French school of painters, and to their English counterparts who came to the fore with the foundation of the New English Art Club in 1886.[8] As in France, the term was very quickly extended to ways of writing which were thought to possess the qualities popularly attributed to the painters—to works that were spontaneous and rapidly executed, that were vivid sketches rather than detailed, finished, and premeditated compositions.[9] The literary use of the term remained even more casual and descriptive; although Stephen Crane was widely categorised as an "impressionist,"[10] and in 1898 a reviewer of Conrad's first collection of short stories, *Tales of Unrest*, described him as an "impressionistic realist,"[11] there was little talk of impressionism as a literary movement until considerably later.

It was Ford Madox Ford who gave wide currency to the view that he and Conrad, like Flaubert and Maupassant, had been writers of impressionist fiction. This view was expounded in Ford's 1913 essay "On Impressionism," which sees the distinctive trait of "the Impressionist" as giving "the fruits of his own observations alone";[12] but it is Ford's memoir of Conrad which gives his fullest account of literary impressionism. The memoir was published after Conrad's death, and so we do not know whether Ford's statement there that Conrad "avowed himself impressionist"[13] would have been contradicted by Conrad if communication had been possible. Edward Garnett immediately registered an emphatic protest,[14] but later critics such as Joseph Warren Beach[15] and Edward Crankshaw[16] applied the term to Conrad, and he is now ensconced in literary history as an impressionist.

Conrad certainly knew something about pictorial and literary impressionism, but the indications are that his reactions were predominantly unfavorable.[17] Conrad's tastes in painting, as in music, were distinctly old-fashioned; he apparently disliked Van Gogh and Cézanne, and the only painter he ever mentioned as a model for his own writing was the peasant realist Jean-François Millet: in a letter to Quiller-Couch, Conrad wrote "it has been my desire to do for seamen what Millet (if I dare pronounce the name of that great man and good artist in this connection) has done for peasants."[18] As to literary impressionism, at the very least Conrad probably read a mildly derogatory article on "The Philosophy of Impressionism," which appeared in *Blackwood's Magazine* in May 1898,[19] and presumably knew Garnett's view of Stephen Crane as an artist of "the surfaces of life."

Conrad's own references to Crane's impressionism suggest that he shared Garnett's unsympathetic view of it. Thus, speaking of Crane's story, "The Open Boat," Conrad writes: "He is *the only* impressionist and *only* an impressionist" (*CL* 1: 416). This was in 1897, and Conrad's sense of the limitations of impressionism apparently hardened later; thus in 1900 he praised the "focus" of some Cunninghame Graham sketches, and added: "They are much more of course than mere Crane-like impressionism" (*CL* 2: 242). Conrad was to pay much more favourable public tributes to Crane later; but his early private comments make it clear that, much like Garnett, he thought of impressionism as primarily concerned with visual appearances. This is confirmed by Conrad's usage of the term in *The Mirror of the Sea* (1906). He writes there of a sailor asking "in impressionistic phrase: 'How does the cable grow?' "[20]; here "impressionistic" can only mean describing how things look as opposed to stating what is "really happening."

Perhaps the most distinctive quality of Conrad's own writing, like Crane's and unlike Ford's, is its strong visual sense; and Conrad's insistence in the preface to *The Nigger of the "Narcissus"* that art depends for its success on an "impression conveyed through the senses," is to that extent wholly consistent with impressionist doctrine. So, indeed, is much of the narrative itself, whose technique constitutes an original kind of multiple visual impressionism. This was immediately recognized by Arnold Bennett when he read *The Nigger of the "Narcissus"*; he wrote admiringly to H. G. Wells in 1897 asking: "Where did the man pick up . . . that *synthetic* way of gathering up a general impression and flinging it at you?"[21]

Heart of Darkness is essentially impressionist in one very special and yet general way: it accepts, and indeed in its very form asserts, the bounded and ambiguous nature of individual understanding; and because the understanding sought is of an inward and experiential kind, we can describe the basis of its narrative method as subjective moral impressionism. Marlow's story explores how one individual's knowledge of another can mysteriously change the way in which he sees the world as a whole, and the form of *Heart of Darkness* proposes that so ambitious an enterprise can only be begun through one man trying to express his most inward impressions of how deeply problematic is the quest for—to use Pater's terms—"an outer world, and of other minds." There is a certain kinship between the protagonist of Pater's *Marius the Epicurean* (1885) and Marlow, who comes to believe something fairly close to the "sceptical argument" of Marius; since "we are never to get beyond the walls of this closely shut cell of one's own personality," it follows that "the ideas we are somehow impelled to form of an outer world, and of other minds akin to our own, are, it may be, but a day dream."[22] *Heart of Darkness* embodies more thoroughly than any previous fiction the posture of uncertainty and doubt; one of Marlow's functions is to represent how much a man cannot know; and he assumes that reality is essentially private and individual—work, he comments, gives you "the chance to find yourself. Your own reality—for yourself, not for others—what no other man can ever know. They can only see the mere show, and never can tell what it really means" (85).

The other most distinctively impressionist aspect of Conrad's narrative method concerns his approach to visual description; and this preoccupation with the problematic relation of individual sense impressions to meaning is shown most clearly in one of the minor innovations of his narrative technique.

Long before *Heart of Darkness* Conrad seems to have been trying to find ways of giving direct narrative expression to the way in which the consciousness elicits meaning from its perceptions. One of the devices that he hit on was to present a sense impression and to withhold naming it or explaining its meaning until later; as readers we witness every step by which the gap between the individual perception and its cause is belatedly closed within the consciousness of the protagonist.

In both "The Idiots" and "An Outpost of Progress" the climax of the story is presented in this way. Thus in "The Idiots," when Susan Bacadou jumps over the edge of the cliffs to her death, a seaweed-gatherer merely sees that she "at once vanished before his eyes, as if the islet itself had swerved aside from under her feet" (*Tales of Unrest*, 84). This takes us directly into the observer's consciousness at the very moment of the perception, before it has been translated into its cause, into the term death or suicide, which make the sense-events of the outside world intelligible and communicable to the observer.

There is a much more elaborate version of this device in "An Outpost of Progress." Kayerts, terrified by the delusion that Carlier is coming to shoot him, suddenly hears

> the other push his chair back; and he leaped to his feet with extreme facility. He listened and got confused. Must run again! Right or left? He heard footsteps. He darted to the left, grasping his revolver, and at the very same instant, as it seemed to him, they came into violent collision. Both shouted with surprise. A loud explosion took place between them; a roar of red fire, thick smoke; and Kayerts, deafened and blinded, rushed back

thinking: I am hit—it's all over. He expected the other to come round—to gloat over his agony. He caught hold of an upright of the roof—"All over!" Then he heard a crashing fall on the other side of the house, as if somebody had tumbled headlong over a chair—then silence. Nothing more happened. He did not die. (112–13)

Persuaded that Carlier is still stalking him, Kayerts finally decides to end his suspense and face his doom: "He turned the corner, steadying himself with one hand on the wall; made a few paces, and nearly swooned. He had seen on the floor, protruding past the other corner, a pair of turned-up feet." Even now Kayerts does not decode the visual signs; and it is only when he sees Carlier's untouched revolver that Kayerts at last realizes that "He had shot an unarmed man."

This narrative device may be termed delayed decoding, since it combines the forward temporal progression of the mind, as it receives messages from the outside world, with the much slower reflexive process of making out their meaning. Through this device—here used somewhat crudely—the reader participates in the instantaneous sensations of Kayerts, and is "made to see" that he is too blinded by terror to know what he has done.

This passage seems to be the fullest example of delayed decoding in Conrad until Marlow's appearance in "Youth." Here is Marlow's description of the final explosion on the *Judea*:

The carpenter's bench stood abaft the mainmast: I leaned against it sucking at my pipe, and the carpenter, a young chap, came to talk to me. He remarked, "I think we have done very well, haven't we?" and then I perceived with annoyance the fool was trying to tilt the bench. I said curtly, "Don't, Chips," and immediately became aware of a queer sensation, of an absurd delusion,—I seemed somehow to be in the air. I heard all round me like a pent-up breath released—as if a thousand giants simultaneously had said Phoo!—and felt a dull concussion which made my ribs ache suddenly. No doubt about it—I was in the air, and my body was describing a short parabola.

But short as it was, I had the time to think several thoughts in, as far as I can remember, the following order: "This can't be the carpenter—What is it?—Some accident—Submarine volcano?—Coals, gas!—By Jove! we are being blown up—Everybody's dead—I am falling into the after-hatch—I see fire in it." (22–23)

The text gives a chronological sequence of momentary sensations in the protagonist's mind; and the reader finds it quite natural that there should be a delay before Marlow's brain finally decodes his impressions into their cause: "We are being blown up." Technically the passage is an improvement on that in "An Outpost of Progress," partly because it is done through concrete impressions of the outside world, and partly because there is nothing arbitrary in our being put into the protagonist's consciousness, since, as was not the case with Kayerts, we are in Marlow's mind throughout. Conrad's mastery of the device is also shown by the way he uses it for a comic effect; the very slowness of the decoding makes us smile at Marlow's impercipience—his initial blaming the carpenter, for instance, and the odd contrast between the pedantic precision of "my body was describing a short parabola" with the wild chaos of what is actually happening.

BY THE TIME Conrad came to write *Heart of Darkness*, then, he had developed one narrative technique which was the verbal equivalent of the impressionist painter's attempt to render visual sensation directly. Conrad presented the protagonist's immediate sensations, and thus made the reader aware of the gap between impression and understanding; the delay in bridging the gap enacts the disjunction between the event and the observer's trailing understanding of it. In *Heart of Darkness* Conrad uses the method for the most dramatic action of the story, when Marlow's boat is attacked, just below Kurtz's station. Marlow, terrified of going aground, is anxiously watching the cannibal sounding in the bows just below him: "I was looking down at the sounding-pole, and feeling much annoyed to see at each try a little more of it stick out of that river, when I saw my poleman give up the business

suddenly, and stretch himself flat on the deck, without even taking the trouble to haul his pole in" (109).

As in the "Youth" passage, Marlow's initially inexplicable visual
impression is accompanied by his irritation at an apparently gratuitous change in the normal order of things. Here, however, the
effect is duplicated: "At the same time the fireman, whom I could
also see below me, sat down abruptly before his furnace and
ducked his head. I was amazed." Only now does the cause of
these odd changes in posture begin to emerge: "Then I had to
look at the river mighty quick, because there was a snag in the
fairway. Sticks, little sticks, were flying about—thick: they were
whizzing before my nose, dropping below me, striking behind me
against my pilot-house." But it is only when Marlow has finished
attending to his duty as captain, and negotiated the next snag,
that his understanding can finally decode the little sticks: "We
cleared the snag clumsily. Arrows, by Jove! We were being shot
at!"

Meanwhile the pilgrims, and, to Marlow's fury, even his helmsman, have started "squirting lead" into the bush. Marlow is navigating and catching occasional glimpses of "vague forms of men"
through the shutterhole of the pilot-house, when his attention
is suddenly deflected:

> Something big appeared in the air before the shutter, the rifle
> went overboard, and the man stepped back swiftly, looked at
> me over his shoulder in an extraordinary, profound, familiar
> manner, and fell upon my feet. The side of his head hit the
> wheel twice, and the end of what appeared a long cane clat-
> tered round and knocked over a little camp-stool. It looked as
> though after wrenching that thing from somebody ashore he
> had lost his balance in the effort. The thin smoke had blown
> away, we were clear of the snag, and looking ahead I could
> see that in another hundred yards or so I would be free to
> sheer off, away from the bank; but my feet felt so warm and
> wet that I had to look down. The man had rolled on his back
> and stared straight up at me; both his hands clutched that
> cane. It was the shaft of a spear . . . He looked at me anxiously,

gripping the spear like something precious, with an air of being afraid I would try to take it away from him. (111–12)[23]

A third sudden and unfamiliar action is enacted through the protagonist's consciousness, and the delay in his decoding of it makes the reader simultaneously experience horror and sardonic amusement. Amusement, because we feel a certain patronizing contempt for those who do not understand things as quickly as we do, and because there is a gruesome comedy in the mere visual impression of the helmsman's "air of being afraid I would try to take [the spear] away from him." This macabre note has already been prepared for: if the poleman lies down, and then the fireman sits down, it is only natural that Marlow should assume that the dead helmsman's recumbent posture must be just a third example of the crew's deserting their duty just for their personal safety.

Still, the passage is obviously not primarily comic. Conrad's main objective is to put us into intense sensory contact with the events; and this objective means that the physical impression must precede the understanding of cause. Literary impressionism implies a field of vision which is not merely limited to the individual observer, but is also controlled by whatever conditions—internal and external—prevail at the moment of observation. In narration the main equivalents to atmospheric interference in painting are the various factors which normally distort human perception, or which delay its recognition of what is most relevant and important. First of all, our minds are usually busy with other things—Marlow has a lot to do just then, and it is only natural that he should be annoyed by being faced with these three new interferences with his task of keeping the boat from disaster. Secondly, our interpretations of impressions are normally distorted by habitual expectations—Marlow perceives the unfamiliar arrows as familiar sticks. Lastly, we always have many more things in our range of vision than we can pay attention to, so that in a crisis we may miss the most important ones—in this case that the helmsman has been killed. Conrad's method reflects all these difficulties in translating perceptions into causal or conceptual

terms. This takes us deeply into the connection between delayed
decoding and impressionism: it reminds us, as Michael Levenson
has said, of the precarious nature of the process of interpretation
in general; and since this precariousness is particularly evident
when the individual's situation or his state of mind is abnormal,
the device of delayed decoding simultaneously enacts the objective and the subjective aspects of moments of crisis. The method
also has the more obvious advantage of convincing us of the
reality of the experience which is being described; there is nothing
suspiciously selective about the way it is narrated; while we read
we are, as in life, fully engaged in trying to decipher a meaning
out of a random and pell-mell bombardment of sense impressions.

THE ATTEMPT TO TRANSCRIBE the process of individual perception was one of the most widely diffused tendencies in all the
arts during the period between 1874, the date of the first Impressionist exhibition in Paris, and 1910, the date of the exhibition
of new painting in London for which Roger Fry coined the term
Post-Impressionism. Conrad's device of delayed decoding represents an original narrative solution to the general problem of
expressing the process whereby the individual's sensations of the
external world are registered and translated into the causal and
conceptual terms which can make them understandable to the
observer and communicable to other people. More generally,
Marlow's emphasis on the difficulty of understanding and com-
municating his own individual experience aligns *Heart of Darkness*
with the subjective relativism of the impressionist attitude. Nevertheless, it is very unlikely that Conrad either thought of himself
as an impressionist or was significantly influenced by the impressionist movement. Conrad wanted to pay as much attention to
the inside as to the outside, to the meaning as to the appearance;
and this is one of the reasons why, in the last analysis, he is so
different both from the French Impressionists and from Pater,
Crane, or Ford.

Behind this difference is another which gives a unique quality
to the impressionist elements in Conrad. For Conrad, the world
of the senses is not a picture but a presence, a presence so intense,

unconditional, and unanswerable that it loses the fugitive, hy-
pothetical, subjective, and primarily aesthetic qualities which it
usually has in the impressionist tradition. Ramon Fernandez, in
one of the very few indispensable essays on Conrad, remarks that
his way of describing the external world is the exact opposite of
traditional narrative description such as Balzac's: Conrad's art, he
writes, "does not trace the reality before the man, but the man
before the reality; it evokes experiences in their subjective entirety
because the impression is the equivalent of the entire perception,
and because the whole man experiences it with all the powers of
his being." Conrad's "great originality," Fernandez concludes, "is
to have applied this impressionism to the knowledge of human
beings."[24]

Notes

1. Quoted by Jean Renoir in *Renoir, My Father*, trans. Randolph and
Dorothy Weaver (Boston and Toronto, 1958), p. 174.

2. *The Common Reader* (London, 1938), pp. 148–49.

3. Jacques Lethèye, *Impressionnistes et Symbolistes devant la presse* (Paris,
1959), p. 63.

4. Jean Leymarie, *Impressionism*, trans. J. Emmons, 2 vols. (Lausanne,
1955), 2: 28.

5. E. H. Gombrich, *The Story of Art*, 12th ed. (London, 1972), p. 406.

6. Bk. I., "Of the Understanding," Pt. 1, sect. i.

7. 2nd ed. (New York, 1841), p. 188.

8. See Holbrook Jackson, "British Impressionists," in *The Eighteen-
Nineties* (London, 1939), pp. 240–50.

9. See OED, and Todd K. Bender, "Literary Impressionism: General
Introduction," in *Preliminary Papers for Seminar #8*, distributed for the Modern Language Association Annual Meeting, 1975 (University of Wiscon-
sin, Madison, 1975), pp. 1–21.

10. By Edward Garnett, for instance, in an 1898 essay reprinted in
Friday Nights (London, 1922).

11. Cited by Bruce E. Teets and Helmut Gerber, eds., *Joseph Conrad:
An Annotated Bibliography of Writings about Him* (De Kalb, Ill., 1971), p. 16.

12. Reprinted in *Critical Writings of Ford Madox Ford*, ed. Frank MacShane
(Lincoln, Nebr., 1964), p. 37.

13. Ford, *Joseph Conrad: A Personal Remembrance* (London, 1924), p. 6.

14. *Nation and Athenaeum* 36 (1924): 366–68.

15. In *The Twentieth-Century Novel* (New York, 1932), Conrad and Lawrence are categorised under Impressionism; Joyce comes under Post-Impressionism, Virginia Woolf under Expressionism.

16. Crankshaw writes: "The label will do as well as any other" (*Joseph Conrad: Some Aspects of the Art of the Novel*, [1936; reprinted New York, 1963], p. 9).

17. Conrad visited Marguerite Poradowska in the Paris apartment of her cousin, Dr. Paul Gachet, close friend of Van Gogh and Cézanne, and found his collection "nightmarish" (René Rapin, *Lettres de Joseph Conrad à Marguerite Poradowska* [Geneva, 1966], p. 87).

18. Frederick R. Karl and Laurence Davies, eds., *The Collected Letters of Joseph Conrad* (Cambridge, 1983–), 1: 430–31 (henceforth abbreviated *CL*).

19. By C. F. Keary, no. 991, pp. 630–36.

20. *The Mirror of the Sea*, in Dent's Collected Edition of the Works of Joseph Conrad (London, 1946–55), p. 21. All references to Conrad's works are to this collected edition.

21. Norman Sherry, ed., *Conrad: The Critical Heritage* (London, 1973), p. 82.

22. Walter Pater, *Marius the Epicurean* (London, 1939), pp. 106, 110.

23. Beerbohm hit off Conrad's use of delayed decoding for the climax of his story. The protagonist is "silenced by sight of what seemed to be a young sapling sprung up from the ground within a yard of him—a young sapling tremulous, with a root of steel" (*A Christmas Garland*, [London, 1950], p. 133). The closest analogy seems to be this passage, although Jocelyn Baines says that "Max Beerbohm based his witty parody of Conrad in *A Christmas Garland*" on "Karain" and "The Lagoon" (*Joseph Conrad: A Critical Biography* [London, 1960], p. 190); and Addison C. Bross argues, in "Beerbohm's 'The Feast' and Conrad's Early Fiction," (*Nineteenth-Century Fiction* 26 [1971]: 329–36), for "An Outpost of Progress" as a closer source.

24. "L'Art de Conrad," *Nouvelle Revue Française* 12 (1924): 732; conveniently available in English in *The Art of Joseph Conrad*, ed. Robert W. Stallman (East Lansing, Mich., 1960), pp. 8–13.

Narratological Parallels in Joseph Conrad's *Heart of Darkness* and Francis Ford Coppola's *Apocalypse Now*

LINDA COSTANZO CAHIR

◆　◆　◆

T HE THEME OF Joseph Conrad's *Heart of Darkness* is, as his
character Charles Marlow states, the "fascination of the
abomination" (31). The novella is a frame-story, wonderfully en-
tangled by a narrative within a narrative, a flashback within a
flashback, a series of quotes within quotes. It is a *bildungsroman*, an
initiation into darkness and chaos, calmly framed by a prologue
and an epilogue.

Heart of Darkness opens with an unnamed narrator's account of
an evening spent aboard the yawl *Nellie*. He and four other men
had to wait at the estuary of the Thames for the turn of the tide
that would carry their boat down the river. Like Chaucer's Pilgrims, Conrad's characters (in this frame portion of the story) are
identified by their professions only; and they, too, passed the time
in story-telling. The narrator relates to us one tale that was told
to them that evening: the Sailor's story, or Marlow's tale. The
largest portion of *Heart of Darkness* is the narrator's verbatim recording and recounting of Marlow's story as told to him that
evening aboard the *Nellie*. Marlow's tale, actually told to us by

the narrator, is recited in Marlow's own voice; consequently, Marlow's narrative, every single thing that he says throughout *Heart of Darkness*, is placed in ongoing quotation marks.

Thus, Marlow's tale, seemingly spoken in Marlow's voice, is voiced, instead, by this unnamed narrator. His presence is so subtle that either we never really notice him or we soon forget that Conrad has positioned this disembodied voice between Marlow and us. Conrad causes something wonderfully magical to happen when we read *Heart of Darkness*. The mediating narrative voice, actually always present, vanishes and we believe that we are alone, face to face, in absolute solitude with Charles Marlow.

Critics have debated at length the significance of this narratological structure. This paper contends that Conrad's narrative structure is inherently cinematic. The recording eye of Conrad's anonymous narrator functions much in the same way as the camera functions in a film.[1] Both interpose themselves (near-invisibly) between the teller and the listener; both function as narrators who control what we hear and what we see; and both are subtle, ongoing structuring presences which somehow fade from our consciousness. The recording eye of the camera and Conrad's interposed voice both function as narrative devices that create the *illusion* of an unmediated relationship between the tale teller and the tale hearer. Perhaps both function as a warning: No interpersonal communication can ever be fully unmediated.

Thus, the structure of Conrad's narrative is, at the very least, empathic to the very nature of film. Francis Ford Coppola seemed alert to this in *Apocalypse Now*, his contemporary version of Conrad's *Heart of Darkness*. Much in the same way as Conrad's narrator retells Marlow's story, Coppola's camera retells Benjamin Willard's tale. Although superficial details may change, the substance of the tale each tells is timeless, unalterable, and ongoing. Charlie Marlow understood this, and tells us so by prefacing his tale of the Belgian Congo with a reference to "when the Romans first came here, nineteen hundred years ago . . . to face the darkness" (30–31). Man's fascination with the abomination, his initiation into the heart of darkness is the same whether the descent is made by a Roman journeying up the Thames, an Englishman up the Congo, or an American up the Nung.

The atemporality of that journey and the compelling need the initiate has to tell and retell his story are assumptions inherent in both Conrad's novel and Coppola's film. Although the "story" told by the novel is quite different from the "story" told by the film, their "narratives" are surprisingly similar. The theoretical distinction between the two, the story and the narrative, is explained by Gérard Genette:

> I propose, without insisting on the obvious reasons for my choice of terms, to use the word *story* for the signified or narrative content (even if this content turns out, in a given case, to be low in dramatic intensity or fullness of incident), to use the word *narrative* for the signifier, statement, discourse or narrative text itself, and to use the word *narrating* for the producing narrative action and, by extension, the whole of the real or fictional situation in which that action takes place. (27)

Thus, the *story* is the fictive account, the "who, what, when, and where" of the work; while the *narrative* is the text, itself, the particular structure, the specific manner in which (i.e., "how") the "story" is presented. Thus, Conrad's "story" is set in nineteenth-century Belgian Congo and centers on Charles Marlow, an experienced sailor who has been hired by a European trading company as captain of one of their steamboats. His primary responsibility is to transport the ivory, collected in Africa, back to the European company. In the course of his travels, Captain Marlow journeys upriver and meets the infamous Mr. Kurtz, a man who the trading concern believes has grown far too rapacious, and is taking company-owned ivory as his own.

In stark contrast to the novel, Coppola's "story" is set in twentieth-century Southeast Asia and focuses on Captain Benjamin Willard, a hired assassin in the American Army. *Apocalypse Now* tells the story of Willard's complicity in the Vietnam War, and his willingness to "Terminate with extreme prejudice" a fellow American Army officer: Colonel Walter E. Kurtz, a distinguished Operations Commander in the Special Forces, a man considered "one of the most outstanding officers this country's produced" (i.e., he graduated from West Point at the top of his class, held an M.A. from Harvard, and had been awarded "about a thousand [military] medals").

Thus, Coppola's and Conrad's *stories* are radically different; yet, the *narrative* of each is splendidly similar. Both *Heart of Darkness* and *Apocalypse Now* are frame-stories with mediating narrators. In each the mediating narrator is simultaneously present and not present in the text. In both works, the tale proper is narrated in first person retrospect and the pattern of tale telling is remarkably similar.

In both the novel and the film, our first view of the protagonist (Marlow/Willard) is that of a man radically altered by a past experience. Each tale proper begins with the protagonist's explanation of how he got the appointment which necessitated his excursion up a river. Each river excursion is distinguished by three scheduled stops (a number rich in mythic significance); the third and last stop for each is the soul-altering confrontation with the mysterious Kurtz. Additionally, each narrative uses similar patterns of symbology and each employs the effects of sound and lighting in similar ways.

Heart of Darkness begins (and ends) in a circumscribed space, on the yawl *Nellie*. The opening scene, one of considerable placidity, is a meditative moment. "The day was ending in a serenity of still and exquisite brilliance. The water shone pacifically; the sky, without a speck, was a benign immensity of unsustained light" (28). In the center of this serenely lighted placidity, Charlie Marlow sits, "his arms dropped, the palms of hands outwards, resembl[ing] an idol." He has "sunken cheeks, a yellow complexion, a straight back, [and] an ascetic aspect" (28). We are cued early on: clearly, Marlow is not like the others (the Lawyer, the Director, the Accountant) aboard the *Nellie*. The scene is a conspiracy of visual images, sounds, and lighting; it seems to have been created supra-verbally (quite an accomplishment considering that the medium is the novel). The calm and orderly serenity apparent outside of Marlow creates an effective contrast to the tumultuous chaos within him.

Apocalypse Now begins with that tumultuous chaos. A series of discordant images that dissolve, one into the other, and a haunting point-counterpoint of sound cue us that the inner life of Benjamin Willard's memories is being given outward expression. The scene is a visual and aural stream of consciousness. The fecund greenness of palm trees streams into the lethal green of wartime's noxious gases; the pointed fronds of the palm leaves conjure the fronds of helicopter blades. The sound of the blades subtly intrudes upon and punctuates the existential purr of The Doors's apocalyptical tune, "The End." The Doors's song ironically comments on the fade-in to the letters and photograph lying beside the bed in Willard's hotel room (also a circumscribed space): they are from his wife whose petition for divorce announces the end of their marriage. The sequence of dissolves climaxes in a view of Willard's face. He opens his eyes and we are cued: clearly, Willard is not like the others, the Lawyers, the Directors, the Accountants seated in front of him, listening to his tale in the movie theater. Watching and listening, we are privileged to his thoughts even before Willard speaks; and, like the opening of *Heart of Darkness, Apocalypse Now* begins with a supra-verbal meditative moment, focalized through the protagonist.

Both works shift, at this point, from the meditative to the expository as the protagonist of each explains the details of how he came to make his river journey. The manner in which each text manipulates this shift is, arguably, similar. It is done through both narration and lighting. In each, we move from darkness to light. In *Heart of Darkness* Marlow begins his tale at sunset, in a moment of "brooding gloom." (This nightfall is our first introduction to darkness.) In the opening of *Apocalypse Now*, "brooding gloom" characterizes Willard's darkened hotel room. In both texts the transition back in time, prompted in each by Marlow's/Willard's narrative voice, takes us to a world brightly lit, yet macabre; a strange world of distorted, dark figures who live in a deceiving world of light.

In *Heart of Darkness* these macabre figures inhabit the "Company's offices," a place of "desolation" and "dead silence." The double doors of the company's inner office have as sentries two "women, one fat and the other slim, [who] sit on straw-bottomed chairs, knitting black wool" (35); Conrad tells us that their function is "guarding the door of Darkness." Reminiscent of Charles Dickens's Madame Defarge (who knitted during the French Revolution's public beheadings), the two make a morbid duo. There is "something ominous in the atmosphere," we are told; and the morbidity is given full expression in the guise of the jovial company doctor who asks Marlow's permission, "in the interest of science, to measure [his] cranium." The doctor further explains that he likes to get the measurements of all "of those going out there." When Marlow asks if he also does so upon their return, the doctor remarks that he "never see[s] them" again. It takes a moment for the significance of the scene to register: the doctor's private interest and delight is in measuring the heads of the damned.

The heads of the damned are a symbol that recurs in *Apocalypse Now*. Our first view of Captain Benjamin Willard is a head shot, as is our first sight (a photograph) of Colonel Walter E. Kurtz. The previous officer assigned to "relieve Kurtz of his post" shot himself in the head before completing his mission.[2] Like Marlow, Willard is ushered into the Company's (i.e., the U.S. Army's) inner offices by two attendants. As in *Heart of Darkness* there is "something ominous in the atmosphere," and images, which take a moment to register, are fraught with horror: fleshy roast beef, rare, is aggressively stabbed and cut; prawns (still with *their* heads) form a grotesque swarm on a platter; and the tape recorder which plays Kurtz's peculiar musings was made by Sony, a Japanese company.[3] Japan, once America's great war enemy, has become America's (and the U.S. Army's) commercial comrade. The image is a nasty ribbing: wars are not fought for timeless and eternal values, but for political or commercial expediency.

At this point, Marlow and Willard, both captains in their Companies, are sent on their assignments. Both are to travel up a river and stop at outposts where they will collect Company materials (in Marlow's case ivory, in Willard's information). Ultimately, each must continue his journey to the furthest point upstream, find Kurtz, and relieve him of his post. The company office where each man gets his assignment is a considerable distance away from his river destination.

Marlow's first stop is at the government seat at the mouth of the river. Here we see, in trenchant detail, the horrors of imperialism. Enslaved natives are bound, one to the other, by iron collars and chains. "A lot of people, mostly black and naked, moved about like ants" (42). Marlow realizes that these prisoners, literally being worked to death, "were not enemies, they were not criminals." They were victims of an unconscionable, imperial system which transformed men into "black shadows of disease and starvation, lying confusedly in the greenish gloom" (44). In the midst of this suffering, Marlow meets "a white man . . . in an unexpected elegance of . . . a high starched collar, white cuffs, a light alpaca jacket, snowy trousers, a clear necktie, and varnished boots" (45). This "miracle" is the Company's chief accountant.

Marlow stays at this station for ten days, then with "a caravan of sixty men" makes "a two-hundred-mile tramp" to the Central Station. Along the way, Marlow witnesses "empty land . . . burnt grass" and "several abandoned villages." At the Central Station, Marlow learns that his steamer has been damaged and that it will take several months for the repairs to be made.

In *Apocalypse Now* Coppola compresses these two distinct stops into one, and action which takes several months to complete in the novel is condensed into two days in the film. Willard's first stop is to rendezvous with the Air Cavalry, his escorts to the Nung River. Like Marlow's first stop, Willard's is characterized by the horrors of imperialism. In order to acquire and maintain authority over a tiny village, the United States employs its formidable war machinery. The machinery looks absurdly indomitable when counterpoised against the straw huts and the women and children who populate the scene. (It's like using a sledgehammer to kill a butterfly.) Natives, apparently unarmed, are facelessly butchered. They scurry (like ants) "confusedly in the greenish gloom" (Conrad 44). The camera's narrating eye pans the battlefield, which is green with fecund foliage and green with noxious gas, only to "accidentally" come upon an American news team filming the campaign. In a satirically barbed moment, we see the reporter (Francis Ford Coppola himself) standing amid the gross confusion and attempting to direct the "real" war that his team is filming. The reporter/director yells at the befuddled Willard, "Don't look at the camera, don't look at the camera. Just go by as if you're fighting." The scene confirms our worst fears; the evening news really is *cinéma vérité*.

The scene is a madman's burlesque, a burlesque made more absurd when the U.S. Air Cavalry's own "miracle" emerges in the form of Captain Kilgore (Robert Duvall). Like Conrad's tidy Company accountant, Kilgore moves (in his neatly creased shirt, cavalry hat, and yellow ascot) unscathed and unsmudged through the explosive horror. His job is to transport Willard and his team safely to the mouth of the Nung. However, like Charlie Marlow waiting at the second outpost for his steamship to be repaired, Benjamin Willard has a problem that threatens to hinder his boat's progress. There are only two points where enough water can be drawn to enter the Nung, and "both are hot." They belong to the Viet Cong. Kilgore's job is to choose the better of the two sites, launch a successful assault, and deliver Willard's boat safely to its destination. He does so. Choosing the site because it's a remarkably good beach for surfing, Kilgore commands an air attack in which an impassioned, lethal, and crazed choreography of helicopters all move to the madly inspiring "Flight of the Valkyries." The scene shows us man at his most cruel, arrogant, and ignominious; and we sit watching: transfixed, fascinated, and, perhaps, even a little delighted by it all.

The scene is crucial, both in Conrad's text and in Coppola's, because it asserts concerns fundamental to each author: What are the moral implications of imperialism? What is acceptable human conduct? And do we all harbor a secret "fascination with the abomination"? For both Willard and Marlow the river journey becomes an exploration of these very questions. The journey upstream (a movement to the deepest interior, symbolic of the psychological journey made by Marlow/Willard) is characterized by stops which become progressively more feral, more untamed, and more irrational.

Both Willard and Marlow make two scheduled stops before reaching Kurtz's inner station. Marlow visits the government seat and the outer station; Willard has a rendezvous with Captain Kilgore and stops to refuel, where he comes upon a bizarre attempt at a USO show, staged in the midst of a war-torn jungle. Additionally, both Willard and Marlow make significant unscheduled stops, stops which Marlow condenses in his description: "Sometimes we came upon a station, close by the bank, clinging to the skirts of the unknown, and the white men rushing out of a tumbledown hovel . . . seemed very strange" (67).[4] Coppola recreates this same moment, the experience of a station which "clings to the skirts of the unknown," in Captain Willard's stop at the last Army outpost along the river.

The scene begins with the image of living bodies, swirling in a Dantesque pool of water and crying out to be saved. The movement of light and darkness is a quick and ongoing cycle, a spook house strobe effect created by gunfire intermittently lighting the night. The soundtrack is an eerie mix of exploding bombs, human cries, and ghostly music. Willard, attempting to find the Commanding Officer, crouches down into a "tumbledown," sandbag "hovel." But, there is no C.O.; chaos has no order. Willard is witness to the purgatory of Sisyphus, where each day the condemned must rebuild a bridge that is destroyed anew each night. Like Marlow, Willard finds this stop "very strange," very strange indeed.

The entire journey, to varying degrees, becomes a very strange quest, a gradual initiation into the dark world of the enigmatic Kurtz. But nothing that preceded it could have prepared the initiate for his experience at Kurtz's inner station.

In both texts, the novel and the film, the approach to Kurtz's station occurs during a thick fog. Behind "the blind whiteness of the fog," the crew hears eerie human cries, "modulated in savage discord." Marlow claims that "it seemed as though the mist itself had screamed, so suddenly, and apparently from all sides at once,

did this tumultuous and mournful uproar arise"; and that the
"sheer unexpectedness of it made [his] hair stir under [his] cap"
(73). In the film, Captain Willard shows us this same response;
it's registered on his face, and we can almost see the hairs on his
head move beneath his helmet. The natives are trying to scare
Willard/Marlow and the crew because they do not want to lose
their revered Kurtz. Their attempt at coercion continues. Out of
the opaque air comes a thick volley of intimidating "little sticks,"
which turn to lethal arrows when Marlow's/Willard's boat fires
back at the shore. In the exchange the black helmsman (Phillips,
the voice of reason in the film) is killed. Coppola, following in
Conrad's tradition, realizes that the initiation into darkness cannot be accompanied by reason; no one can be at the helm on
this journey.

In mythic tradition the initiate is often given a guide, a seer
of sorts who never completes the spiritual journey himself. This
mythic pattern is enacted in both Conrad's and Coppola's works.
The guide, a deranged Russian in Conrad's text and a crazed
American photojournalist (Dennis Hopper) in Coppola's, escorts
Marlow/Willard to Kurtz's station. In both the film and the novel,
the perimeter of Kurtz's compound is decorated with the same
ornamentation: human heads. We are cued: a threshold beyond
the pale is about to be crossed; only the stouthearted should
attempt such passage.

Marlow crosses the threshold, and meets with Kurtz, the force
revered by the natives as a man/god. Conrad's text hints at rites
performed by Kurtz, but these rituals remain unspoken, vague.
We know that the rituals have deified Kurtz in the natives' eyes,
but the rites are so shocking that Marlow, in retrospect, decides
not to report them. Critic Stephen A. Reid suggests that the
rituals involve human sacrifice and subsequent consumption of a
portion of the sacrificial victim; he cites those passages in Frazer's
The Golden Bough which discuss these rituals as performed by the
natives in the Congo.

Coppola also cites *The Golden Bough*, by positioning it among the
books we see on Kurtz's shelf. He includes two other works which
focus on the mythic pattern of death and rebirth: the Bible and

Jessie L. Weston's *From Ritual to Romance*. Coppola's use of intertextuality grows even more complex. Kurtz recites a portion of T. S. Eliot's poem "The Hollow Men." Eliot's 1922 poem *The Waste Land* borrows largely from the Bible, Frazer, and Weston, and shows us the horror of an infertile, barren land, void of the rejuvenating power of a hero/god. (Kurtz's kingdom is a fecund jungle, burgeoning with life.) Eliot's poem "The Hollow Men" pays intertextual homage to Conrad's *Heart of Darkness* by taking from the novel the line "Mistah Kurtz—he dead" as its epigram. The great horror of "The Hollow Men" begins at this epigram; Kurtz is dead and the poem shows us the consequences, a world in which Kurtz, and men like him, no longer exist. Eliot argues, and I believe that Conrad and Coppola do also, that if Marlow and Willard are not Kurtz's spiritual sons, then the unregenerating death of men like Kurtz, no matter how morally terrifying their manifestation was, is the greatest horror; it leaves us with nothing except a world of hollow men.

The horror of this world of hollow men is at the core of both Conrad's novel and Coppola's film; and Kurtz stands, in both works, as the hollow man's antithesis. Kurtz, in his morally terrifying manifestation and his god-like acousmatic voice, is invested with greatness: he understands existence in all its antipathy. Terrified and repelled, he forced himself to look into the very heart of darkness, to participate fully in the dualism, the good and the evil, of Being. To call Kurtz, himself, good or evil, heroic or rapacious, is to miss the point. He is a man forever altered by a dark satori, by an understanding of the ubiquitous nature of darkness.

Both Willard and Marlow, arguably Kurtz's spiritual sons, undergo the same realization. Both men look full face at the great abomination, at the dark ambiguity of Being. Each confronts moral terror in the form of human conduct pushed beyond decent limits; and each is profoundly altered by the experience.

Joy Gould Boyum argues that "in substituting Willard for Marlow, a madman for a sane one," Coppola creates a character incapable of "any shock of recognition," a man unable to "know evil when he sees it" (114). She argues that there is no discovery for Willard; he's a "murderer confronting a murder, a madman face to face with madness—it amounts only to a tautology." Thus, for Boyum, *Apocalypse Now* is a film "without a moral center." She asserts that, in contrast to Willard, Marlow is a man who has returned from the river journey "with his sanity and moral perspective intact." He invites "our trust and identification." In her view, the book-to-screen transition of *Heart of Darkness* is a faulty one.

But, *Heart of Darkness*, itself, is a book with no moral center; Marlow's great lesson is that existence, itself, has no moral heart. He has not sustained the river experience with his "moral perspective intact," unaltered. In the end, he is a changed man, vastly isolated and tremendously different from those aboard the *Nellie*. Marlow is forever alienated in his wisdom.

In the end, Willard, too, is isolated by his newly acquired knowledge. While Boyum sees Willard as unchanging, immoral, and insane, I hold that Colonel Kurtz's perception of him is far more fitting. Kurtz describes the Benjamin Willard who first arrives at his compound as "an errand boy sent by grocery clerks to collect a bill." By the end Willard is wiser. He has been changed, humbled by his confrontation with the darkness inherent in Kurtz, in himself, in existence.

Thus, the separate tales of Benjamin Willard's and Charlie Marlow's river journeys follow similar narrative patterns and arrive at similar truths. Coppola's *Apocalypse Now* is a structural and a thematic analogue to Conrad's *Heart of Darkness*, possibly because, in his authorial wisdom, Coppola understood that technique and theme, structure and meaning are inseparable entities. To tell a story differently is to tell a different story. Ultimately, it seems, Conrad and Coppola tell the same tale.

Notes

1. For a clear and cogent explanation of the camera as "the equivalent of a narrator, a cinematic storyteller itself" see Joy Gould Boyum's *Double Exposure*, 38.

2. Both texts structure a foreboding mood in similar ways; in each the protagonist's predecessor has committed suicide. Captain Willard is told about the death by Phillips, the pilot of the Navy patrol boat; in *Heart of Darkness* the pilot of the French steamer that transports Marlow tells him that Marlow's predecessor had "hanged himself."

3. Another reference to *Heart of Darkness* is subtly present in this scene in the form of two *ivory* tusks that point like daggers at the Sony recorder. Later, we learn that the Army's code name for the Kurtz mission is "Ivory."

4. Conrad's language here is what Jean-Paul Sartre terms "foreshortening," or the compressing into a single sentence any event that happened multiple times. Sartre (writing on Orson Welles's *Citizen Kane*) suggests that filmmakers also "foreshorten," through their "curious attempt to give certain images the quality of the frequentative" (Magny 22). In *Apocalypse Now* Coppola invests certain images (i.e., the movement of the water in the river, the cycle of day and night, Willard's eyes, helicopters, cattle, and photographs) with this frequentative quality. It is curious to note that as early as 1940 Orson Welles wanted to make *Heart of Darkness*. Welles's plan was to keep the camera "constantly in the place of the hero, showing us things as they appear to him, without ever being allowed to see him except when he looks at himself in a mirror" (Magny 23).

Works Cited

Boyum, Joy Gould. *Double Exposure: Fiction into Film*. New York: Universe Books, 1985.

Chatman, Seymour. *Story and Discourse: Narrative Structure in Fiction and Film*. Ithaca, N.Y.: Cornell University Press, 1978.

Conrad, Joseph. *Heart of Darkness*. New York: Penguin, 1983.

Genette, Gérard. *Narrative Discourse: An Essay in Method*. Translated by Jane E. Lewin. Ithaca, NY: Cornell University Press, 1980.

Jacobs, Diane. "Coppola Films Conrad in Vietnam." In *The English Novel and the Movies*, edited by Michael Klein and Gillian Parker. New York: Frederick Ungar. 1981.

Kimbrough, Robert, ed. Joseph Conrad, *Heart of Darkness* New York: Norton, 1971.

Magny, Claude-Edmonde. *The Age of the American Novel: The Film Aesthetics of Fiction between the Two World Wars*. Translated by Eleanor Hochman. New York: Frederick Ungar, 1972.

Reid, Stephen A. "The 'Unspeakable Rites' in *Heart of Darkness.*" *Modern Fiction Studies* 9, no. 4 (Winter 1963–64): 347–56.

Rising, Catherine. *Darkness at Heart: Fathers and Sons in Conrad*. New York: Greenwood Press, 1990.

The Exclusion of the Intended from Secret Sharing in Conrad's *Heart of Darkness*

NINA PELIKAN STRAUS

◆　◆　◆

I N A S T I R R I N G but sketchy essay entitled "Finding Feminist Readings: Dante-Yeats," Gayatri Spivak writes that "feminist alternative readings might well question the normative rigor of specialist mainstream scholarship through a dramatization of the autobiographical vulnerability of their provenance." Such autobiographical dramatization, Spivak points out, has already begun in the work of Jacques Derrida and other male critics, but "the privilege of autobiography to counter the rigor of theoretical sanctions is accessible to very few of the world's women" (47).

The feminist reader's access to a text like Conrad's *Heart of Darkness* is especially problematic in the terms Spivak considers. Not only is the tale concerned with a kind of mainstream male experience associated with traditional Western high art (penetration into a female wilderness, confrontation with monstrosity, male rites of passage, life at the "edge"), but those who write about it may be tempted to ally themselves with the heroic consciousness that Conrad presents. The feminist reader, in contrast, is apt to be more skeptical about and alienated from this masculinist tradition, and her access to Conrad's text may be so inhibited that her commentary is thrown off its most responsive and useful center. Her pleasure-in-the-text in Roland Barthes' sense may be rendered uneasy. Her understanding of Marlow or Kurtz may produce not psychic plenitude but psychic penury. The question of the reader-participator's sense of self in imagined contexts obtrudes, and in reading *Heart of Darkness* she becomes aware of a particular kind of ambiguity. Even if the sexism of Marlow and Kurtz is part of the "horror" that Conrad intends to disclose, the feminist reader cannot but consider that the text is structured so that this horror—though obviously revealed to male and female reader alike—is deliberately hidden from Kurtz's Intended. If *Heart of Darkness* is one of the *Ur*-texts of modernist high art by which our reading (and teaching) habits are tested, it is a text which makes us tend to distinguish between women *inside* texts and women outside texts, between women as fictive characters and women as living readers. Conrad's tale thus opens several difficult questions: must the woman reader neutralize awareness of her gender so that her reading becomes "objective" (non-autobiographical) in the way that male readings supposedly are? Is this neutralization in any way a complicity with the sexism of "mainstream commentary"? Might not the disclosure of her own autobiographical vulnerability throw light on *Heart of Darkness* as an example of how high art functions, or on the question of why, in Spivak's words, "the traditions and conventions of art are so brutally sexist" (60)?

Not only is the feminist reader traumatized by decades of nearly exclusive male commentary surrounding *Heart of Darkness*, but she may recognize that her own literary response is influenced by this traumatization. She may not be able to take the starting point of her own reading for granted; she may confess, as Spivak does in another context, to the necessity of self-scrutiny regarding the "intractable starting points" of any literary investigation, to the inevitability of deconstructing her own reading, and to the fact that "in disclosing complicities the critic-as-subject is herself complicit with the object of her criticism" ("Draupadi," 382–83). The deliberate installation of an autobiographical response in her own commentary can thus be posited as a way of investigating the repressed irritation that *Heart of Darkness* produces as a type of highly artistic intimidation. But it is not only Conrad as artist towards which this investigation is aimed; it is also aimed at the mainstream critics whose own autobiographical resonances are hidden within supposedly objective commentary, and finally at those radical critics who insist on the infinitely regressing "openness" of *Heart of Darkness.*

   Although the woman reader may attempt to take as much pleasure in Conrad's art as does the male reader, this pleasure is aborted by the fact that Marlow presents a world distinctly split into male and female realms—the first harboring the possibility of "truth" and the second dedicated to the maintenance of delusion. "Truth," then, is directed at and intended for men only. As Edward Said suggests, "the Conradian encounter is not simply between a man and his destiny . . . but . . . it is the encounter between speaker and hearer. Marlow is Conrad's chief invention for this encounter, Marlow with his haunting knowledge that a man such as Kurtz or Jim 'existed for me, and after all it is only through me that he exists for you.' The chain of humanity—'we exist only in so far as we hang together'—is the transmission of actual speech" (176). Marlow speaks in *Heart of Darkness to* other men, and although he speaks *about* women, there is no indication that women might be included among his hearers, nor that his existence depends upon his "hanging together" with a "humanity" that includes the second sex. The contextuality of Conrad's tale, the deliberate use of a frame to include readers as hearers, suggests the secret nature of what is being told, a secrecy in which Conrad seems to join Marlow. The peculiar density and inaccessibility of *Heart of Darkness* may be the result of its extremely masculine historical referentiality, its insistence on a male circle of readers. This *donnée* is not arbitrary: it determines what Hans Jauss calls the reader's reception, his "horizon of expectation." If the impact of a literary work can be described by referring to the "frame of reference of the reader's expectation" which develops in "the historical moment of its appearance and from a previous understanding of the genre, from the forms and themes of already familiar works" (11, 14), the degree to which the woman reader feels herself excluded from worlds familiar to men is the degree to which her reading will be "pulled from the straight and made to alter its clear vision in deference to external authority" (Woolf 77), or alternately, will be pulled towards the practice of feminist terrorism that mistakenly argues that sexist high art is not high art because it is sexist.

No doubt that the artistic conventions of *Heart of Darkness* are brutally sexist, but this is only the beginning of a larger recognition of the ways in which sexism has so profoundly conventionalized and obscured itself in literature and in literary commentary. An awareness of the different autobiographical vulnerabilities of male and female readers encountering *Heart of Darkness* is warranted by the fact that Marlow/Conrad discriminates between male and female views of the world, and by the fact that both mainstream and radical critics tend to agree that the novel involves "irreconcilable points of view in sexually stereotyped characters" (Thompson 461) and "sets women, who are out of it, against men who can live with the facts" (Miller 47). This is not to suggest that a woman reader cannot identify with Kurtz or Marlow any more than she can identify with the African woman or the Intended, but that her response to the Strong Poet who is both Conrad and Marlow involves a self-defensiveness and self-consciousness that the male commentator probably does not experience. It is Conrad's text itself that stimulates the notion that the psychic penury of women is a necessary condition for the heroism of men, and whether or not *Heart of Darkness* is a critique of male heroism or is in complex complicity with it, gender dichotomy is an inescapable element of it.

Because "truth" in *Heart of Darkness* is the possession of men and is hidden "luckily" from the text's women, the male critic who apprehends this truth, no matter how abominable or ironic, may be enlarged by it. For him, Spivak's question—"how is the figure of the woman used to achieve this psychotherapeutic plenitude in the practice of the poet's craft?" ("Dante-Yeats," 48)— may be answered by referring to age-old literary and sexual conventions. Gordon Thompson argues, for example, that for Marlow "woman is the spiritual potential in man's life" (541–42) and that Conrad is "less interested in the truth or illusion of feminine vision than he is in the impact of that vision on a man seeking meaningful action" (461). Not only are women readers kept in their places within the mainstream criticism to which Thompson makes his addition, but the more radical criticism offered, for example, in J. Hillis Miller's *"Heart of Darkness* Revisited" (1985) casts itself in a mode of skepticism towards Conrad's text whereby doubt is given a status that pays little attention to feminist perceptions. Describing Conrad's text as an apocalyptic parody, Miller argues that "male practicality and idealism reverse, however. They turn into their opposites because they are hollow at the core. They are vulnerable to the horror. They *are* the horror" (47). By reducing male heroism to the horror of emptiness, Miller seems to detonate the feminist critic's contention that male criticism is self-serving. Yet Miller, like Thompson, can be argued to have penetrated that circle of discourses which Said so astutely recognizes as the Conradian encounter. In complicity with the exemptions literary greatness may claim, the commentator inscribes traces of his (perhaps fantasized) autobiography by analyzing and attaching himself to the Strong Poet whose disclosure of horror's meaning certifies the high art of his text. As Annette Kolodny suggests in a reference to the work of Harold Bloom, this inscribing of the critic's closeness to the author is a "pleasure his (intended and mostly male) readership will take in the discovery that their own activity replicates the psychic adventures of The Poet, every critic's *figura* of heroism" (47).

This kind of critical activity and the psychotherapeutic plenitude it achieves for the commentator is most apparent in the Norton Critical Edition of *Heart of Darkness* (1963). Though revised in 1971—with the addition of a single essay by a female commentator, and this dating back to 1955—it remained the model. And it clearly suggests the extent to which criticism can be a form of covert autobiography, without the vulnerable consciousness of being so. Indeed, the degree to which the (all male) commentators understand Marlow or Kurtz is the degree to which they can identify the nature of their heroism. No matter how the meaning of *Heart of Darkness* is defined—as a quest within, as a journey to a mythic underworld, as apocalypse, as a critique of imperialism or of Western civilization—the standard commentary centers upon the secret sharings of male characters whose isolation from female language or experience evokes (if not sanctions) the dream of a homocentric universe.

The inhabitants of this universe are not confined to fictional characters or their authors; they include the commentator writing in the masculinist tradition—a tradition, as Geoffrey Hartman reminds us, that provides us with "a definite term for the man who is so much greater than we are, not morally perhaps but in mode of being—Nietzsche would have said he stands beyond good and evil" and "he is the hero" (68). The pleasure of identifying oneself, no matter how humbly, with either the character's or the author's heroism is the pleasure of entering a circle of communications about high art to which the concerns of women or women's questions are subordinated. The mainstream critic thus replicates the pattern of the text he describes; his literary method is to stress the formal and aesthetic ingredients at the expense of its sexist resonances; to exclude the possibility of woman's intended views just as Marlow excludes the Intended from sharing in the views his tale discloses. Designed to camouflage the autobiographical origins of its commentary, the Norton essays sustain the masculinist myths they are said to analyze. Stewart Wilcox lyrically summarizes the standard analysis which transforms misogyny into heroism or rationalizes Conrad's aesthetic "function" for women as morally necessary:

> As a foil to Kurtz's Intended, the native girl signifies his passionate involvement with Time and the flesh. Adorned with the ivory of his unholy quest, "She was savage and superb, wild-eyed and magnificent. . . . And in the hush that had fallen suddenly upon the whole sorrowful land, the immense wilderness, the colossal body of the fecund and mysterious life seemed to look at her, pensive, as though it had been looking at the image of its own tenebrous, passionate soul." . . . What is more to the present purpose, however, is the functions of

the Intended and the native girl in *Heart of Darkness.* . . . [Marlow
says:] "We must help them to stay in that beautiful world of
their own, lest our [world] get worse." The emphasis here is
up on moral contrast . . . [The Intended is] "one of those creatures that are not the playthings of Time." The one is a partner
in Kurtz's plunge into Satanic, unspeakable rites; the other an
exemplar of the Fidelity to which man must cling for salvation.
Because Kurtz could neither trust in nor be trusted by any
other human being he is forever lost to both women, lost to
both the flesh and the spirit. (217–18)

Disregarding the contradictions in this passage (Kurtz is both pas-
sionately involved with the flesh and lost to it), it is clear that
the facile opposition of the native girl's "flesh" and the Intended's
"spirit" functions here to sustain the commentator's sense of
plenitude. As long as the woman of light and the woman of
darkness retain their significations as binary opposites, there will
be (for male commentator as well as male character) Satanic
pleasuring and danger on the one hand and a dutifully sanctioned
Fidelity on the other. The answer to Spivak's question becomes
possible here: woman is exploited as a signifier, fictively adjusted
to conform to the commentator's need to identify himself with
characters who have access to *both* light and darkness, whose exclusive incorporation of the dual limitations represented by
Kurtz's women (indeed, beyond their good and evil) is the sign
of heroism itself. This psychic dependence on the contrasting
images of women is never acknowledged, however; and the use
of women as one-dimensional objects is rationalized as necessary
for "moral contrast" and the aesthetic (high art) properties of the
tale. If moral contrast is a necessary component of high art, it
apparently does not strike the male commentator that this morality is immoral—that it justifies sexism and racism—nor that
this contrast between soulless flesh and fleshless soul is a jarring
note of psychologically reductive simplicity in a text which, when
referring to male characters, is psychologically dense.

   The tactics by which mainstream critics of *Heart of Darkness*
sustain their masculinist brotherhoods do not necessarily depend

on the unquestioning misogyny illustrated in the Norton edition. Those who address the Woman Question more directly, who are aware of Conrad's gynophobia (described so persuasively by Bernard Meyer), nevertheless approach this question in terms that evade the issue of why the high art of *Heart of Darkness* must be so "brutally sexist." While some mainstream critics discover rationalizations for excluding women from their consideration by describing female characters as embodying such allegories as Fidelity or Wilderness, others like Ian Watt treat the problem of Kurtz's Intended by referring to Conrad's critique of "society" as though society were a neutral phenomenon in which sexism and patriarchal self-empowering were non-existent:

> It therefore follows that, merely by allotting women a leisure role, society has in effect excluded them from discovering reality; so it is by no choice or fault of hers that the Intended inhabits an unreal world.
>
> Marlow's opinion of leisured women makes them negative examples of the idea that work is the basis of the individual's sense of reality; but it also makes them positive examples of the complementary idea of the danger of relying on words. . . . [The Intended] is armoured by the invincible credulity produced by the unreality of the public rhetoric. (244–45)

Watt's linkage of the Intended's exclusion from "reality" with her susceptibility to "public rhetoric" is persuasive here, but his autobiographical vulnerability is exposed in the phrase "work is the basis of the individual's sense of reality." Because the Intended does not work, the argument runs, she is doomed to a delusive innocence. Because Marlow (and Watt) do work, they are both, as Conrad's character and Conrad's critic, installed in a world from which the Intended and all leisurely women are excluded. "Society" here is given no etiology, but the Intended's exclusion from Reality is. Whereas the cause of woman's inhabiting "an unreal world" is clearly specified, the reason why "society" allots her such a role does not appear to interest the commentator. Although Conrad's text suggests that men's society would be threatened if women were allowed access to the male-dominated realm of work where horrifying secrets are discovered, Watt's reading is based on deliberate and traditional omission of this possibility. The notion of "work" as a heroic enterprise is taken for granted, just as the idea that "society" is responsible for female unreality can be presented as unquestionable fact. The possibility that the "psychological power compulsion of men" originated "the primacy of sexual oppression over all other forms in society" (Mitchell 178) does not complicate the smooth assertion of contrasts in Watt's analysis. The final payoff of this analysis is that the commentator can afford to be generous to the Intended and to leisured women in general, confirming that "it is not by chance or fault of hers" that she is deluded and excluded.

The issues of sexism and racism have been discussed in recent studies of Conrad, particularly by Edward Said, Karen Klein, Sandra Gilbert, Susan Brodie, and Ruth Nadelhaft, among others. However, it seems dubious to argue that Conrad knew well what he wrote in *Heart of Darkness*, and that women are excluded from the circle of readers not *by him*, but by the speaker Conrad seeks to expose. Nadelhaft argues that in *Almayer's Folly* and *An Outcast of the Island* "women, frequently half-breeds, represent the clearest means of challenging and revealing Western male insularity and domination" (242–43). Certainly Winnie Verloc in *The Secret Agent* and Miss Haldin of *Under Western Eyes* are evoked with a complexity quite different from the treatment of the Intended or the African woman in *Heart of Darkness*. But these texts are not about a Congo wilderness in which "the stillness of an implacable force brood[s] over an inscrutable intention"; they do not insist that the "savage" woman is "like the wilderness itself, with an air of brooding over an inscrutable purpose." They do not close in their last pages with the teller of the tale confronting one woman while thinking about the other, placing the dark figure over the light figure like a transparency as though this layering replicated the mysterious obscurity of the "truth" itself:

> I shall see this eloquent phantom as long as I live, and I shall
> see her too, a tragic and familiar Shade, resembling in this

gesture another one, tragic also, and bedecked with powerless charms, stretching bare brown arms over the glitter of the infernal stream, the stream of darkness. (78)

In *Heart of Darkness* Conrad's impressionistic metaphors work with a looseness of association that suggests the inscribing of unconscious or at least dream-like condensations regarding women. The savage woman, condensed into Wilderness, presides over the "infernal" horror and mystery; and the Intended, emblem of society, is nothing less than another kind of horror—another inscrutable "intention" that Marlow defends himself against through his specious complicity with her need to describe Kurtz as having a "noble heart." It is possible that the images of women in *Heart of Darkness* are thus immobilized in order to suggest a critique of Marlow's heroism—a critique of his delusion that "what saves us is efficiency"—which attaches Marlow to the destructive coil of the imperialist venture itself. Yet the narrator who tells us that "Marlow was not typical," that "to him the meaning of an episode was not inside like a kernel but outside, enveloping the tale which brought it out only as a glow brings out a haze," is also (as J. Hillis Miller suggests) describing his own literary method. That this method depends on the production of "haze," of deliberate ambiguity, makes the question of Conrad's intentions for his tale difficult to adjudicate. What can be analyzed, however, is the effect of Conrad's words on various readers; and it is the contention of this essay that these words are understood differently by feminist readers and by mainstream male commentators. In the possible paranoia that this text generates for certain women readers, the production of literary "haze" seems to function not only to hide something from Marlow, but from Conrad himself. The "horror" of the wilderness/society polarity suggests the difficulty Conrad, along with his surrogate spokesman, has in finding a clear place to stand in relation to them—a difficulty, moreover, which replicates the difficulty of the male's standing in relation to both "wild" and civilized women. Whether Marlow is intended to be a parody of a wiseman or whether he is, as the last paragraph of the tale indicates, meant

to preside as Conrad's "meditating Buddha," the Conradian encounter is between men and men, or at the most, between men
and women who are willing to suspend their womanliness far
enough to forever disassociate themselves from the women characters in *Heart of Darkness.*

As receiver, "foil," "moral contrast," or emblem of "armoured
unreality," the Intended is reserved for the role of white lady in
the tower, just as Marlow, among the other roles he plays, is
reserved for the role of heroic deliverer of that lady. As in the
Romance of the Rose, literary convention demands that Marlow as
hero must penetrate the thorny thicket that surrounds the lady,
in this case the "sepulchral city" with its "people hurrying
through the streets to filch a little money . . . to dream their insignificant and silly dreams." The form Marlow's heroism takes is
that of rescuing the Intended from "inner truth." The lie Marlow
offers her is understood to be a form of chivalric, albeit ironic,
sacrifice, cryptically underscoring an ideology that defines a protective lie as a moral act. We are meant to see Marlow grit his
teeth as he does it; he, like Prometheus, risks the wrath of the
Gods: "It seemed to me that . . . the heavens would fall upon my
head." Unlike Prometheus, however, Marlow brings truth to men
by virtue of his bringing falsehood to women. Heroic maleness is
defined precisely in adverse relation to delusional femininity. And
Marlow's power to incorporate both the "truth" of "darkness"
and the necessary illusions of "light" is exactly what separates
him from those deluded others incapable of grasping his psychic
plenitude.

Psychotherapeutic plenitude is thus reserved for those who can
identify with Marlow, and through Marlow, with Kurtz. For a
woman reader to do so is to court self-degradation, and this is
not a problem specific to *Heart of Darkness* but also to Yeats and
Dante and to much of what constitutes the canon of high art.
At the end of Conrad's tale Seymour Gross reminds us, "The
transformation has been complete: 'the benign immensity of un-
stained light' has become 'the heart of an immense darkness.'
Now [the narrator], like Marlow, will be set apart from all those
who do not know the truth" (202). And it is clear that for Gross,

as well as Watt and the host of male critics who are able to identify the imaginative autobiography of their masculinity with Marlow's, this set-apartness, this full psychic cup engineered by transcending "good and evil," is what they expect from reading and analyzing *Heart of Darkness*.

A woman's experience of the text is quite different. Whether the woman "armors" herself as Watt describes with the "public rhetoric" of female purity and "Fidelity," and thus attempts to identify with the Intended; or whether the reader psychically en-acts a "flight from womanhood," to use Karen Horney's words (211)—a flight which an identification with Marlow or Kurtz might entail—the woman reader has no access to the sense of pleasure or plenitude which male critics display in their readings of *Heart of Darkness*. A third possibility for the woman reader is to identify with Kurtz's savage queen, that mirror of wilderness, that earth mother in bangles in whose body the white man seeks to bury his civilization's discontents. The queen's image, though vi-sually full, is psychically void and nearly inhuman; for it is ex-plicitly allied with that abominable darkness described by Marlow, essentialized in Kurtz's voice; and Conrad's text offers no woman's voice or variant female version of wilderness to the reader. In terms of the autobiographical impulse which we have argued here to be an unexpungeable element in criticism, the brown queen offers nothing to the feminist reader but the possible dream of regression.

Of the three alternatives, none is full; each suggests the deg-radation of the other; and high art seems nearly to be defined by its propensity to stimulate the woman reader to abandon her own concerns. Goethe's revolutionary question, "What is it for *me*?" seems clearly answered in terms of women: it is *not* for you; it is not *intended* to be for you. Implied here is the curious semantic puzzle that might also be one of the conventions of a language which tells lies to women about herself: You are the INTENDED. How can an INTENDED have INTENTIONS?

At this point, Spivak's third question: "what, then, does a woman do with the reactionary sexual ideology of high art?" becomes inexorable. If such art is traditionally the occasion for

the male critic to sustain archetypal autobiography through conventional language techniques that mask the subjective resonance
of his commentary so that it appears to be "objective," then a
radical feminist criticism of high art would remove the mask to
disclose the particular delusions intrinsic to a particular literary
work.

In one sense psychoanalysis has already done this, if we are to
take Freud's rather mocking description of the hero in "The Poet
and Day-Dreaming" as the measure of modern de-mystification:

> There is one very marked characteristic in the productions of
> these writers which must strike us all: they all have a hero
> who is the centre of interest, for whom the author tries to
> win our sympathy by every possible means, and whom he
> places under the protection of a special providence . . . The feel-
> ing of security with which I follow the hero through his dan-
> gerous adventures is the same as that with which a real hero
> throws himself into the water to save a drowning man, or
> exposes himself to the fire of the enemy while storming a
> battery. It is this very feeling of being a hero which one of our
> best authors has well expressed in the famous phrase, 'Nothing
> can happen to me!' [trans.] It seems to me, however, that the
> significant mark of invulnerability very clearly betrays—His
> Majesty the Ego, the hero of all day-dreams and novels. (50–
> 51)

No doubt Freud is prone to literary reductiveness here, yet the
passage foreshadows his later discussions of narcissism. For Freud
was to discover in this heroic "nothing can happen to me!" the
roots of a narcissistic paranoia and melancholy. Although Marlow
is often presented as one who, after Kurtz's death, comes back to
Brussels heroically carrying the psychic load (if not dead body)
of his secret sharer in order to somehow deliver its remains to
the Intended, the thing the woman reader can "do" is to note
how contingent Marlow's mental state is upon the decision he
makes to lie to the Intended, to decide that the truth about Kurtz

is "too dark" to reveal to her, and to harbor within himself a mystery he will reveal much later only to those "man" enough to take it.

Mourning for Kurtz, nearly driven "mad" by his revelations in the Congo, Marlow's self-reproaches are oddly passionate and each one of them is connected to Kurtz:

> And then they very nearly buried me.
>
> However, as you see, I did not go to join Kurtz there and then. . . . I remained to dream the nightmare out to the end, and to show my loyalty to Kurtz once more. Destiny. My destiny! Droll thing life is—that mysterious arrangement of merciless logic for a futile purpose. The most you can hope from it is some knowledge of yourself—that comes too late—a crop of unextinguishable regrets. (71)

Speaking of his near death, Marlow tells his hearers: "I was within a hair's-breadth of the last opportunity for pronouncement, and I found with humiliation that probably I would have nothing to say. This is the reason why I affirm that Kurtz was a remarkable man. . . . He had summed up—he had judged. 'The horror!' He was a remarkable man. . . . he had stepped over the edge, while I had been permitted to draw back my hesitating foot. . . . Better his cry . . ." (72).

Better than what? Marlow never tells. Better than Marlow's "having nothing to say," and obviously better than the Intended's hysterical "I loved him—I loved him. . . . I want—something!" But the point is that Marlow's self-disgust colors all he sees: the "intruders" in the "sepulchral city" whose "bearing, which was simply the bearing of commonplace individuals going about their business in the assurance of perfect safety, was offensive to me like the outrageous flautings of folly in the face of a danger it is unable to comprehend." Marlow "totter[s]" about the streets, finds the official who comes for Kurtz's papers "darkly menacing," has a vision of Kurtz "on the stretcher, opening his mouth voraciously, as if to devour all the earth with all its mankind." And in these images of being devoured, in the sense that Marlow is set apart with Kurtz from the "commonplace," a glimpse of Marlow's narcissistic dream emerges. Censored and distorted by the language of romantic agony, Marlow's language is nonetheless immersed in what Freud calls "narcissistic identification" where "the object" (Kurtz) "has been set up in the ego itself."

> He lived then before me; he lived as much as he had ever lived—a shadow insatiable of splendid appearances, of frightful realities; a shadow darker than the shadow of the night, and draped nobly in the folds of a gorgeous eloquence. The vision seemed to enter the house with me—the stretcher, the phantom-bearers, the wild crowd of obedient worshippers, the gloom of the forests, the glitter of the reach between the murky bends, the beat of the drum, regular and muffled like the beating of a heart—the heart of a conquering darkness. It was a moment of triumph for the wilderness, an invading and vengeful rush which, it seemed to me, I would have to keep back alone for the salvation of another soul. (74–75)

Freud argues that in narcissistic identification, which is closer to homosexual object-choice than to the heterosexual kind, the self-reproaches and regrets are in the service of "repelling an undesirably strong homosexual impulse.... The subject ... strikes with a single blow at his own ego and the loved and hated object" (*Introductory Lectures*, 426–27).

Marlow's language—intertwining descriptions of Kurtz's "abject pleadings" with his "gorgeous eloquence" and with Marlow's own "humiliation" and suspicion that "perhaps all truth, and all sincerity, are just compressed into that inappreciable moment of time in which we step over the threshold of the invisible"— suggests what Freud calls narcissistic "ambivalence." For it is clear that Marlow's identification with Kurtz is of a violently passionate kind; it leads to self-loathing, to the shadowing of self called depression, to an urge to escape from this state itself—an urge Marlow articulates in his "there remained only his memory and his Intended—and I wanted to give that up, too." There are glimpses in the text's imagery of Marlow's wish to be swallowed by Kurtz, to "join" him in death, and finally to be "rush[ed]" and invaded by the wilderness which Kurtz embodies. Finally, in the passage quoted above, a particular movement of psychic energy is dramatized: a vision of Kurtz appears to Marlow, intensifies ("enter[ed] the house with me") and blossoms into savage rites for a dying god. In images which compound terror with desire (sexual energy with violence, if you will), the climactic moment is described in terms of the "beating of a heart." It is at that climactic and visionary moment of excitement when Marlow's identification with Kurtz is most intense that Marlow decides to "keep back" what he knows, the depth of what he feels, from the Intended.

Marlow's rationalization comes quickly, is perhaps hardly noticeable to the reader who accepts as heroic Marlow's decision to lie. The morality of "salvation of another soul" is intrinsic to the conventions of high art from the story of Jesus through Joyce's *Ulysses*. But whom does such morality save here? Does not Marlow save himself, at this crucial moment of memory, hate, and desire, from the disclosure of a knowledge that is "too dark" for him to bear? "Not the least of the ironies of *Heart of Darkness*," suggests David Thorburn in *Conrad's Romanticism*, "is Marlow's blindness to the fact that his comments about Kurtz's harlequin exactly describe his own responses to Kurtz and to the task of telling about him. His evasive account, as Guerard has shown, approaches Kurtz only reluctantly, postponing the climactic encounter with obsessive ingenuity. Like the harlequin, Marlow, his life filled with Kurtz, is yet 'jealous of sharing with any the peculiar blackness of that experience'" (143). Having gone this far in explaining the nature of Marlow's relation to Kurtz, both Thorburn and Guerard stop. The connection between Marlow's "blindness" and his final encounter with the Intended does not interest these critics, for the Intended is not considered as in any way part of the text's problem. Whether Marlow is trustworthy or blinded, he is understood to heroically deliver the Intended from "darkness," and his capacity to deliver insinuates his link to a more traditional heroism.

It is clear that Marlow prefers Kurtz's cry of "the horror" to the Intended's cry of "I loved him." For "horror" is the secret password in the brotherhood of men who "know." Frederick Karl comes very close to acknowledging that there is less a moral question involved than an aesthetic one, one that has to do with the conventions of art per se. "Kurtz: death: ivory: art are intermingled. He is ivory" (459 n.). To take this one step further towards the questions posed in this essay, the woman reader might notice that *Heart of Darkness* is *about* art's relation to horror—that the excitement and mystery of horror, the "fascination of the abomination" is the revelation that Marlow offers to his brotherhood of "hearers" who constitute both his mates inside the text and his mates outside of it. If for Conrad/Marlow, art is inextricably linked with a horror which only men can experience, it is finally this art-horror that Marlow must "keep back alone" from the Intended who is woman.

If Marlow's sense of horror is unmasked to reveal his love for Kurtz, his love for Kurtz's "cry" which is his art, then the woman reader comes closer to understanding the motive for Marlow's behavior with the Intended. So deeply impressed is Marlow with Kurtz's ability to "cry" and "say" something about the "profound riddle of life" that Marlow incorporates this riddle and these words of horror which embody it. He comes not only to possess these words but to jealously guard them; and finally, faced with the task of symbolically rendering Kurtz unto the Intended, Marlow cannot bear to share him with her.

To answer Spivak's question more directly: what the woman reader can "do" is to recognize that in *Heart of Darkness* women are used to deny, distort, and censor men's passionate love for one another. Projecting his own love onto the form of the Intended, Marlow is able to conceal from himself the dark complexity of his own love—a love that strikes him with horror—for Kurtz. This is not to claim that the conventions of high art are homosexual, but rather to suggest that Marlow's relation to Kurtz as his commentator is a paradigm of the relation of the male critic's relation to the Strong Poet. That a homocentric loyalty exists (a loyalty to the sexist nightmare of one's choice) is not surprising, for it confirms the relations of love between

men who are each other's "narcissistic objects"; or to put it another way, whose enterprise as readers and critics (hearers-
speakers) affirms the greatness of the one and the possessive attempt to appropriate that greatness by the other.

The "psychotherapeutic plenitude" of which Spivak speaks
may therefore be a result of gender identification. This suggests
that high art is in some way a confirmation of the one gender's
access to certain secrets (in this case the secret conjunction of art
and horror) which would be both deconstructed and demystified
if the Intended had access to it. Could Marlow's truth be dramatized without the Intended's contrasting delusion? Would such
notions as romantic agony and the secret experience of "inner
truth" be able to be named if there were not a nameless one who
is "allotted" (to use Watt's word) to a world of merely outer or
"public rhetoric"? The guarding of secret knowledge is thus the
undisclosed theme of *Heart of Darkness* which a woman reader can
discover. Marlow's protectiveness is no longer seen in the service
of woman's deluded desires, but serves the therapeutic end of
keeping the woman/Intended mute. The male hearers of Marlow's tale never hear the Intended's name. She remains in the
stereotypically convenient world of "she." She lacks that one distinguishing feature of the beloved, which is that she is absolutely
individual to the one who loves her. The Intended is thus thrice
voided or erased: her name is never spoken by Kurtz, by Marlow,
or by Conrad; and it is determined that it will never be spoken
by Conrad's commentators.

The erasure of the Intended represents a final stage in the
development of the brutally sexist conventions of high art.
Dante's Beatrice and Yeats' Maud have faces, voices, and names.
But Conrad's Intended is no more than a "pale head, floating
towards me in the dusk." What this figure achieves, as perhaps
few other female characters in fiction do, is what could nicely be
called negative capability but which is psychologically symbolic
of the male's need for an infinite receptivity and passivity. Male
heroism and plenitude depend on female cowardice and emptiness. Dante creates truth and embodies it; when Maud shrieks
from the lectern, Yeats is unmanned. Because the female figure's

psychic penury is so valuable in asserting the heroism of the Strong Poet and the Strong Poet's character, the male commentator (who serves both) is filled with pleasure—a pleasure so therapeutic that it subverts his capacity to discover *on what terms* Marlow is a hero or a coward.

Because the woman reader is not so "filled," she is in the position to insist that Marlow's cowardice consists of his inability to face the dangerous self that is the form of his own masculinist vulnerability: his own complicity in the racist, sexist, imperialist, and finally libidinally satisfying world he has inhabited with Kurtz.

Lionel Trilling, in a discussion from *Sincerity and Authenticity*, makes this clear when he notes that "Marlow accords to Kurtz an admiration and loyalty which amounts to homage, and not, it would seem, despite of his deeds but because of them" (106). If this loyalty to Kurtz is constituted by Marlow's knowledge that the "black shadows of disease and starvation," the trophy fence of shrunken human heads, the "rapacious folly" and fascinating "abomination" are all Kurtz's creations, then Marlow's lie to the Intended is neither heroic nor protective so much as self-deluded. It serves not the Intended but Marlow's own subconscious intentions.

Although a woman cannot, since Henry James, distort the Strong Poet's *donnée* nor re-write his ending, as Samuel Johnson was impelled to do in the case of *King Lear*, she can register her radical protest against the continual romanticization of a work like *Heart of Darkness*, and against the ongoing critical insistence that this work is in some way moral. Art is not moral. High art may be especially immoral. Its province is pleasure, "psychotherapeutic plenitude." The question for the future is: whose pleasure does it serve? Does *Heart of Darkness* become less authentic, less finally recognizable as the truth of our times, when it is recognized that it is less the comprehensive human Id that is disclosed than a certain kind of male self-mystification whose time is passing if not past? The cultural context in which a woman character can be exploited in the ways Conrad's Intended is exploited cannot be affirmed in a humanist criticism without embarrassment to both men and women. What this leads to is the degree to

which feminist commentary on literature is central to the enterprise all readers share. One would hope that the exposure of male
autobiographical vulnerability in the choosing of literary canons,
in the perpetuating of certain myths about what constitutes morality, will contribute to the confidence that women commentators and women novelists are seeking. The privilege of *conscious*
autobiographical dramatization on a woman commentator's part
must become less rare. Perhaps new artistic conventions will be
created thereby, conventions which are able to serve both art *and*
truth.

Works Cited

All quotations from *Heart of Darkness* are taken from Joseph Conrad, *Heart of Darkness*. Norton Critical Edition, edited by Robert Kimbrough. New York: W.W. Norton, 1963.

Brodie, Susan Lundvall. "Conrad's Feminine Perspective." *Conradiana* 16 (1984): 141–54.
Freud, Sigmund. *Introductory Lectures on Psychoanalysis*. Edited and translated by Lytton Strachey. New York: W.W. Norton, 1966.
————. "The Relation of the Poet and Daydreaming." *Creativity and the Unconscious: Papers on the Psychology of Art, Literature, Love, Religion.* Edited by Benjamin Nelson. New York: Harper and Row, 1958, pp. 44–54.
Gilbert, Sandra. "Rider Haggard's Heart of Darkness." *Partisan Review* 50 (1983): 444–53.
Gross, Seymour. "A Further Note on the Function of the Frame in *Heart of Darkness*." In Joseph Conrad, *Heart of Darkness*, edited by Robert Kimbrough. New York: W.W. Norton, 1963, pp. 199–202.
Hartman, Geoffrey. *Beyond Formalism: Literary Essays*. New Haven: Yale University Press, 1970.
Horney, Karen. *Feminine Psychology*. New York: W.W. Norton, 1967.
Jauss, Hans Robert. "Literary History as a Challenge to Literary Theory." *New Literary History* 2 (1970): 25–28.
Karl, Frederick. *Joseph Conrad: The Three Lives: A Biography*. New York: Farrar, Straus and Giroux, 1979.
Klein, Karen. "The Feminist Predicament in Conrad's *Nostromo*." In *Brandeis Essays in Literature*, edited by John H. Smith. Waltham, Mass.: Dept.

of English and American Literature, Brandeis University, 1983, pp. 101–16.

Kolodny, Annette. "A Map for Rereading: Gender and the Interpretation of Literary Texts." In *The New Feminist Criticism: Essays on Women, Literature and Theory*, edited by Elaine Showalter. New York: Pantheon Books, 1985, pp. 46–62.

Meyer, Bernard. *Joseph Conrad: A Psychoanalytic Biography.* Princeton, N.J. Princeton University Press, 1967.

Miller, J. Hillis. "*Heart of Darkness* Revisited." In *Conrad Revisited*, edited by Ross C. Murfin. University: University of Alabama Press, 1985, pp. 31–50.

Mitchell, Juliet. *Woman's Estate.* New York: Pantheon Books, 1971.

Nadelhaft, Ruth. "Women as Moral and Political Alternatives in Conrad's Early Novels." In *Theory and Practice of Feminist Literary Criticism*, edited by Gabriela Mora and Karen S. van Hooft. Ypsilanti, Mich.: Bilingual Press, 1982, pp. 242–55.

Said, Edward. "The Text, the World, the Critic." In *Textual Strategies: Perspectives in Post-Structuralist Criticism*, edited by Josue V. Harari. Ithaca, N.Y.: Cornell University Press, 1979, pp. 161–88.

Spivak, Gayatri Chakrovorty. "Draupadi" by Mahasveta Devi. Translated with a Foreword by Gayatri Spivak. *Critical Inquiry* 8 (1981): 381–402.

———. "Finding Feminist Readings: Dante-Yeats." In *American Criticism in the Post-Structuralist Age*, edited by Ira Konigsberg. Ann Arbor: University of Michigan Press, 1982, pp. 42–65.

Thompson, Gordon. "Conrad's Women." *Nineteenth-Century Fiction* 32 (1978): 442–65.

Thorburn, David. *Conrad's Romanticism.* New Haven: Yale University Press, 1974.

Trilling, Lionel. *Sincerity and Authenticity.* Cambridge, Mass.: Harvard University Press, 1972.

Watt, Ian. *Conrad in the Nineteenth Century.* Berkeley: University of California Press, 1979.

Wilcox, Stewart C. "Conrad's 'Complicated Presentations' of Symbolic Imagery." In Joseph Conrad, *Heart of Darkness*, edited by Robert Kimbrough. New York: W.W. Norton, 1963, pp. 211–18.

Woolf, Virginia. *A Room of One's Own.* New York: Harcourt Brace and World, 1957.

Heart of Darkness Revisited
The African Response

RINO ZHUWARARA

◆   ◆   ◆

T HE STANDING OF Joseph Conrad as a major novelist of his time has been for a long time unassailable. F. R. Leavis certainly regards Conrad as rightfully belonging to the "Great Tradition" of English literature—minor misgivings notwithstanding. It is argued that he is one of those artists who have extended the frontiers of the novel and created more space and more possibilities for the exploration and depiction of human experience. This view is confirmed by David Daiches who in his book *The Novel and the Modern World* acknowledges the technical possibilities heralded by Conrad's multiple points of view in the art of storytelling. Albert Guerard's assessment of Conrad's work is in the same vein but at times uncomfortably specific. He regards *Heart of Darkness* as being "among the half-dozen greatest short novels in the English language" (Guerard 9). This commendation is in fact far from being an eccentric one uttered by an overenthusiastic critic. F. R. Leavis, who is generally a rigorous and censorious critic, writes that "*Heart of Darkness* is, by common consent, one of Conrad's best things" (Leavis 174).

On the other hand, the African response to some of Conrad's work has been at best mixed and at other times openly hostile. Here is how one of the most influential novelists and critic-*cum*-thinkers describes his reaction to Conrad:

> In the works of Joseph Conrad, which I studied as a special paper, I had seen how the author had used a variety of narrative voices at different times and places in the same novel with tantalising effect. With Conrad the same event could be looked at by the same person at different times and places; and each of these multiple voices could shed new light on the event by supplying more information, more evidence, or by relating other episodes that preceded or followed the event under spotlight. *Nostromo* was my favourite but on the whole I found Conrad's vision limited. (Ngugi 76)

Ngugi wa Thiong'o is, like David Daiches, fascinated by the way in which Conrad handles the technical aspects of creative writing but somewhat critical of his vision. Similarly, that doyen of the African novel in English, Chinua Achebe, admits that Conrad is "a great stylist of modern fiction" and a good story-teller (Achebe 2)—in a sense a writer who has produced a serious and therefore permanent literature. But Achebe's positive comment is qualified in the same essay by a vigorous and relentless attack on *Heart of Darkness* in particular. It is a novel, he argues with passion, which "eliminates the African as human factor and parades in the most vulgar fashion, prejudices and insults from which a section of mankind has suffered untold agonies" (Achebe 10).

Indeed Achebe's indignant comments echo those of another African scholar, Michael Echeruo. In a critical work specifically devoted to Joyce Cary's fiction, Echeruo digresses momentarily to make a disdainful swipe at *Heart of Darkness*. He writes: "*Heart of Darkness*, ultimately, reveals the mind of an imperial Europe at its day's end: it reveals nothing about the character of Africa itself" (Echeruo, *Joyce Cary*, 5).

Why, the reader may ask, is the African reader vehemently critical of *Heart of Darkness*? The text seems to elicit an unusual degree of criticism especially from highly influential voices from the African continent. Is it a failure, on the part of the African reader and writer, to appreciate the subtleties of an acclaimed European masterpiece or is it that African readers are victims of a prejudiced and wilful misreading of the novel? This article is an attempt to account for the African reaction to the novel in the process of underlining the following:

i) The fact that in *Heart of Darkness* Conrad sets out to question the nature of man in a specific historical context characterized by imperialism.

ii) That what starts off as a subversion of the ideals of imperialistic discourse is in turn subverted by an artistic process which becomes too dependent on stereotypes of the time, especially when Marlow starts sailing up the Congo River.

iii) That these stereotypes are part of a long-standing tradition which has been harmful to blacks for centuries.

It is helpful to recall that Conrad wrote *Heart of Darkness* barely thirteen years after the Berlin Conference of 1884 had officially sanctioned the partition of Africa into specific spheres belonging to various European powers. These powers did not bother at all to consult the inhabitants of the African continent; neither were they concerned about the ethical basis of their momentous decision. Had famous missionaries such as David Livingstone and well-known travellers like Henry Morton Stanley not made it obvious that Africa was a vast continent waiting to be blessed with the virtues of the Christian gospel as well as the benefits of Western trade and commerce? Apart from the writings of David Livingstone and others, Europe had an opportunity to whet its curiosity with the writings of Stanley whose books had obliging titles such as *Through the Dark Continent* (1878) and *In Darkest Africa* (1890). Soon Europe assumed an Adamic role which entailed banishing the darkness of Africa, giving new names to its features and people, and taming the African wilderness into a garden bereft of the proverbial biblical snake. Often the rhetoric of imperialism became indistinguishable from that of the Christian gospel, and so messianic as to gloss over the economic interests of those involved. Alongside this historical phenomenon there developed in Europe a literature which, consciously or unconsciously, was aimed at justifying the whole process of colonization and empire-building as a noble undertaking.

Writing about the nature and function of popular literature in Britain at the turn of the last century, David Daniell has this to say in his essay titled "Buchan and 'The Black General.' "

> It becomes aggressively, and defensively imperialistic. It leaves the Christian family ambience and becomes all male and public school: military values invade and take over stories; white dominates black with cool superiority of a god—now in the name of something called civilisation . . . Between 1880 and 1900 a hundred children's journals were founded, over half of them devoted to 'manly' adventure for boys—privileged boys at public school, preparing to be officers in the armed forces. (Dabydeen 141)

Indeed, the narrator in Rider Haggard's *King Solomon's Mines* (1885) claims that his narrative is an adventure story for his mischievous son at home. It is a story in which the aristocratic values of Europe represented by Sir Henry Curtis and those of the military represented by Captain Good triumph over the values of a superstitious and gullible African people. Africa becomes a playground for Europeans keen to exhibit their manhood and superiority in the face of a challenging environment. Similarly in John Buchan's *Prester John* (1910) we witness how David Crawford together with his fellow whites subdue a legendary African general, Laputa, thus all the more vindicating the superiority of whites over blacks. Both *King Solomon's Mines* and *Prester John* are adventure stories shamelessly Eurocentric and racist. In the penultimate chapter of *Prester John* Crawford defines the white man's burden in Africa as follows:

> I knew then the meaning of the white man's duty. He has to take all risks, reckoning nothing of his life or his fortunes, and

well content to find his reward in the fulfilment of his task. That is the difference between white and black, the gift of responsibility, the power of being in a little way a King, and so long as we know this and practise it, we will rule not in Africa alone but wherever there are dark men who live only for the day and their own bellies. (Buchan 230)

Considering the fact that *Prester John* and *King Solomon's Mines* have been, over time, accorded the status of minor classics, and made into films, it can be argued that they typify the kind of popular fiction which touched the hearts and excited the imaginations of many European citizens who would have been condemned to a routine and rather drab existence. Such a literature becomes a vicarious rite of passage for those entering into their phase of manhood. More importantly, however, such books spurred many into embracing the cause of imperialism in Africa and other parts of the world.

The publication of *Heart of Darkness* in 1902 can be seen as an integral part of the development of that literature spawned by the European expansion into other parts of the world. In fact there is a way in which *Heart of Darkness* has elements of an Edwardian adventure story. Marlow himself is driven into Africa by his desire to fulfil a childhood dream about the Congo. By the time he returns he is an entirely different man—he has grown up! Kurtz himself sets out for Africa as an archetypal figure representing those departments of civilization in which Europe is perceived as having taken a lead over the dark peoples of the world. Rumor has it that Kurtz is a musician, an orator, a poet-*cum*-painter, an agent of science and progress, and a trading official into the bargain. According to fragmentary bits of information which reach Marlow, Kurtz has the talent and the will-power, in fact everything which Europe could give to such a man of destiny. As such Kurtz becomes the embodiment of those ideals which imperialism often proclaimed as part of its Crusade to civilize savage continents. For Kurtz, Africa is part of a challenging frontier to be tamed and controlled.

What almost rescues *Heart of Darkness* from becoming a political romance in the Rider Haggard school of imperialist propaganda is the inherently skeptical and ruthlessly questioning stance assumed by Marlow right from the beginning of his journey to Africa. In addition there is an attempt by Conrad to distance himself from Marlow through a careful narrative strategy. Unlike the unreturned Kurtz of the earlier journey, Marlow is disdainful and scathing in his attitude towards these very ideals cherished by the European public. He is taken aback upon discovering that his brainwashed aunt regards him as:

> Something like an emissary of light, something like a lower sort of apostle. There had been a lot of such rot let loose in print and talk just about that time, and the excellent woman, living right in the rush of all that humbug, got carried off her feet. She talked about "weaning those ignorant millions from their horrid ways," till, upon my word, she made me quite uncomfortable. I ventured to hint that the company was run for profit. (Conrad 39)

It can be argued here that Marlow as an artistic creation enjoys the insight of Conrad, the writer who visited the Congo in 1890, and had an opportunity to see for himself Leopold II's Congo Free State. It must have become obvious to Conrad that there was a gap between the discourse of imperialism with all its clichés and idealistic sentiments and the actual sordid business of exploiting Africa. Also there is the biographical fact that Conrad himself grew up in a part of Poland dominated by Russia and, as such, he did not find it easy to share the European euphoria about empire—more so when his numerous journeys to what John McClure calls "the raw edges of the empire" (Dabydeen 154) had enabled him to see the whole business of empire from a slightly different angle.

One passage which reveals more clearly the attitude of Marlow, and perhaps that of Conrad himself, towards imperialism is often cited by critics. Marlow stumbles upon dying blacks in Africa and says:

> They were not enemies, they were not criminals, they were nothing earthly now,—nothing but black shadows of disease

and starvation, lying confusedly in the greenish gloom. Brought from all the recesses of the coast in all the legality of time contracts, lost in uncongenial surroundings, fed on unfamiliar food, they sickened, became inefficient, and were allowed to crawl away and rest. (Conrad 44)

Being confirmed by Marlow at this instance is the fact that whites in Africa are not pilgrims of progress as is claimed by the protagonists of *King Solomon's Mines*. Often they are actors in a barbaric and destructive drama which inflicts untold havoc on the very inhabitants of a continent which the rhetoric of imperialism claims to redeem. Far from being "pilgrims," "apostles," and "emissaries of light," they are, ironically, a callous and vicious lot propelled by base motives of selfishness and greed. In other words, the supposedly heroic deeds celebrated in the boy's adventure story are revealed as fraudulent, often with consequences horrifying to look at. Marlow's comments at this stage are a direct indictment of imperialism: the blacks become the proverbial victims they have always been in history, trampled upon by the wheels of empire.

What seems to have interested and fascinated Conrad, however, is not so much the fate of the non-white as a victim of imperialism but rather, what became of the character and fate of the so-called superior race the moment it left the shores of a supposedly "civilized" Western world and came face to face with the dark people of an alien culture and environment. In the stock drama churned out by the Haggards and Buchans of the pro-imperialist world, that point of contact and conflict with other races becomes an opportunity to vindicate white supremacy. As for Conrad, that moment is fraught with perilous contradictions and disabling anxieties. For instance, the moment Kurtz reaches the interior of Africa, he becomes a ruthless ivory collecting brute. His passion for ivory becomes a demonic obsession which knows no moral boundaries. He raids the locals with the supreme confidence of a god. Far from spreading the seeds of European civilization in a supposedly dark and malevolent wilderness, Kurtz becomes a sinister figure—indeed an integral part of the very darkness he is meant to banish from Africa. The messianic zeal and idealism often displayed in the boys' adventure story, and which we initially identify with Kurtz, is brutally undercut. That impressive and more or less romantic public profile which Kurtz enjoys in Europe and with those who know him from a distance is pitilessly undermined by what Marlow discovers about him in Africa. He becomes a sinister and resounding mockery of those ideals which man has always parroted, often as an unwitting justification of his own latent and selfish needs.

The implication of the degeneration which takes place in Kurtz is that the moment he leaves Europe with its restraining order and civilizing influences he becomes overwhelmed by the forces of darkness which have always lurked beneath European civilization itself right from those centuries predating Roman influence in Britain. His convictions and ideals dwindle into embarrassing sentiments rudely cast aside by the beast in him. One can even claim that by hinting at the darkness which Europe still harbors in its breast and which the nineteenth- and early twentieth-century European reader was readily prone to see in the otherness of non-whites, Conrad is deliberately assaulting the all too often simplistic moral inanities of imperialistic discourse with its insistence on the crude dichotomies between darkness and light, black and white, savage and civilized. This is more evident in that even Europe is associated with metaphors suggesting incipient darkness and death. In *Heart of Darkness*, the Manichean mode of perception and expression becomes destabilized as conventional symbolic language becomes invested with uncustomary associations. The color of ivory and the sinister resonance it acquires in this novel is a good example here.

If it is accepted that the symbolic role of Kurtz is to question and subvert European modes of perception and thinking, the question that arises pertains to the consistency and effectiveness with which this is done in *Heart of Darkness*. Put another way, to what extent does *Heart of Darkness* succeed in undercutting and displacing the popular ideas and prejudices of its Edwardian readership? Does this novel succeed in creating enough space for new thinking to take root, for new attitudes and feelings to emerge? To address these questions, we have to examine the mode in which the spiritual disintegration of Kurtz is described. Marlow continues:

> The wilderness had patted him on the head and behold, it was like a ball, an ivory ball; it had caressed him, and lo!, he had withered; it had taken him, and got into his veins, consumed his flesh, and sealed his soul to its own by the inconceivable ceremonies of some devilish initiation. (Conrad 84)

In order for Conrad to describe the intangible but real world of the spirit associated with the moral decay of Kurtz, he transforms Africa into an active, symbolic persona possessing those anarchic Dionysian energies which are forever locked in combat against the Apollonian principles underpinning Western civilization. Africa and its ivory become an objective correlative acting out the role of a demonic Vampire which is pitiless in its hold over the seduced and hapless Kurtz.

One way of regarding the role which Conrad assigns to Africa is to take the continent as merely an appropriate setting on which to dramatize the moral dissolution of Kurtz—it is an environment whose supposed wilderness is meant to perform a small task—that is, elicit the darkness deeply buried within the heart of the protagonist himself. On the other hand, African readers are painfully conscious of the wicked archetypal role often assigned to the so-called frontier societies which are non-white. Here is how Richard Slotkin describes the stereotypical role of the native Indian in the psyche of North American whites:

> They are our ecological link with our biota—the organic environment which we strive to *repudiate* and *destroy* . . . the flooding tide full of turmoil and whirlpools of the unconscious; or id, or the dark forces of the blood . . . the actual savage environment that reason and order and human relationships can penetrate but cannot control. (Slotkin 18)

In a sense Africa and its inhabitants are reduced into a threatening symbol which, like the symbolic role of the Indians, harbors an anarchic potential which the civilized world has striven to "repudiate and destroy."

It appears as if critics such as Frederick R. Karl, Albert Guerard, F. R. Leavis and others have been quite content to regard the symbolic role assigned to the Congo as appropriate in expressing the darker and more menacing side of European culture. Such an artistic process appears to them as a helpful and indeed a legitimate free play of the imagination which singles out Conrad as a genius. However, most of those African readers who have been on the receiving end of imperialism find such a symbolic role unfortunate in the extreme. If we take into account the politics and attitudes of Conrad's readers at the turn of the last century, readers whose imaginations were steeped in theories of racial superiority of whites over blacks, the symbolic darkness of Africa and its supposed barbarism and savagery are the very stuff which the empire builder and the purveyor of popular imperialist literature needed most. Conrad's desire to underline the existence of what John McClure calls a "radical moral and epistemological darkness" (Dabydeen 162) in terms inherently African and black is counterproductive in that it confirms the pernicious myths which were cherished by missionaries, explorers, and empire builders who sought to establish a European presence in Africa in one form or other. Far from subverting the simplistic moral categories of imperialistic discourse Marlow's perception of Africa confirms the worst about Africa.

Conrad himself seems to have been aware of the over-dramatization of evil and sought to justify it in the following terms:

> "*Heart of Darkness* is experience, too; but experience pushed a little (and only very little) beyond the actual facts of the case for the *perfectly legitimate*, I believe, purpose of bringing it home to the minds and bosoms of the readers." Its theme "had to be given a *sinister* resonance, a tonality of its own, a continued vibration that, I hoped, would hang in the air and dwell on the ear after the last note had been struck." (Daiches 7)

By implying that his fictional process is ultimately rooted in the actual experience of his visit to the Congo in 1890, Conrad is in fact insisting that his narrative be seen as a credible version of the white experience in the Congo. One cannot quarrel about his assessment of the calibre of those fortune-seekers who flocked to the Congo during the latter part of the nineteenth century. Marlow is right in exposing the crassness and moral vacancy of those who descended upon Africa like vultures. The history of Leopold II in his Congo Free State is testimony enough. However, it is when Conrad tries to create what he calls "a sinister resonance" that he lapses into a controversial process of myth-making which denies blacks a recognizable humanity. In a letter to Elsie Martindale (Mrs. Ford Madox Ford) Conrad confessed: "What I distinctly admit is the fault of having made Kurtz too symbolic or rather symbolic at all. But the story being mainly a vehicle for conveying a batch of personal impressions I gave free rein to my mental laziness and took the line of least resistance" (Karl 28). Frederick R. Karl regards the somewhat self-effacing comments by Conrad as referring to the "tardiness of Kurtz's vitality." One can actually argue here that the line of least resistance entailed a reliance on ready-made images and stereotypes about Africa which ultimately overshadow the anti-imperialistic thesis implicit in Marlow's original stance. The symbolic and pre-historical Africa of his novel naturally demands a protagonist who operates at a symbolic level, too.

Thus the Congo which Conrad visited is skillfully transformed into a primeval terrain which Marlow claims to be "the beginnings of the world when vegetation rioted on the earth and the big trees were Kings" (Conrad 66). It is a pre-historic Africa peopled by cannibals with filed teeth addicted to superstition and weird ceremonies of the devil. Unlike Marlow, the "pilgrims," and the Russian who converse in a respectable and recognizable language, the African is reduced to an almost pre-verbal creature whose dialect is a hotch-potch of "screeches," "howls," "babbles of uncouth sounds," and "grunting phrases": sometimes the blacks merge with the environment as part of the flora and fauna;

at other times they become part of a weird and sinister mood—a menacing presence. The evocation of this sinister world is so vivid and so new as to transport the reader into a nightmarish world inhabited by alien species bearing the shape of humans. It is a riveting poetic conjuration of sinister images intimating the outlines of a world inhabited by a lunatic breed of primeval blacks and a few stray whites. The sensational character of this world with its shifting moods and elusive certainties has dazzled Western readers no end. But for the black reader, that bewitching success of Conrad places his identity beyond the pale of human civilization—that is, in the minds of people whose societies have not hesitated in the past to wield excessive power over the African's fate in an unfair way.

Even Marlow, whose point of view is central in the novel, and who seems to be morally awake and conscious of the moral travesties which abound, cannot help but betray his own prejudice against blacks. Those who assist the white buccaneers are regarded by Marlow as "reclaimed" or "improved specimens" or "poor devils." Marlow, who alone could provide that yardstick by which readers can judge those around him, makes it clear that he prefers the "black cannibals" rather than the "improved specimens" who, according to his prejudice, are often guilty of forgetting their natural position in the scheme of things. He describes the black fireman as follows: "to look at him was as edifying as seeing a dog in a parody of breeches and a feather hat, walking on his hind legs" (Conrad 70). Such a description speaks volumes about his antipathy towards blacks. In fact instead of being seen as part of the human family, the black man is projected as being much nearer the animal world.

When Conrad deliberately opts for a version of Africa based on myths and prejudices of his age rather than one based on his experiences in the Congo of the 1890s, he is in fact pandering to the predilections of a readership whose imagination and sensibility have been for a long time indisposed towards anything black and anyone non-white. The stereotypical roles of Aaron in Shakespeare's *Titus Andronicus* (1590) and the daughters of Niger in Ben Jonson's *Masque of Blackness* (1605) come to mind here. More disturbing is that antipathy towards non-whites was rooted in a theology of an earlier era and the pseudo-science of the Victorian period. Brian Street writes:

> The central ordering device for a long time prior to the nineteenth century Britain was the concept of "a chain of being," whereby nature was taken to be a unified whole, ranked in a hierarchy from angels to insects. In the nineteenth century this essentially theological notion was adapted to scientific descriptions of nature and refined by Darwinian theories of evolution. The application of evolutionary theory to the ladder meant that researchers could expect to find examples of earlier stages of their developments by examining living contemporary societies. The comparative method enabled travellers and scientists alike to examine living creatures and fellow men for evidence of their own past. (Dabydeen 97)

Thus when Marlow describes the black assistants on the boat as belonging to the "beginnings of time" he is in fact invoking as well as eliciting the concurrence of a seemingly valid evolutionary paradigm which underpins what Michael Echeruo has dubbed the "conditioned imagination." In such a paradigm, those who hail from the "dark" continent occupy a position perilously close to the bestial world, which Europe has long since left behind. By regarding blacks as primitive primates Marlow is in fact suggesting the incalculable and normally unbridgeable gulf separating Europe from dark, primitive Africa. The latter becomes an indispensable existential condition of absurdity against which we can measure the monumental distance which Kurtz has had to cover during his fall from the topmost rung of the ladder of civilization. His fall becomes complete the moment he embraces the moral abyss conceived as being inherently a Congolese phenomenon.

Of primary significance is the way darkness is described as being epistemologically African, a phenomenon whose perils may catch up with the unwary European of the likes of Kurtz. The fact that Kurtz is engulfed by darkness does not necessarily mean that darkness has become an oppressive part of Europe: the darkness remains a potent threat rather than the overwhelming nightmare that it is in the Africa of Conrad's narrative. As such the image of darkness remains an African burden and Kurtz is simply part of an ominous cautionary tale which Europe has to heed if it is to keep the ever-threatening terrors of the wilderness at bay. Put in another way, the process of identifying Europe with darkness is done in a teasingly tentative manner so as to be weaker than the process of imbuing Africa with a menacing darkness. At this level Kurtz's darkness together with that of the lesser "pilgrims" is exceptional while that of the blacks is typical. In a sense Marlow's narrative is banking on the concurrence of the popular imagination of the period which dismissed black cultures in distant lands as backward. What Conrad does is to succumb to the habitual myth-making process which automatically identifies the outward color of the black man with the worst of moral associations. In *The Nigger of the Narcissus* for instance, Conrad is eager to go for the blackness he sees in Jimmy Wait and to make him a menacing symbol whose diseased and disabling enigmatic presence becomes the yardstick by which we can assess the moral health or lack of it of the whole crew.

It is quite tempting to those who have enjoyed reading *Heart of Darkness* in the past to point out that it is no use for the African reader to get worked up ninety years after the book was published: after all the Africa of *Heart of Darkness* is a mythical one and, as such, illuminates very little about the realities of Africa of the 1890s. The only problem here is that in the history of black people myth and reality have often collided very much to the detriment of the children of Africa. For instance a well known powerful gentleman of culture, Lord Chesterfield, argued in a letter to a son of his who was probably troubled about the morality of the slave trade: "blacks are little better than lions, tigers, leopards and other wild beasts which that country produces in great numbers." He went on to argue that blacks had no arts, sciences and systems of commerce and, as such, it was acceptable "to buy a great many of them to sell again to advantage in the West Indies" (Dabydeen 29). In other words Conrad is peddling myths about blacks which have been manipulated in the past by those who sought to exploit them for material gain.

An interesting stereotype which some critics have positively commented upon at the expense of the rather lifeless presence of Kurtz's Intended is centered on the savage African woman. She is a personification of the whole continent and is described as follows:

> She walked with measured steps, draped in striped and fringed clothes, treading the earth proudly with a slight jingle and flash of barbarous ornaments. She had brass leggings to the knees, brass wire gauntlets to the elbow, a crimson spot on her tawny cheek, innumerable necklaces of glass beads on her neck; bizarre things, charms, gifts of witch-men, that hung about her, glittered and trembled at every step. She must have had the value of several elephant tusks upon her. She was savage and superb, wild-eyed and magnificent; there was something ominous and stately in her deliberate progress. And in the hush that had fallen suddenly upon the whole sorrowful land, the immense wilderness, the colossal body of the fecund and mysterious life seemed to look at her, pensive, as though it had been looking at the image of its tenebrous and passionate soul. (Conrad 101)

Here the African woman symbolizes a barbaric magnificence: she is majestically alluring yet with a gaudiness which is gratuitously repellent; she is the ivory which beckons fortune seekers, but only to destroy the morally unwary. Her vitality is as seductive as it is sinfully corrosive: it is part of that sexuality hinted at by the words "passion," "mysterious," and "fecundity," but a sexuality which is demonic and therefore morally dangerous. Later in the narrative Kurtz is said to have been part of unspeakable sexual deeds of a lurid and debauched nature. As Karl claims, her "demanding display of sex" is provocatively tempting but fatal to the likes of Kurtz, who lacks restraint. She is the darkness which awakens the primeval instincts in Kurtz and as such, part of the black peril which casts a dark menacing shadow across the width and breadth of the whole land. In a way she becomes an African version of the legendary *femme fatale*, the proverbial temptress of the African wilderness.

According to the metaphysical language of the narrative, the fall of Kurtz is a moral crime caused by his singular lack of restraint. Unlike Captain Good who rejects the gentle but equally tempting black beauty, Foulata of *King Solomon's Mines*, Kurtz goes native the moment he embraces the savage African woman and indulges in sexual orgies of an inexpressible and abominable kind. In falling from grace he dramatizes the extent to which imagination, vitality, resolute will-power, and restraint—all qualities identified with the construction of a European civilization and with Kurtz—can easily be destroyed by those primeval instincts which have always hounded man. These instincts can express themselves through an unbridled lust for sex, an unrestrained greed for wealth, and a passion for a godlike power over other fellow creatures.

Given a chance to choose between the rather pale and lifeless Intended and the savage African mistress, the reasoning part in Kurtz would opt for the former: but of course the anarchic beast in him opts for the seductive but vengeful African mistress and in doing so he loses his soul in the Faustian manner. Incidentally, even the language of the story becomes very scriptural at this point. In other words, in spite of the assiduously cultivated sense of mystery and vagueness which Leavis describes correctly as being achieved through an "adjectival insistence," one senses the crude outline of a morality play of the medieval period embedded in the novella, but of course rendered in the cynical idiom of a theologically more uncertain nineteenth- and twentieth-century environment. The African mistress embodies those regressive primeval instincts which, in the story, overwhelm the idealism of the ambitious Kurtz. Evil, this time, triumphs over good.

It can be argued that as an artist Conrad is entirely free to offer us a mythical version of Africa, as long as this version suits his artistic purposes. Unfortunately for Africans, the cliché-ridden description of the savage mistress with her dark and tempting sexuality is part of a long-standing stereotype in which blacks are perceived as possessing a lustfulness and bestiality associated with the animal Kingdom. According to Ruth Cowhig, the belief in the excessive sexuality of blacks "was encouraged by the widespread belief in the legend that blacks were descendants of Ham in the Genesis story punished for their sexual excess by their blackness" (Dabydeen 1). Black as a color becomes a symbolic badge proclaiming the moral condition of a whole people. Consequently, the unspeakable sexual excesses of which Kurtz is accused become credible once they are identified within an African context as Conrad does here successfully. On the other hand very few people would deny the fact that such sexual stereotyping has been very harmful to black-white relations on a global scale. One can cite the abysmal black-white relations and the lynching which went on during as well as immediately after the slavery period in the Deep South of the United States. Fear of miscegenation and other numerous sexual horrors of an abominable and unspeakable type haunted the white settlers in Southern Africa so much that statute books were filled with laws forbidding sex relations between blacks and whites. The fate of Mary Turner in Doris Lessing's *The Grass is Singing* comes to mind here. So the sexual stereotyping that is related to the savage mistress is far from being a harmless exercise of the imagination. Together with other historical factors, such a sexual image has been very successful in needlessly widening the racial and cultural gulf separating whites from blacks and much damage has been done to both races, but more so to the blacks who are noted historically for their powerlessness and vulnerability.

Apart from the rather raw and unmediated process of stereotyping Africa and its blacks, a process which denies them a recognizable social order, there is also a certain moral inconsistency which is bound to puzzle many an African reader. One of the crimes which Kurtz is alleged to have committed is that, according to Marlow, "he had taken a high seat amongst the devils of the land—I mean literally" (Conrad 85). By projecting the African as a sub-human primate devilish in character, Marlow violates a sense of poetic justice which the blacks would rightfully regard as owed to them. In Marlow's narrative the African native is in fact the victim of a double injury: the historical victim of the European buccaneers who brutalize him during the nineteenth century and the hapless victim of an artistic process which, while condemning imperialism, uses him and abuses him in the same breath. This not only indicates a contradiction in Marlow's character but also the limitations of a writer without a clear moral standpoint or alternative.

If the fortune-seeker is gaining materially from his exploitation of the African, there is practically no way the likes of Marlow can persuade him to desist from such an exercise since he has pronounced the black people to be devils. Christian history, of which the so-called "pilgrims" are part, has never been very accommodating to devils of any kind—be they real or metaphorical. A good example here is the Papal Bull which authorized the opening of one of the first black slave markets in Lisbon in the first decade of the sixteenth century (p'Bitek 3). The reason given for such an unprecedented act was that slavery would redeem blacks from the evils of paganism. Even the cult of African savagery and primitivism which Conrad's so-called masterpiece needs so desperately for its success is not the harmless affair as it might look from a distance. Here is how one of the holy fathers proposed to solve the problem of darkness and African primitivity almost at the same time that Conrad was writing his book:

> "Father Biehler is so convinced of the hopelessness of regenerating the Hashonas," wrote Lord Grey from Chishawasha in January 1897, "whom he regards as the most hopeless of mankind . . . that he states that the only chance for the future of the race is to exterminate the whole people, both male and female, over the age of 14! This pessimistic conclusion," Grey continued, "I find it hard to accept." (Ranger 3)

The presumed African darkness seems to have elicited a whole gamut of human feelings, especially in Europeans, ranging from the most noble to the frighteningly ignoble. Kurtz, with his chilling utterance "Exterminate all the brutes!" is a good example, and Marlow too. The latter's anti-imperialistic stance becomes more muted the moment he begins his long-awaited journey up the river Congo. In fact Marlow's anti-imperialistic discourse becomes subordinate to the imperatives of a story which, so one can argue, degenerates into a sensational melodrama. As the language becomes more abstract and metaphysical, the very victim of imperialism is, by a strange twist of logic, turned into a devil and, as such, he becomes a scapegoat as well as the author of his own misfortunes. It may sound old-fashioned and simplistic but it needs saying nevertheless: there is something of a moral untidiness that sits at the heart of Conrad's masterpiece. This has all to do with the moral conception of the whole story. Conrad makes Marlow equivocate on a very crucial moral issue here and this makes him remain as ethnocentric and self-centered as the pilgrims of whom he is so disdainful. Marlow is simply incapable of acknowledging the humanity of those blacks conscripted by the forces of history to take part in an imperialist drama. The grossly exaggerated and luridly sensational barbarism associated with Africa is very much the kind of stuff characteristic of the boys' adventure story of the Victorian era—and this is the genre which the novel promises to outgrow at the beginning!

It is interesting to observe that Chinua Achebe's bitter criticism of *Heart of Darkness* and Michael Echeruo's unceremonious dismissal of it ironically betray the importance they both attach to the novel. In fact *Heart of Darkness* is placed, both historically and imaginatively, at a strategic position from which African writers and scholars can ponder the magnitude of their predicament as they try to communicate across cultures. Conrad's metaphor of darkness, with all its ironic implications, is, ultimately, based on a pejorative and fundamental oversimplification of a whole continent which Africans know has never been that simple or mysterious either. They also share the painful knowledge that Conrad is harping on myths which are ultimately rooted in and originating from societies whose relationship with Africa has hardly been based on what is truthful and mutually beneficial. These are societies associated with conquests of other parts of the world during the seventeenth century, societies which embarked on slavery during the seventeenth and eighteenth centuries and spearheaded the imperialism of the nineteenth century. Throughout these centuries myths about Africa have either grown or diminished in relation to the economic role assigned to the inhabitants of the continent at a particular time in history.

In addition, anyone familiar with the emergence and growth of modern African literature will know that one of the factors which has inspired African writers, thinkers, and even politicians is the desire to address a whole battery of stereotypes about blacks which have remained lodged at the centre of the Western imagination. In 1965 at Leeds University, Achebe said:

> I would be quite satisfied if my novels (especially the ones I set in the past) did no more than teach my readers that their past—with all its imperfections—was not one long night of savagery from which the first Europeans acting on God's behalf delivered them. (Achebe 30)

One of the factors which sparked off Achebe's creativity was his encounter with Joyce Cary's *Mister Johnson*—a book which, unfortunately, perpetuates some of the myths propagated by Conrad's book. One can even go so far as to say that ideas associated with Negritude, African Personality, and indeed African nationalism itself have much to do with the desire on the part of the African to confront and refute a long-standing tradition of abuse against blacks.

It is important to underline the fact that there is no evidence to suggest that Conrad tried to justify imperialism. The opposite seems to be more probable in fact. However, his rather lazy overdependence on metaphors and stereotypes which in history have been used to justify the physical and spiritual mutilation of nonwhites cannot be counted as the strength of a great artist. Shakespeare may have initially accepted such stereotyping of black people in *Titus Andronicus* but towards the end of the same play the humanity of Aaron comes across in a way which modifies somewhat the earlier stereotype. In *Othello* the image of the black general transcends the prejudices of the Elizabethan era so as to enhance and extend our own vision of humanity. The same applies to the *Merchant of Venice*—a play in which stereotypes about Jews are indirectly questioned by the nature of the human interactions on the stage. As for Kurtz, he may be humanized by Africa and come to recognize his own hollowness, but that Africa remains physically and morally grotesque. The fact is Conrad allowed the prejudiced and popular imagination of his time to run away with his story of the Congo and in the process he prevented a whole continent from occupying its rightful place in the human family. His treatment of the Congolese setting and its people can only harden the racist attitudes of his European audience. It is a paradoxical achievement that in order for Conrad to revitalize Europe spiritually he has to dehumanize and distort Africa beyond recognition first. His handling of the African dimension of his story amounts to a very cheap way of entertaining a jaded Europe afflicted by self-doubts; but, ultimately, every broad-minded reader has to come to terms with a story notable for its harsh exclusions and embarrassing racism.

Some critics have argued that the image of Africa portrayed in *Heart of Darkness* is Marlow's version. It is true insofar as through Marlow's ironic inconsistencies Conrad seems to have placed the whole sin of Europe on Marlow's shoulders. For instance, while trying to detach himself from the sin of his people, Marlow becomes deeply steeped in their prejudices and ends up regarding blacks like any other white man of his time. There is no moral lesson to learn from him as regards the European attitude to Africa. Ultimately, however, readers have to talk about the author's vision as it is revealed in the text, and it is a vision which, while critical of imperialism, reinforces unpalatable stereotypes about Africa. The moral revulsion of both Marlow and his author, Conrad, at the sordid nature of imperialism is not strong enough to transcend racial boundaries. There is an element of the Brabantio of *Othello*'s world in both of them—that pseudo-liberalism in which racism is never far beneath the surface. It is only fair to state that Conrad remained as much a racist as his European tradition allowed him, a tradition within which a philosophical spokesman like Hegel could declare with disarming confidence:

Africa proper, as far as History goes back, has remained—for all purposes of connection with the rest of the world—shut up; it is the Gold-land compressed within itself—the land of childhood, which lying beyond the days of self-conscious history, is enveloped in the dark mantle of Night.

The negro as already observed exhibits the natural man in his completely wild and untamed state. We must lay aside all thought of reverence and morality—all, that we call feeling—if we would rightly comprehend him; there is nothing harmonious with humanity to be found in this type of character …[Africa] has no movement or development to exhibit. (Quoted in Lamming 31–2)

Hegel remains one of the most exciting minds to contribute to the development of Western philosophy, yet one wonders if his greatness can be reconciled with the nauseating opinions he displays in the instance above. So much for the prejudices and ignorance which have been dutifully handed down to numerous Western generations as acquired wisdom! By the same token, *Heart of Darkness* can be called great, but one wonders at what price! The novel has been accorded the status of a classic in the Western world but such a status is based on its capacity to peddle racist myths in the guise of good fiction.

Conrad's novel presents, regrettably, a powerful convergence of most of those stereotypes which have been bandied about in regard to the nature and status of black people in the world. These stereotypes concern their supposed ignorance and barbarism, their assumed simple-mindedness, their being childish and childlike, their irrationality and excessive lustfulness and their animal-like status—to name only a few. African writers and thinkers have been laboring under the burden of such false images for a long time, and it would be surprising if anyone familiar with the suffering and history of black people can label *Heart of Darkness* a masterpiece when it distorts a whole continent and its people. There is a terrible parallel here between the economic rape which Africa suffered and the artistic loot that Conrad gets away with!

In conclusion, it is interesting to note that *Heart of Darkness* betrays the fallibility of some of the so-called great writers and critics. As for African scholars and general readers, it is important to know that texts which are canonized as classics need not be regarded as such by all peoples at all times. These texts are rooted in specific societies at specific points in history and can sometimes, in a most unexpected way, nourish the very prejudices which any society in its right mind should struggle against. More significantly, writers such as Joseph Conrad can help to start a debate about the fate of the oppressed, but, ultimately, they cannot be a substitute for the voices of the oppressed themselves. The discourse of liberation belongs to them. Finally, it is of vital importance that future generations of Africans are sensitized to how peoples of other nations perceive Africa. Only then can they be well placed to relate to other races in a meaningful way.

Works Cited

Achebe, Chinua. *Hopes and Impediments.* London: Heinemann, 1988.
Buchan, John. *Prester John.* London: Nelson and Sons, 1910.
Conrad, Joseph. *Heart of Darkness.* 1902. London: Penguin, 1989.
Dabydeen, David, ed. *The Black Presence in English Literature.* Manchester: Manchester University Press, 1985.
Daiches, David. *White Man in the Tropics: Two Moral Tales.* New York: Harcourt, Brace and World, 1962.
Echeruo, Michael. *The Conditioned Imagination from Shakespeare to Conrad: Studies in, the Exo-Cultural Stereotype.* London: Macmillan 1987.
———. *Joyce Cary and the Novel of Africa.* London: Longman, 1973.
Karl, Frederick R., ed., *Joseph Conrad: Collection of Criticism.* New York: McGraw-Hill, 1975.
Guerard, Albert. *Conrad the Novelist.* Cambridge, Mass.: Harvard University Press, 1978.
Lamming, George. *The Pleasures of Exile.* London: Michael Joseph, 1960.
Leavis, F. R. *The Great Tradition.* London: Chatto and Windus, 1973.
Ngugi wa Thiong'o. *Decolonising the Mind.* 1981. Harare: Zimbabwe Publishing House, 1987.

p'Bitek, Okot. *African Religions in Western Scholarship*. Nairobi: East African Literature Bureau, 1970.

Ranger, Terence. *Revolt in Southern Rhodesia 1896–7; A Study in African Resistance*. London: Heinemann, 1967.

Slotkin, Richard. *Regeneration Through Violence: The Mythology of the American Frontier, 1600–1860*. Middleton, Conn.: Wesleyan Press, 1973.

Jungle Fever

DAVID DENBY

◆   ◆   ◆

"WHO HERE COMES from a savage race?" Professor James Shapiro shouted at his students.

"We all come from Africa," said the one African-American in the class, whom I'll call Henry, calmly referring to the supposition among most anthropologists that human life originated in sub-Saharan Africa. What Henry was saying was that there are no racial hierarchies among peoples—that we're all "savages."

Shapiro smiled. It was not, I thought, exactly the answer he had been looking for, but it was a good answer. Then he was off again. "Are you natural?" he roared at a girl sitting near his end of the seminar table. "What are the constraints for you? What are the rivets? Why are you here getting civilized, reading Lit Hum?"

It was the end of the academic year, and the mood had grown agitated, burdened, portentous. In short, we were reading Joseph Conrad, the final author in Columbia's Literature Humanities (or Lit Hum) course, one of the two famous "great books" courses that have long been required of all Columbia College undergraduates. Both Lit Hum and the other course, Contemporary Civi-

243

lization, are devoted to the much ridiculed "narrative" of Western culture, the list of classics, which, in the case of Lit Hum, begins with Homer and ends, chronologically speaking, with Virginia Woolf. I was spending the year reading the same books and sitting in on the Lit Hum classes, which were taught entirely in sections; there were no lectures. At the end of the year, the individual instructors were allotted a week for a free choice. Some teachers chose works by Dostoyevski or Mann or Gide or Borges. Shapiro, a Shakespeare scholar from the Department of English and Comparative Literature (his book *Shakespeare and the Jews* was published by Columbia University Press in 1996), chose Conrad.

The terms of Shapiro's rhetorical questions—savagery, civilization, constraints, rivets—were drawn from Conrad's great novella of colonial depredation, *Heart of Darkness,* and the students, almost all of them freshmen, were electrified. Almost a hundred years old, and familiar to generations of readers, Conrad's little book has lost none of its power to amaze and appall: it remains, in many places, an essential starting point for discussions of modernism, imperialism, the hypocrisies and glories of the West, and the ambiguities of "civilization." Critics by the dozen have subjected it to symbolic, mythological, and psychoanalytic interpretation; T. S. Eliot used a line from it as an epigraph for "The Hollow Men," and Hemingway and Faulkner were much impressed by it, as were Orson Welles and Francis Ford Coppola, who employed it as the ground plan for his despairing epic of Americans in Vietnam, *Apocalypse Now.*

In recent years, however, Conrad—and particularly *Heart of Darkness*—has fallen under a cloud of suspicion in the academy. In the curious language of the tribe, the book has become "a site of contestation." After all, Conrad offered a nineteenth-century European's view of Africans as primitive. He attacked Belgian imperialism and in the same breath seemed to praise the British variety. In 1975, the distinguished Nigerian novelist and essayist Chinua Achebe assailed *Heart of Darkness* as racist and called for its elimination from the canon of Western classics. And recently Edward W. Said, one of the most famous critics and scholars at Columbia today, has been raising hostile and undermining questions about it. Certainly Said is no breaker of canons. But if Conrad were somehow discredited, one could hardly imagine a more successful challenge to what the academic left has repeatedly deplored as the "hegemonic discourse" of the classic Western texts. There is also the inescapable question of justice to Conrad himself.

WRITTEN IN A LITTLE MORE than two months, the last of 1898 and the first of 1899, *Heart of Darkness* is both the story of a journey and a kind of morbid fairy tale. Marlow, Conrad's narrator and familiar alter ego, a British merchant seaman of the eighteen-nineties, travels up the Congo in the service of a rapacious Belgian trading company, hoping to retrieve the company's brilliant representative and ivory trader, Mr. Kurtz, who has mysteriously grown silent. The great Mr. Kurtz! In Africa, everyone gossips about him, envies him, and, with rare exception, loathes him. The flower of European civilization ("all Europe contributed to the making of Kurtz"), exemplar of light and compassion, journalist, artist, humanist, Kurtz has gone way upriver and at times well into the jungle, abandoning himself to certain . . . practices. Rifle in hand, he has set himself up as god or devil in ascendancy over the Africans. Conrad is notoriously vague about what Kurtz actually does, but if you said "kills some people, has sex with others, steals all the ivory," you would not, I believe, be far wrong. In Kurtz, the alleged benevolence of colonialism has flowered into criminality. Marlow's voyage from Europe to Africa and then up-river to Kurtz's Inner Station is a revelation of the squalors and disasters of the colonial "mission"; it is also, in Marlow's mind, a journey back to the beginning of creation, when nature reigned exuberant and unrestrained, and a trip figuratively *down* as well, through the levels of the self to repressed and unlawful desires. At death's door, Marlow and Kurtz find each other.

Rereading a work of literature is often a shock, an encounter with an earlier self that has been revised, and I found that I was initially discomforted, as I had not been in the past, by the famous manner—the magnificent, alarmed, and (there is no other word) throbbing excitement of Conrad's laboriously mastered English.

Conrad was born in czarist-occupied Poland; though he heard English spoken as a boy (and his father translated Shakespeare), it was his third language, and his prose, now and then, betrays the propensity for high intellectual melodrama and rhymed abstraction ("the fascination of the abomination") characteristic of his second language, French. Oh, inexorable, unutterable, unspeakable! The great British critic F. R. Leavis, who loved Conrad, ridiculed such sentences as "It was the stillness of an implacable force brooding over an inscrutable intention." The sound, Leavis thought, was an overwrought, thrilled embrace of strangeness. (In Max Beerbohm's parody: "Silence, the silence murmurous and unquiet of a tropical night, brooded over the hut that, baked through by the sun, sweated a vapour beneath the cynical light of the stars. . . . Within the hut the form of the white man, corpulent and pale, was covered with a mosquito-net that was itself illusory like everything else, only more so.")

Read in isolation, some of Conrad's sentences are certainly a howl, but one reads them in isolation only in criticism like Leavis's or Achebe's. Reading the tale straight through, I lost my discomfort after twenty pages or so and fell hopelessly under Conrad's spell; thereafter, even his most heavily freighted constructions dropped into place, summing up the many specific matters that had come before. Marlow speaks:

> "Going up that river was like travelling back to the earliest beginnings of the world, when vegetation rioted on the earth and the big trees were kings. An empty stream, a great silence, an impenetrable forest. The air was warm, thick, heavy, sluggish. There was no joy in the brilliance of sunshine. The long stretches of the waterway ran on, deserted, into the gloom of overshadowed distances. On silvery sandbanks hippos and alligators sunned themselves side by side. The broadening waters flowed through a mob of wooded islands. You lost your way on that river as you would in a desert and butted all day long against shoals trying to find the channel till you thought yourself bewitched and cut off for ever from everything you had known once—somewhere—far away—in another existence

perhaps. There were moments when one's past came back to one, as it will sometimes when you have not a moment to spare to yourself; but it came in the shape of an unrestful and noisy dream remembered with wonder amongst the over- whelming realities of this strange world of plants and water and silence. And this stillness of life did not in the least resem- ble a peace. It was the stillness of an implacable force brooding over an inscrutable intention." (35–36)

In one sense, the writing now seemed close to the movies: it revelled in sensation and atmosphere, in extreme acts and gro- tesque violence (however indirectly presented), in shivering enig- mas and richly phrased premonitions and frights. In other ways, though, *Heart of Darkness* was modernism at its most intellectually bracing, with tonalities, entirely contemporary and distanced, that I had failed to notice when I was younger—immense pride and immense contempt; a mood of barely contained revolt; and sar- donic humor that verged on malevolence:

"I don't pretend to say that steamboat floated all the time. More than once she had to wade for a bit, with twenty can- nibals splashing around and pushing. We had enlisted some of these chaps on the way for a crew. Fine fellows—cannibals—in their place. They were men one could work with, and I am grateful to them. And, after all, they did not eat each other before my face: they had brought along a provision of hippo- meat which went rotten and made the mystery of the wilder- ness stink in my nostrils. Phoo! I can sniff it now. I had the Manager on board and three or four pilgrims [white traders] with their staves—all complete. Sometimes we came upon a station close by the bank clinging to the skirts of the unknown, and the white men rushing out of a tumble-down hovel with great gestures of joy and surprise and welcome seemed very strange, had the appearance of being held there captive by a spell. The word 'ivory' would ring in the air for a while—and on we went again into the silence, along empty reaches, round the still bends, between the high walls of our winding way, reverberating in hollow claps the ponderous beat of the stern-wheel." (36–37)

Out of sight of their countrymen back home, who continue to cloak the colonial mission in the language of Christian charity and improvement, the "pilgrims" have become rapacious and cruel. The cannibals eating hippo meat practice restraint; the Europeans do not. That was the point of Shapiro's taunting initial sally: "savagery" is inherent in all of us, including the most "civilized," for we live, according to Conrad, in a brief interlude between innumerable centuries of darkness and the darkness yet to come. Only the rivets, desperately needed to repair Marlow's pathetic steamboat, offer stability—the rivets and the ship itself and the codes of seamanship and duty are all that hold life together in a time of moral anarchy. Marlow, meeting Kurtz at last, despises him for letting go—and at the same time, with breathtaking ambivalence, admires him for going all the way to the bottom of his soul and discovering there, at the point of death, a judgment of his own life. It is perhaps the most famous death scene written since Shakespeare:

> "Anything approaching the change that came over his features I have never seen before and hope never to see again. Oh, I wasn't touched. I was fascinated. It was as though a veil had been rent. I saw on that ivory face the expression of sombre pride, of ruthless power, of craven terror—of an intense and hopeless despair. Did he live his life again in every detail of desire, temptation, and surrender during that supreme moment of complete knowledge? He cried in a whisper at some image, at some vision—he cried out twice, a cry that was no more than a breath:
> "The horror! The horror!' " (68)

Much dispute and occasional merriment have long attended the question of what, exactly, Kurtz means by the melodramatic exclamation "The horror!" But surely one of the things he means is his long revelling in "abominations"—his own internal collapse. Shapiro's opening questions set up a reading of the novella that interrogated the Western civilization of which Kurtz is the supreme representative and of which the students, in their youthful way, were representatives as well.

WHEN SHAPIRO ASKED the class why they thought he had chosen *Heart of Darkness*, hands were going up before he had finished his question.

"You chose it because the whole core curriculum is embodied in Kurtz," said Henry, who had answered Shapiro's earlier question. "We embody this knowledge, and the book asks, Do we fall into the void—do we drown or come out with a stronger sense of self?"

Henry had turned the book into a test of the course and of himself. Conrad had great personal significance for him, which didn't surprise me. An African-American from Baltimore, Henry, in his sophomore year at Columbia, had evolved into a fervent Nietzschean, and, though Conrad claimed to dislike Nietzsche, this was a Nietzschean text. The meaning of Henry's life—his personal myth—required (he had said it in class many times) challenge, struggle, and self-transcendence. He was tall and strong, with a flattop "wedge" haircut and a loud, excited voice. Some months after this class, he got himself not tattooed but *branded* with the insignia of his black Columbia fraternity—an act of excruciating irony unavailable to members of the master race. Kurtz, however horrifying, was an exemplar for him as for Conrad's hero, Marlow.

A freshman of Chinese descent from Singapore, who was largely reared on British and Continental literature, also saw the book as a test for Western civilization. But, unlike Henry, she hated the abyss. Kurtz was a seduced man, a portent of disintegration. "Can we deal with the knowledge we are seeking?" she asked. "Or will we say, with Kurtz, 'The horror'?" For her, Kurtz's outburst was an admission of the failure of knowledge.

And many others made similar remarks. All of a sudden, at the end of the course, the students were quite willing to see their year of education in Western classics as problematic. Their reading

of "the great books" could be affirmed only if it was simultaneously questioned. No doubt Shapiro's rhetorical questions had
shaped their responses, but still their intensity surprised me.

"The book is a kind of test," said a student from the Washington, D.C., area, who was normally a polite, bland schoolboy
type. "Does its existence redeem the male hegemonic line of culture? Does it redeem education in this tradition?" By which I
believe that he also meant to ask, "Could the existence of such
a book redeem the crimes of imperialism?" That, at any rate, was
my question.

The students were in good form, bold and free, and as the
class went on they expounded certain points in the text, some of
them holding the little paperback in their hands like preachers
before the faithful. All year long, Shapiro had struggled to get
them to read aloud, and with some emotional commitment to
the words. And all too often they had droned, as if they were
reading from a computer manual. But now they read aloud spontaneously, and their voices were alive, even ringing.

"For this course, it's a kind of summing up, isn't it?" Shapiro
said. "We began with the journey to Troy."

"It has a resemblance to all the journeys through Hell we've
read," said a student I will call Alex, a thin, ascetic-looking boy,
the son of a professor. He cited the voyages to the underworld
in the *Odyssey* and the *Aeneid*, and he cited Dante, whom Conrad,
in one of his greatest moments, obviously had in mind. Marlow
arrives at one of the trading company's stations, a disastrous ram-
shackle settlement of wrecked machinery and rusting rails, and
there encounters, under the trees, dozens of exhausted African
workers who have been left to die. "It seemed to me I had stepped
into the gloomy circle of some Inferno," he says.

> "They were dying slowly—it was very clear. They were not
> enemies, they were not criminals, they were nothing earthly
> now, nothing but black shadows of disease and starvation lying
> confusedly in the greenish gloom. Brought from all the reces-
> ses of the coast in all the legality of time contracts, lost in
> uncongenial surroundings, fed on unfamiliar food, they sick-

ened, became inefficient, and were then allowed to crawl away and rest. These moribund shapes were free as air—and nearly as thin. I began to distinguish the gleam of the eyes under the trees. Then glancing down I saw a face near my hand. The black bones reclined at full length with one shoulder against the tree, and slowly the eyelids rose and the sunken eyes looked up at me, enormous and vacant, a kind of blind, white flicker in the depths of the orbs which died out slowly. The man seemed young—almost a boy—but you know with them it's hard to tell. I found nothing else to do but to offer him one of my good Swede's ship's biscuits I had in my pocket. The fingers closed slowly on it and held—there was no other movement and no other glance. He had tied a bit of white worsted round his neck—Why? Where did he get it. Was it a badge—an ornament—a charm—a propitiatory act? Was there any idea at all connected with it. It looked startling round his black neck this bit of white thread from beyond the seas.

"Near the same tree two more bundles of acute angles sat with their legs drawn up. One, with his chin propped on his knees, stared at nothing in an intolerable and appalling manner. His brother phantom rested its forehead as if overcome with a great weariness; and all about others were scattered in every pose of contorted collapse, as in some picture of a massacre or a pestilence." (20–21)

Despite the last sentence, which links the grove of death to ancient and medieval catastrophes, there is a sense here, as many readers have said, of something unprecedented in horror, something new on earth—what later became known as genocide. It is one of Conrad's bitter ironies that at least some of the Europeans forcing the Congolese into labor are "liberals" devoted to the "suppression of savage customs." What they had perpetrated in the Congo was not, perhaps, planned slaughter, but it was a slaughter nonetheless, and some of the students, pointing to the passage, were abashed. Western man had done this. We had created an Inferno on earth. *Heart of Darkness*, written at the end of the nineteenth century, resonates unhappily throughout the twentieth. Marlow's shock, his amazement before the sheer strangeness of the ravaged human forms, anticipates what the Allied liberators of the concentration camps felt in 1945. The answer to the question "Does the book redeem the West?" was clear enough: No book can provide expiation for any culture. But if some crimes are irredeemable, a frank acknowledgment of the crime might lead to a partial remission of sin. Conrad had written such an acknowledgment.

That was the heart of the liberal reading, and Shapiro's students rose to it willingly, gravely, ardently—and then, all of a sudden, the class fell into an acrimonious dispute. Alex was not happy with the way Shapiro and the other students were talking about Kurtz and the moral self-judgment of the West. He thought it was glib. He couldn't see the book in apocalyptic terms. Kurtz was a criminal, an isolated figure. He was not representative of the West or of anything else. "Why is this a critique of the West?" he demanded. "No culture celebrates men like Kurtz. No culture condones what he did." There was general protest, even a few laughs. "O.K.," he said, yielding a bit. "It can be read as a critique of the West, but not *only* of the West."

From my corner of the room, I took a hard look at him. He was as tight as a drum, dry, a little supercilious. Kurtz had nothing to do with *him*—that was his unmistakable attitude. He denied the connection that the other students acknowledged. He was cut off in some way, withholding himself. Yet I knew this student. I had seen him only in class, but there was something familiar in him that irked me, though exactly what it was I couldn't say. Why was he so dense? The other students were not claiming personal responsibility for imperialism or luxuriating in guilt. They were merely admitting participation in an "advanced" civilization that could lose its moral bearings.

Henry, leaning back in his chair—against the wall, behind Alex, who sat at the table—insisted on an existential reading. "Kurtz is an Everyman figure," he said. "He gets down to the soul, below the layers of parents, religion, society."

Alex hotly disagreed. They were talking past each other, offering different angles of approach, but there was an edge to their

voices which suggested an animus that went beyond mere dis-
agreement. There was an awkward pause, and some of the students stirred uneasily. I had never seen these two quarrel in the
past, and what they said presented no grounds for anger, but
when each repeated his position, anger filled the room. Shapiro
tried to calm things down, and the other students looked at one
another in wonder and alarm. The argument between Alex and
Henry wasn't about race, yet race unmistakably hovered over it.
In a tangent, Henry brought up the way Conrad, reflecting European assumptions of his time, portrayed the Africans as wild
and primitive. He started to make a case similar to Achebe's
(whose hostile essay is included in the current Norton Critical
Edition of the text), then stopped in midsentence, abruptly abandoning his position. In our class on *King Lear* and at other times
over the past several months, he had argued explicitly as a black
man. But at that moment he wasn't interested. A greater urgency
overcame him—not the racial but the existential issue, his own
pressing need for identification not just as an African-American
but as an embattled man. "Good and evil are conventions," he
said. "They collapse under stress." And this, he insisted, was true
for everyone.

"The book is also about the *difference* between good and evil,"
Alex retorted. "Everyone *judges* Kurtz." But this is not correct.
Marlow judges Kurtz; Conrad judges Kurtz. But back in Brussels
he is mourned as an apostle of enlightenment.

I looked a little closer. Alex was like the fabled "wicked son"
in the Passover celebration, the one who says to the others "Why
is this important to *you?*"—denying a personal connection with
an event of mesmerizing significance. I knew him, all right. A
pale, narrow face, a bony nose surmounted by glasses, a paucity
of flesh, a general air of asexual arrogance. He was very bright
and very young. Of all the students in Shapiro's class, he was—
I saw it now—the closest to what I had been at eighteen or
nineteen. He was incomparably more self-assured and articulate,
but I recognized him all too well. And I was startled. The middle-
aged reader, uneasy with earlier versions of himself, little expects
his simulacrum to rise up as a walking ghost.

Henry sat sheathed in a green turtleneck sweater, dark glasses, and a baseball cap; I couldn't see his expression. But Shapiro's was clear: he was not happy. He had perhaps gone a little too far with his rhetorical questions, striking sparks that threatened to turn into a conflagration, and he quickly moved the conversation in a different direction, getting the students to explicate Conrad's use of the word "darkness." Conrad lets us know that even England—where Marlow sits, telling his story—used to be one of the dark places of the earth. For a while, teacher and students explicated the text in a neutral way. All year long, Shapiro had gone back and forth between analyzing the structure and language of the books and attacking the students' complacencies with rhetorical questions. But sober analysis wasn't what he wanted, not of this text, and he soon returned to the complicity of the West, and even the Western universities, in a policy that King Leopold II of the Belgians—the man responsible for some of the worst atrocities of colonial Africa—always referred to as noble and self-sacrificing.

"How else would you guys be civilized except for 'the noble cause'?" Shapiro said. "You guys are all products of the noble cause. Columbia's motto, translated from the Latin, is 'In Thy light shall we see light.' That's the light that is supposed to penetrate the heart of darkness, isn't it?"

"But enlightenment comes only by way of darkness," said Henry, still at it, and Alex demurred angrily again—no darkness for him—and for a terrible moment I thought they were actually going to come to blows. The women in the class, who for the most part had been silent during these exchanges, were appalled and afterward muttered angrily, "It's a boy thing, macho showing off. 'Who's the biggest intellectual?' " True, but maybe it was also a race thing. Though Shapiro restored order, something had broken, and the class, which had begun so well, with everyone joining in and expounding, had come unriveted.

IS *HEART OF DARKNESS* a depraved book? The following is one of the passages Chinua Achebe deplores as racist:

"We were wanderers on a prehistoric earth, on an earth that wore the aspect of an unknown planet. We could have fancied ourselves the first of men taking possession of an accursed inheritance, to be subdued at the cost of profound anguish and of excessive toil. But suddenly as we struggled round a bend there would be a glimpse of rush walls, of peaked grass-roofs, a burst of yells, a whirl of black limbs, a mass of hands clapping, of feet stamping, of bodies swaying, of eyes rolling under the droop of heavy and motionless foliage. The steamer toiled along slowly on the edge of a black and incomprehensible frenzy. The prehistoric man was cursing us, praying to us, welcoming us—who could tell? We were cut off from the comprehension of our surroundings; we glided past like phantoms, wondering and secretly appalled, as sane men would be before an enthusiastic outbreak in a madhouse. We could not understand because we were too far and could not remember because we were travelling in the night of first ages, of those ages that are gone, leaving hardly a sign—and no memories.

"The earth seemed unearthly. We are accustomed to look upon the shackled form of a conquered monster, but there—there you could look at a thing monstrous and free. It was unearthly and the men were . . . No they were not inhuman. Well, you know that was the worst of it—this suspicion of their not being inhuman. It would come slowly to one. They howled and leaped and spun and made horrid faces, but what thrilled you was just the thought of their humanity—like yours—the thought of your remote kinship with this wild and passionate uproar. Ugly. Yes, it was ugly enough, but if you were man enough you would admit to yourself that there was in you just the faintest trace of a response to the terrible frankness of that noise, a dim suspicion of there being a meaning in it which you—you so remote from the night of first ages—could comprehend." (37–38)

Achebe believes that *Heart of Darkness* is an example of the Western habit of setting up Africa "as a foil to Europe, a place of negations . . . in comparison with which Europe's own state of spiritual grace will be manifest." Conrad, obsessed with the black skin of Africans, had as his real purpose the desire to comfort Europeans in their sense of superiority: "*Heart of Darkness* projects the image of Africa as 'the other world,' the antithesis of Europe and therefore of civilization, a place where man's vaunted intelligence and refinement are finally mocked by triumphant bestiality." Achebe dismisses the grove-of-death passage and others like it as "bleeding-heart sentiments," mere decoration in a book that "parades in the most vulgar fashion prejudices and insults from which a section of mankind has suffered untold agonies and atrocities in the past and continues to do so in many ways and many places today," and he adds, "I am talking about a story in which the very humanity of black people is called in question."

Chinua Achebe has written at least one great novel, *Things Fall Apart* (1958), a book I love and from which I have learned a great deal. Yet this article on Conrad (originally a speech delivered at the University of Massachusetts, Amherst, in 1975, and revised for the third Norton edition of the novel in 1987 and reprinted as well in Achebe's 1988 collection of essays, *Hopes and Impediments*) is an act of rhetorical violence, and I recoiled from it. Achebe regards the book not as an expression of its time or as the elaboration of a fictional situation, in which a white man's fears of the unknown are accurately represented, but as a general slander against Africans, a simple racial attack. As far as Achebe is concerned, Africans have struggled to free themselves from the prison of colonial discourse, and for him reading Conrad meant reentering the prison: *Heart of Darkness* is a book in which Europeans consistently have the upper hand.

Reading Achebe, I wanted to argue that most of the students in the Lit Hum class—not Europeans but an American élite—had seen *Heart of Darkness* as a representation of the West's infamy, and hardly as an affirmation of its "spiritual grace." I wanted to argue as well that everything in *Heart of Darkness*—not just the spectacular frights of the African jungle but everything, including the city of Brussels and Marlow's perception of every white character—is rendered sardonically and nightmarishly as an experi-

ence of estrangement and displacement. Conrad certainly describes the Africans gesticulating on the riverbank as a violently
incomprehensible "other." But consider the fictional situation!
Having arrived fresh from Europe, Marlow, surrounded by jungle,
commands a small steamer travelling up the big river en route
to an unknown destiny—death, perhaps. He is a character in an
adventure story, baffled by strangeness. Achebe might well have
preferred that Marlow engage the Africans in conversation or, at
least, observe them closely and come to the realization that they,
too, are a people, that they, too, are souls, have a destiny, spiritual
struggles, triumphs and disasters of selfhood. But could African
selfhood be described within this brief narrative, with its extraordinary physical and philosophical momentum, and within Conrad's purpose of exposing the "pitiless folly" of the Europeans?
Achebe wants another story, another hero, another consciousness.
As it happens, Marlow, regarding the African tribesmen as savage
and incomprehensible, nevertheless feels a kinship with them. He
recognizes no moral difference between himself and them. It is
the Europeans who have been demoralized.

But what's the use? Though Achebe is a novelist, not a scholar,
variants of his critique have appeared in many academic settings
and in response to many classic works. Such publications as *Lingua
Franca* are often filled with ads from university presses for books
about literature and race, literature and gender, literature and
empire. Whatever these scholars are doing in the classroom, they
are seeking to make their reputations outside the classroom with
politicized views of literature. F. R. Leavis's criterion of greatness
in literature—moral seriousness—has been replaced by the moral
aggressiveness of the academic critic in nailing the author to
whatever power formation existed around him. *Heart of Darkness*
could indeed be read as racist by anyone sufficiently angry to
ignore its fictional strategies, its palpable anguish, and the many
differences between Conrad's eighteen-nineties consciousness of
race and our own. At the same time, parts of the academic left
now consider the old way of reading fiction for pleasure, for
enchantment—my falling hopelessly under Conrad's spell—to
be naïve, an unconscious submission to political values whose

nature is disguised precisely by the pleasures of the narrative. In some quarters, pleasure in reading has itself become a political error, rather like sex in Orwell's *1984*.

AS MUCH AS Conrad himself, Edward W. Said is a self-created and ambiguous figure. A Palestinian Christian (from a Protestant family), he was brought up in Jerusalem and Cairo, but has built a formidable career in America, where he has assumed the position of the exiled literary man in extremis—an Arab critic of the West who lives and works in the West, a reader who is at home in Western literature but makes an active case for non-Western literature. Said loathes insularity and parochialism, and has disdained "flat-minded" approaches to reading. Over the years, he has gained many disciples and followers, some of whom he has recently chastised for carrying his moral and political critiques of Western literature to the point of caricature. Said has repeatedly discouraged any attempt to "level" the Western canon.

His most famous work is the remarkable *Orientalism* (1978), a charged analysis of the Western habit of constructing an "exotic" image of the Muslim East as an aid to controlling it. In 1993, Said published *Culture and Imperialism* as a sequel to that book, and part of his intention is to bring to account the great European nineteenth- and twentieth-century writers, examining and judging them as a way of combatting the notion—still alive today, Said says—that Europeans and Americans have the right to govern the inhabitants of the Third World.

Most imaginative writers of the nineteenth century, Said maintains, failed to connect their work, their own spiritual practice, to the squalid operations of colonialism. Such writers as Austen, Carlyle, Thackeray, Dickens, Tennyson, and Flaubert were heroes of culture who either harbored racist views of the subject-people then dominated by the English and the French or merely acquiesced in the material advantages of empire. They took empire for granted as a space in which their characters might roam and prosper; they colluded in evil. Here and there, one could see in their work shameless traces of the subordinated world: a sugar plantation in Antigua whose earnings sustain in English luxury a landed family (the Bertrams) in Austen's *Mansfield Park*; a central character in Dickens's *Great Expectations* (the convict Magwitch) who enriches himself in the "white colony" of Australia and whose secret bequest turns Pip, the novel's young hero, into a "London gentleman." These novels, Said says, could not be fully understood unless their connections to the colonial assumptions and practices in the culture at large were analyzed. But how important, I wonder, is the source of the money to either of these novels? Austen mentions the Antigua plantation only a few times; exactly *where* the Bertrams' money came from clearly did not interest her. And if Magwitch had made his pile not in Australia but in, say, Scotland, by illegally cornering the market in barley or mash, how great a difference would it have made to the structural, thematic, and metaphorical substance of *Great Expectations*? Magwitch would still be a disreputable convict whom Pip would have to reject as a scoundrel or accept as his true spiritual father. Were these novels, as literature, seriously affected by the alleged imperial nexus? Or is Said making lawyerlike points, not out of necessity but merely because they can be made? Indeed, one begins to suspect that a work like *Mansfield Park* is useful to Said precisely because it's such an outlandish example. For if Jane Austen is heavily involved in the creation of imperialism, then every music-hall show, tearoom menu, and floral arrangement is also involved. The West's cultural innocence must be brought to the bar of justice.

In the end, isn't Said's thesis a vast tautology, an assumption that imperialism did, indeed, receive the support of a structure that produced . . . imperialism? By Said's measure, few writers would escape censure. Proust? Indifferent to French exploitation of North African native workers. (And where did the cork that lined the walls of his bedroom come from? Morocco? The very armature of Proust's aesthetic contemplation partakes of imperial domination.) Henry James? Failed to inquire into the late-nineteenth-century industrial capitalism and overseas expansion that made possible the leisure, the civilized discourse, and the spiritual anguish of so many of his characters. James's celebrated refinement was as much a product and an expression of American imperialism as Theodore Roosevelt's pugnacious jingoism. And so on.

When Said arrives at *Heart of Darkness* (a book he loves), he asserts that Conrad, as much as Marlow and Kurtz, was enclosed within the mind-set of imperial domination and therefore could not imagine any possibilities outside it; that is, Conrad could imagine Africans only as ruled by Europeans. It's perfectly true that *Heart of Darkness* contains a few widely spaced and ambiguous remarks that appear to praise the British variety of overseas domination. But how much do such remarks matter against the overwhelming weight of all the rest—the awful sense of desolation produced by the physical chaos, the death and ravaging cruelty everywhere? What readers remember is the squalor of imperialism, and it's surely misleading for Said to speak of *Heart of Darkness* as a work that was "an organic part of the 'scramble for Africa,' " a work that has functioned ever since to reassure Westerners that they had the right to rule the Third World. If we are to discuss the question of the book's historical effect, shouldn't we ask, on the contrary, whether thousands of European and American readers may not have become *nauseated* by colonialism after reading *Heart of Darkness*? Said is so eager to find the hidden power in *Heart of Darkness* that he underestimates the power of what's on the surface. Here is his summing up:

> Kurtz and Marlow acknowledge the darkness, the former as he is dying, the latter as he reflects retrospectively on the meaning of Kurtz's final words. They (and of course Conrad) are ahead of their time in understanding that what they call "the darkness" has an autonomy of its own, and can reinvade and reclaim what imperialism has taken for *its* own. But Marlow and Kurtz are also creatures of their time and cannot take the next step, which would be to recognize that what they saw, disablingly and disparagingly, as a non-European "darkness" was in fact a non-European world *resisting* imperialism so as one day to regain sovereignty and independence, and not, as Conrad reductively says, to reestablish the darkness. Conrad's tragic limitation is that even though he could see clearly

that on one level imperialism was essentially pure dominance
and land-grabbing, he could not then conclude that imperialism had to end so that "natives" could lead lives free from
European domination. As a creature of his time, Conrad could
not grant the natives their freedom, despite his severe critique
of the imperialism that enslaved them. (33–34)

I have read this passage over and over, each time with increasing disbelief. It's not enough that Conrad captured the soul of
imperialism, the genocidal elimination of a people forced into
labor: no, his "tragic limitation" was his failure to "grant the
natives their freedom." Perhaps Said means something fragmentary—a tiny gesture, an implication, a few words that would
suggest the liberated future. But I still find the idea bizarre as a
suggested improvement of *Heart of Darkness*, and my mind is
flooded with visions from terrible Hollywood movies. *Mist slowly
lifts from thick, dark jungle, revealing a rainbow in the distance; Kurtz, wearing
an ivory necklace, gestures to the jungle as he speaks to a magnificent-looking
African chief. "Someday your people will throw off the colonial oppressor. Someday
your people will be free."*
   Dear God, a vision of *freedom?* After the grove of death?
Wouldn't such a vision amount to the grossest sentimentality?
Instead of doing what Said wants, Conrad says that England, too,
has been one of the dark places of the earth. Throughout the
book, he insists that the darkness is in all men. Conrad is as stern,
unyielding, and pessimistic as Said is right-minded, positive, and
banal.
   Achebe indulges a similar sentimentality. Conrad, he says, was
so obsessed with the savagery of the Africans that he somehow
failed to notice that Africans just north of the Congo were creating great works of art—making the masks and other art works
that only a few years later would astound such painters as Vla-
minck, Derain, Picasso, and Matisse, thereby stimulating a new
direction in European art. "The point of all this," Achebe writes,
"is to suggest that Conrad's picture of the people of the Congo
seems grossly inadequate."
   But Conrad certainly did not offer *Heart of Darkness* as "a picture

of the people of the Congo," any more than Achebe's *Things Fall Apart*, set in a Nigerian village, purports to be a rounded picture of the British overlords. Conrad, as much as his master, Henry James, was devoted to a ruthless notion of form. Short as it is— only about thirty-five thousand words—*Heart of Darkness* is a mordantly ironic tale of rescue enfolding a philosophical meditation on the complicity between "civilization" and savagery. Conrad practices a narrow economy and omits a great deal. Economy is also a remarkable feature of the art of Chinua Achebe; and no more than Conrad should he be required to render a judgment for all time on every aspect of African civilization.

Achebe wants *Heart of Darkness* ejected from the canon. "The question is whether a novel which celebrates this dehumanization, which depersonalizes a portion of the human race, can be called a great work of art," he writes. "My answer is: No, it cannot." Said, to be sure, would never suggest dropping Conrad from the reading lists. Still, one has to wonder if blaming writers for what they *fail to write about* is not an extraordinarily wrongheaded way of reading them. Among the academic left, literature now inspires restless impatience. Literature excludes: it's about one thing and not another, represents one point of view and not another, "empowers" one class or race but not another. Literature lacks the perfection of justice, in which all voices must be heard, weighed, balanced. European literature, in particular, is guilty of association with the "winners" of history. Jane Austen is culpable because she failed to dramatize the true nature of colonialism; Joseph Conrad is guilty because he *did* dramatize it. They are guilty by definition and by category.

In the end, Achebe's and Said's complaints come down to this: Joseph Conrad lacked the consciousness of race and imperial power which we have today. Poor, stupid Conrad! Trapped in his own time, he could do no more than write his books. A self-approving moral logic has become familiar on the academic left: So-and-so's view of women, people of color, and the powerless lacks our amplitude, our humanity, our insistence on the inclusion in discourse of all people. One might think that elementary candor would require the academy to render gratitude to the older writers for yielding such easily detected follies.

Why am I so angry? A disagreeable essay or book does not spell the end of Western civilization, and liberal humanists, of all people, should be able—even required—to listen to points of view that are contrary to their own. But what Achebe and Said (and a fair number of other politicized critics) are offering is not simply a different interpretation of this or that work but something close to an attack on the moral legitimacy of literature.

"THERE IS NO WAY for me to understand your pain," Henry said the next time the class met, speaking to everyone in general but perhaps to Alex in particular. "Nor is there any way for you to understand mine. The only common ground we have is that we can glimpse the horror."

It was a portentous remark for so young a man, but he backed it up. Launching into a formal presentation of his ideas about *Heart of Darkness,* he rose from his seat behind Alex to speak. At one point, shouting with excitement, he brushed past him— "Watch out, Alex!" he warned—and threw some coins into the air, first catching them and then letting them drop to the table, where they landed with a clatter and rolled this way and that. Everyone jumped. "That's what the wilderness does," he said. "It disperses what we try to hold under control. Kurtz went in and saw that chaos."

Henry had a talent for melodrama. "Chaos" was another Conradian notion, and I shuddered; our first class on Conrad had come close to breaking apart. Today, however, Shapiro had restored civility, beginning the class with a somber speech. Hunching over the long table, his voice low, he said, "I had to feel a little despair the other day." He warned the students against shouting past one another. He spoke very slowly of his own ambivalence in teaching a book that challenges the very nature of Western society. "It's very hard when you teach a course like Lit Hum, which the outside world represents as the normative, or even conservative, view of social values—it's very hard to *find* yourself. As you read Conrad, do you say, 'Am I going to step away from this culture?' Or do you say, 'I'm going to interact with it in some way that recognizes the contradictions and lies that culture tells itself?' "

And Shapiro went on, slowly reestablishing the frame of his class, situating the book in the year's work and in the work of the élite university that sits on a hill above Harlem.

Looking back on our little *Kulturkampf*, I realize now that however much I disliked Achebe's and Said's approach, they helped me to understand what happened in the classroom. Just as Alex fought so angrily to keep Western civilization untouched by the stain of Kurtz's crimes, I initially wanted *Heart of Darkness* to remain impervious to political criticism. In truth, I don't think any political attack can seriously hurt Conrad's novella. But to maintain that this book is not embedded in the world—to treat it innocently, as earlier critics did, as a garden of symbols, or as a quest for the Grail or the Father, or whatnot—is itself to diminish Conrad's achievement. And to pretend that literature has no political component whatsoever is an equal folly.

However wrong or extreme in individual cases, the academic left has alerted readers to the possible hidden assumptions in language and point of view. Achebe and Said jarred me into seeing, for instance, that Shapiro's way with *Heart of Darkness* was also highly political. I will quickly add that the great value of Shapiro's "liberal" reading is that it did not depend on reductive control of the book's meanings: when the class, provoked by Shapiro's questions, broke down, it did not do so along the clichéd lines of whether Conrad was a racist, or an imperialist. On the contrary, an African-American student had read the book seeking not victimization through literature but self-realization through literature, and white and Asian students, with one exception, had tried in their different ways not to accuse the text but to interrogate themselves. Their responses participated in the liberal consensus of a great university, in which the act of self-criticism is one of the highest goals and a fulfillment of Western education itself. A benevolent politics, but politics nonetheless.

Reading Conrad again, one is struck by his extraordinary unease—and by what he made of it. In the end, his precarious situation both inside and outside imperialism should be seen not as a weakness but as a strength. Yes, Conrad the master seaman had done his time as a colonial employee, working for a Belgian company in 1890, making his own trip up the Congo. He had lived within the consciousness of colonial expansion. But if he had not, could he have written a book like *Heart of Darkness*? Could he have captured with such devastating force the peculiar, hollow triviality of the colonists' ambitions, the self-seeking, the greed, the pettiness, the lies and evasions? Here was the last great Victorian, insisting on responsibility and order, and fighting, at the same time, an exhausting and often excruciating struggle against uncertainty and doubt of every kind, such that he cast every truth in his fictions as a mocking illusion and turned his morally didactic tale into an endlessly provocative and dismaying battle between stoical assumption of duty and perverse complicity in evil. Conrad's sea-captain hero Marlow loathes the monstrous Kurtz, yet feels, after Kurtz's death, an overpowering loyalty to the integrity of what Kurtz discovered in his furious descent into crime.

"The horror" was Conrad's burden as man and artist—the violent contraries that possessed him. But what a yield in art! Certainly T. S. Eliot and others understood *Heart of Darkness* to be one of the essential works of modernism, a new kind of art in which the radically disjunctive experiences of the age would find expression in ever more complex aesthetic forms. Seen in that light, the spectacular intricacy of Conrad's work is unimaginable without his participation in the destructive energies of imperialism. It's possible that Achebe and Said understand this better than any Western reader ever could. But great work galls us, drives us into folly; the fervor of our response to it is a form of tribute. Despite his "errors," Conrad will never be dropped from the reading lists. Achebe's and Said's anguish only confirms his centrality to the modern age.

AT THE END OF THE SECOND CLASS, Henry spoke at length of Kurtz's progression toward death and Marlow's "privilege of watching this self encounter itself," and Alex was silent, perhaps humbled. My antagonism toward him eased. I had not much liked myself as a young man, I remembered. Alex had resisted the class consensus, which took some courage, or stubbornness, and if he thought he was absolved of "darkness" he had plenty of time to discover otherwise. In Shapiro's class, liberal humanism had resisted and survived, though the experience had left us all a little shaken. It was hard these days, as Shapiro noted, to find yourself.

"I don't want to say that this is a work that teaches desperation, or that evil is something we can't deal with," Shapiro said. "In some ways, the world we live in is not as dark as Conrad's; in some ways, it is darker. This is not a one-way slide to the apocalypse that we are witnessing. We ourselves have the ability now to recognize, and even to fix and change our society, just as literature reflects, embodies, and serves as an agent of change."

The students were relieved. They wanted reconciliation and peace. And one of them, it seems, had, like Marlow, discovered what he was looking for. He had "found" himself. "We scream at the wilderness, and the wilderness screams back," Henry said, concluding his presentation with a flourish. "There's a tension, and at that point of tension we resolve our nature."

Works Cited

Conrad, Joseph. *Heart of Darkness*. Norton Critical Edition, edited by Robert Kimbrough. New York: W.W. Norton, 1988.
Said, Edward W. *Culture and Imperialism*. London: Chatto & Windham, 1993.

A Chat with Joseph Conrad

CYRIL CLEMENS

❖   ❖   ❖

WHILE I WAS HAVING tea with my late friend Hugh
Walpole in his London apartment at 90 Piccadilly, during
the early 1920s, he asked me if there was anyone I would particularly like to meet during my stay in London.

My reply was that since I had been rereading *Lord Jim* on the
ship coming over I would like very much to meet its author.

"That's easy," returned Walpole, "Jessie and Joseph Conrad are
two of my best friends. It won't be necessary for me to write any
letter of introduction. Just tell them you are a friend of mine
that I sent you along.

"I never cease to marvel at Conrad," mused Walpole. "A youth
in Poland who read Shakespeare and Cervantes and Molière in
translation, and while still in his teens shipped before the mast
on a French vessel that brought him to the Gulf of Mexico.

"Until past forty, Conrad lived the sailor's life, rising in time
to become a captain in the British merchant marine.

"In 1895 *Almayer's Folly* was published, a first novel simply written but with a vast movement and a mood of deep enigmatical

pondering that lends such a subtle charm to all of that master's stories.

"You know in 1896 he abandoned the sea and settled down in England where he has lived ever since," Walpole concluded.

A few days later found me having tea with Conrad at "Oswalds," his delightful home at Bishopsbourne, just outside of Canterbury, Kent, where he lived with his English-born wife and two sons.

"I am pleased to hear that you like *Lord Jim*," Conrad was saying, "for if I have a favorite among my books I believe that is the one. It cost me much pain to produce and that always makes a book sweet to an author.

"But I am obliged to write every book about six times," Conrad added. "First I tumble out a mass of words, incoherent even to myself, but fairly bristling with ideas. Then, laboriously, I straighten them out until I have something like a skeleton to work on.

"Then I pull them this way and that until the events are arranged in order. Then I dive into my characters and try to bring them to life. My last two revisions are usually devoted to polishing up."

When I praised the extraordinary vividness of the shipwreck scene in *Lord Jim*, the novelist answered, "I built it upon fragments of an authentic incident of the sea that I picked up in my wanderings, and the 800 pilgrims bound for Mecca were really on board. Unfortunately the most dramatic incident of that shipwreck did not come to my knowledge until too late to be put in the book.

"When all hope was abandoned, and the ship was expected to founder any minute, the pilgrims put on their grave clothes and disposed themselves in long rows on the deck. There they lay, resigned, and chanting religious songs, until the ship made its final plunge through the waves. What a novelist could have made of that!"

I mentioned that Americans looked upon Conrad as the greatest writer of sea stories, and he answered, "It seems to me that your fellow countrymen imagine I sit here and brood over the sea. That is quite a mistake. I brood, certainly, but I insist, not on the events, but on [their] effect upon the characters.

"In everything I have written there is always one invariable intention, and that is to capture the reader's attention, by securing his interest and enlisting his sympathies for the matter in hand, whatever it may be, within the limits of the visible world and within the boundaries of human emotions.

"The moral side of an industry," Conrad went on, "is the attainment and preservation of the highest possible skill on the part of the craftsman. Such skill, the skill of technique, is more than honesty; it is something wider, embracing honesty, and grace, and clear sentiment.

"A writer's attainment of proficiency, the pushing of his will with attention to the most delicate shades of excellence, is a matter of vital concern. But there is something beyond—a higher point, a subtle and unmistakable touch of love and pride beyond mere skill; almost an inspiration which gives to all work that finish which is almost—which, in fact, *is* art."

I asked, "Is there any particular book, Mr. Conrad, that you are fond of reading over and over again?"

"Indeed there is—a book I first became acquainted with in my youth—Cervantes' inimitable *Don Quixote*. Certain maxims from the work I find myself frequently quoting, such as: 'The brave man carves out his own fortune and every man is the son of his own works.' "

Handing me a cigarette and taking one himself, Conrad continued in his slow, even, well-modulated voice, "I like to reflect on the Spaniard's colorful career. As you are doubtless aware, very little is known of his childhood and youth except that he was born at a small Spanish town in 1547.

"He fought valiantly at the Battle of Lepanto in 1571, and was wounded, losing the use of his left hand. He traveled through Italy, was captured by the Turks in 1575, and after an attempt to escape, was ransomed about 1580.

"Upon his return to Madrid, he completed a pastoral novel, *La Galatea*, and wrote his drama *Numanica*. In 1605 he published the first part of *Don Quixote* which was followed by various minor works, until, angered by the appearance of a spurious sequel, he hastened the completion of the second part which was published in 1615—and none too soon, for he died the year following." Conrad fell silent.

"Is it correct that you knew Stephen Crane?" I asked a little later.

"Yes, he was one of my early friends," returned the novelist. "I met Crane shortly after he came to England to live. I remember he told me that he was born in Newark, New Jersey, and attended Lafayette College and Syracuse University.

"He then served as war correspondent in the Greco-Turkish and Spanish-American wars. Although a few years younger than I, as an author Crane was the senior, and I used to remind him of that now and then with affected humility which always provoked his smiles.

"He had a quiet smile that charmed and frightened one. It made you pause, by something revelatory it cast over his own physiognomy, not like a ray, but like a shadow.

"I often asked myself what it could be, that quality that checked one's care-free mood, and the passage of years has given me the answer. It was simply the smile of a man who is aware that his time will not be long on this earth. For he died in 1900 at twenty-nine."

"What books of Crane do you like best, Mr. Conrad?" I asked.

"Well, my favorite is *The Red Badge of Courage*—an extraordinary example of psychological portraiture, the state of mind of a soldier in action. It is marvelous how vivid Crane made it when he had never been in any kind of warfare himself.

"English friends who read the story when it first came out were willing to bet any amount of money that the author had been an eye-witness of the battle of Chancellorsville, in which Lee and Jackson brilliantly defeated Hooker. Crane was not born until 1871—six years after the Civil War was over.

"A rather neglected book of his that I have always much admired is his *Whilomville Stories*. As you perhaps are aware, these are tales and adventures of American child-life; the misadventures, practical jokes, amusing foibles, and antics of precocious youths of eight and nine, all humorously related. It is a book that has never received anything like the success it deserves.

"Another author from your side of whom I am very fond," Conrad continued, "is Sir Gilbert Parker who was born in Canada in 1862, and educated at Trinity College, Toronto. He moved to England in 1900, and became a member of Parliament for the borough of Gravesend which he represented for almost twenty years.

"As you know he wrote some poetry and many novels. Of the latter I think my favorite is *The Right of Way*, a poignant romance dealing with a brilliant Montreal barrister who wanders, temporarily crazed by dipsomania and an accident, into a French-Canadian village."

I said, "Do you like him for his delineation of character, Mr. Conrad?"

"Yes, that is excellent," returned the novelist, "but some of his nature descriptions are so simply, yet so effectively done. One from *The Right of Way*, I think I can repeat from memory:

> The sweet sun of early spring was shining hard and the snow was just beginning to pack, to hang like a blanket on the branches, to lie like a soft coverlet over all the forest and the fields.
>
> In the distance on the frozen river were saplings stuck up to show where the ice was safe—a long line of poles from shore to shore—and carioles were hurrying across to the village.
>
> Being market-day, the place was alive with cheerful commerce of the habitants. The bell of the parish church was ringing. The sound of it came up distantly and peacefully.

When I said that I rather liked *The Money Master*, Conrad returned, "That is also a favorite of mine. I will never forget the charmingly described little French-Canadian town and the hero Jean Jacques Barbille, miller and money master, who retains his cheerful disposition and trust in God—how often the two go together—despite troubles innumerable.

"The author is a past master at blending pathos with whimsical humor. Nor should one forget that cleverly written *When Valmond Came to Pontiac*, the romance of the arrival of a supposed son of Napoleon into the life of a French-Canadian village."

I said, "I heard from Arnold Bennett that you are writing a novel dealing with some phase of Napoleon's career. Is this correct?"

"Yes," Conrad answered. "Lately, I have been reading a great many books on Napoleon and his times, especially for the years 1813–1814. I have a feeling that I will be able to write some story dealing with the Elba episode.

"If any period of Napoleon's life has been neglected, it would seem to be this. I first became interested in Napoleon when I was a boy in Poland. During my research, I thought more than once of what Napoleon said on one occasion!"

It is more easy for ordinary historians to build upon suppositions, and to stitch hypotheses together, than to relate simply, and march onward with the facts in their possession; but man, and above all the historian, is full of vanity; he must give a fine scope to imagination, he must interest the reader, even at the expense of truth; reputation hangs on this.

"The Corsican is also author of that very wise saying: 'The guilt of many men may be traced to over-affection for their wives.' "

"Do you think that Mark Twain was a good pilot, Mr. Conrad?" I asked.

"Yes, he must have been," replied the novelist. "No man who had not done the actual work could write of steamboat life so vividly and realistically as he did. In the late 1880s when I was a young officer in the British Merchant Marine, I chanced to pick up an old book on a London bookstall for 10 pence. It turned out to be Twain's account of his days on the River.

"There had been considerable talk of him in Europe. Long before that, of course, *Innocents Abroad* had been all the rage.

"But his descriptions of life in America—some of the short

stories as well as the longer books—those are what really count. They have life—American life. They are genuinely authentic."

After taking several puffs on his cigarette, Conrad continued, "The work of Twain's that came closest to my own career was *The Mississippi Pilot*. No, it was not called *Life on the Mississippi*. That is the title, now, certainly.

"But then perhaps it was the first edition, I do not recall at this late date—then it was called *The Mississippi Pilot*. The book had a beastly glazed cover. A cardboard cover, but there was life inside it, and that's what counts!"

When Conrad had reflected a few moments, he resumed, "Yes, discovering Mark Twain gave me the same thrill that I had when I discovered Cervantes and Shakespeare. Each of those authors opened up a new world for me—so stimulating and refreshing. My very first book, *Almayer's Folly: The Story of an Eastern River*, was commenced in 1889, not so very long after I had read *The Mississippi Pilot*.

"While I was in command of a steamer that plied up and down the Congo, and stood straining in the night looking for snags, I thought of Mark Twain's similar experiences on the great Mississippi and of what Mark would have said and thought if he had been working up and down my river. In many ways so different, yet so similar. Yes, indeed, I thought of him very often!"

"Was there any particular passage in *Life on the Mississippi* that you found more arresting than another?" I asked.

"Yes, there was one section that especially appealed to me. In fact, I read and reread it so much that I know it by heart or at least I used to. Let me see if I can repeat it over a quarter of a century."

> Soon a film of black smoke appears above one of those remote points; instantly a Negro drayman, celebrated for his quick eye and prodigious voice, lifts up the "S-t-e-a-m-b-o-a-t a comin!" and the scene changes!
>
> The town drunkard stirs, the clerks wake up, a furious clatter of drays follows, every house and store pours out a human contribution, and all in a twinkling the dead town is

alive and moving—drays, carts, men, boys, all go hurrying
from many quarters to a common center, the wharf.

Assembled there, the people fasten their eyes upon the
coming boat as upon a wonder they are seeing for the first
time. And the boat is rather a handsome sight, too!

She is long and sharp and trim and pretty; she has two tall,
fancy-topped chimneys, with a gilded device of some kind
swung between them; a fanciful pilot house, all glass and "gin-
gerbread" perched on top of the "texas" deck behind them;
the paddle boxes are gorgeous with a picture or with gilded
rays above the boat's name; the boiler-deck, the hurricane-
deck, and the texas deck are fenced and ornamented with clean
white railings; there is a flag gallantly flying from the jackstaff.

"But why go on with something that you, too, must almost
know by heart?"

I said, "How did you enjoy your recent visit to America, Mr.
Conrad?"

"I had a most interesting and pleasant time. I shall never forget
being met in New York by about forty cameras held by as many
men. Although this was a nerve-wracking experience, my reception by the American press was quite remarkable in its friendli-
ness. I stayed with my publisher, Frank Doubleday, who lives on
Long Island.

"One day," Conrad continued, "I gave a talk and pieces of
reading out of my novel *Victory* at the nearby home of Mrs. Curtis
James. Altogether I spoke for about an hour and twenty minutes
and the spacious drawing room must have held about fifty people.
I was told afterward that all the week preceding my talk there
was desperate fighting and plotting among New York society to
secure invitations. I had the lucky inspiration to refuse to accept
any payment.

"After the applause from the audience, which stood up when
I appeared, had died down, I had a moment of positive anguish.
Then I took out the watch that my wife had given me and laid
it on the table, made one mighty effort, and began to speak. That

watch was the greatest comfort to me. All my life I have done very little public speaking."

I asked, "Did you meet any Americans outside of the social set?"

"Yes, there are several whom I recall with keen pleasure," answered Conrad. "One was John W. Davis, recently American ambassador at the Court of St. James. And the other was the celebrated Colonel Edward M. House who gave me some fascinating glimpses of President Woodrow Wilson whose interest in my native Poland I have always appreciated."

Before leaving, I had the satisfaction of telling Joseph Conrad, my host, that Woodrow Wilson had read *Almayer's Folly* when it first appeared in 1895. And he had written a friend, characterizing it as "a book of high simplicity with an epic sweep and an atmosphere of brooding mystery which I find most fascinating."

Suggested Reading

Achebe, Chinua. "An Image of Africa." *Massachusetts Review* 17, no. 4 (1977): 782–94. Reprinted in *Hopes and Impediments: Selected Essays, 1967–87.* London: Heinemann, 1988, pp. 1–13.

Bivona, Daniel. *British Imperial Literature, 1870–1940: Writing and the Administration of Empire.* Cambridge: Cambridge University Press, 1998.

Bloom, Harold, ed. *Joseph Conrad's "Heart of Darkness."* New York and Philadelphia: Chelsea House, 1987.

Brantlinger, Patrick. *Rule of Darkness: British Literature and Imperialism, 1830–1914.* Ithaca, N.Y., and London: Cornell University Press, 1988.

Brooks, Peter. "Un rapport illisible: *Cœur des ténèbres.*" *Poétique* 11, no. 44 (1980): 472–89. Revised and translated as "An Unreadable Report: *Heart of Darkness.*" In Brooks, *Readings for the Plot: Design and Intention in Narrative.* New York: Knopf; Oxford: Clarendon, 1984, pp. 28–63.

Bross, Addison. "Beerbohm's 'The Feast' and Conrad's Early Fiction." *Nineteenth-Century Fiction* 26, no. 3 (Dec. 1971): 329–36.

Clifford, James. "On Ethnographic Self-Fashioning: Conrad and Malinowski." In Clifford, *The Predicament of Culture: Twentieth-Century Ethnography, Literature, and Art.* Cambridge, Mass.: Harvard University Press, 1988, pp. 92–113.

Conrad, Joseph. *The Collected Letters of Joseph Conrad.* Edited by Laurence Davies et al. 6 vols. Cambridge: Cambridge University Press, 1983–.

———. "Geography and Some Explorers." In *Last Essays.* London: Dent, 1926.

———. *Heart of Darkness.* Edited by Robert Kimbrough. New York: Norton, 1988.

Dean, Leonard F., ed. *Joseph Conrad's "Heart of Darkness": Backgrounds and Criticisms.* Englewood Cliffs, N.J.: Prentice-Hall, 1960.

Firchow, Peter Edgerly. *Envisioning Africa: Racism and Imperialism in Conrad's "Heart of Darkness."* Lexington: University Press of Kentucky, 2000.

Ford, Ford Madox. *Joseph Conrad: A Personal Remembrance.* London: Duckworth, 1924.

Galef, David. "On the Margin: The Peripheral Characters in Conrad's *Heart of Darkness.*" *Journal of Modern Literature* 17, no. 1 (Spring 1990): 117–38.

Ghose, Indira. "Conrad's *Heart of Darkness* and the Anxiety of Empire." In *Being/s in Transit: Travelling—Migration—Dislocation,* edited by Liselotte Glage. Amsterdam and Atlanta: Rodopi, 2000, pp. 93–110.

Hamner, Robert, ed. *Joseph Conrad: Third World Perspectives.* Washington, D.C.: Three Continents, 1990.

Hawkins, Hunt. "Conrad's Critique of Imperialism in *Heart of Darkness.*" *PMLA* 94, no. 2 (Mar. 1979): 268–99.

———. "Joseph Conrad, Roger Casement, and the Congo Reform Movement." *Journal of Modern Literature* 9, no. 1 (1981–1982): 65–80.

Hervouet, Yves. *The French Face of Joseph Conrad.* Cambridge: Cambridge University Press, 1990.

Hochschild, Adam. *King Leopold's Ghost.* Boston and New York: Houghton Mifflin, 1998.

Jean-Aubry, G. *Joseph Conrad in the Congo.* Boston: Little, Brown, 1926.

Kaplan, Carola M. "Colonizers, Cannibals, and the Horror of Good Intentions in Joseph Conrad's *Heart of Darkness.*" *Studies in Short Fiction* 34, no. 3 (1997): 323–33.

Knowles, Owen, and Gene M. Moore. *The Oxford Reader's Companion to Conrad.* Oxford: Oxford University Press, 2000.

Lindqvist, Sven. *"Exterminate All the Brutes."* Translated by Joan Tate. New York: New Press, 1996; London: Granta, 1997.

Mongia, Padmini. "The Rescue: Conrad, Achebe, and the Critics." *Conradiana* 33, no. 2 (Summer 2001): 153–63.

Moore, Gene M., ed. *Conrad on Film.* Cambridge: Cambridge University Press, 1997.

Murfin, Ross C., ed. *Joseph Conrad, "Heart of Darkness": A Case Study in Contemporary Criticism.* Boston and New York: Bedford, 1989.

Najder, Zdzisław, ed. *Congo Diary and Other Uncollected Pieces by Joseph Conrad.* Garden City, N.Y.: Doubleday, 1978.

Nakai, Asako. *The English Book and Its Marginalia: Colonial/Postcolonial Literatures after "Heart of Darkness".* Amsterdam and Atlanta: Rodopi, 2000.

Ong, Walter J. "Truth in Conrad's Darkness." *Mosaic: A Journal for the Comparative Study of Literature and Ideas* 11, no. 1 (1977): 151–63.

Parrinder, Patrick. "*Heart of Darkness*: Geography as Apocalypse." In *Fin de Siècle / Fin du Globe: Fears and Fantasies of the Late Nineteenth Century*, edited by John Stokes. London: Macmillan, 1992, pp. 85–101.

Raskin, Jonah. "*Heart of Darkness*: The Manuscript Revisions." *Review of English Studies*, n.s. 18, no. 69 (1967): 30–39.

Shaffer, Brian W. " 'Progress and Civilization and All the Virtues': Teaching *Heart of Darkness* via 'An Outpost of Progress.' " *Conradiana* 24, no. 3 (1992): 219–31.

Sherry, Norman. *Conrad's Western World.* Cambridge: Cambridge University Press, 1971.

Todorov, Tzvetan. "Knowledge in the Void: *Heart of Darkness*." 1975. Translated by Walter C. Putnam III. *Conradiana* 21, no. 3 (Autumn 1989): 161–72.

Watt, Ian. "Conrad's *Heart of Darkness* and the Critics." In Watt, *Essays on Conrad.* Cambridge: Cambridge University Press, 2000. 85–96.

Watts, Cedric. *Conrad's "Heart of Darkness:" A Critical and Contextual Discussion.* Milano: University Mursia Editore, 1977.

———. "*Heart of Darkness*." In *The Cambridge Companion to Joseph Conrad*, edited by J. H. Stape. Cambridge: Cambridge University Press, 1996, pp. 45–62.

White, Andrea. *Joseph Conrad and the Adventure Tradition: Constructing and Deconstructing the Imperial Subject.* Cambridge: Cambridge University Press, 1993.